WAYSIDE SCHOOL
IS FALLING DOWN

LOUIS SACHAR
ILLUSTRATED BY TIM HEITZ

To Emily, Walker, Annie,
Bill, Bobbie, and Corky

1. A PACKAGE FOR MRS. JEWLS

Louis, the **yard** teacher, **frowned**.

The school yard was a **mess**. There were pencils and pieces of paper everywhere. How'd all this **junk** get here? he wondered. Well, I'm not going to pick it up!

It wasn't his job to pick up **garbage**. He was just supposed to pass out the balls during lunch and **recess**, and also make sure the kids didn't kill each other.

He **sigh**ed, then began cleaning it up. He loved all the children at Wayside School. He didn't want them playing on a dirty **playground**.

As he was picking up the pencils and pieces of paper, a large truck drove into the **parking lot**. It **honk**ed its **horn** twice, then twice more.

Louis ran to the truck. "Quiet!" he whispered. "Children are trying to learn in there!" He pointed at the school.

A short man with big, **bushy** hair stepped out of the truck. "I have a package for somebody named Mrs. Jewls," he said.

"I'll take it," said Louis.

"Are you Mrs. Jewls?" asked the man.

"No," said Louis.

"I have to give it to Mrs. Jewls," said the man.

Louis thought a moment. He didn't want the man **disturb**ing the children. He knew how much they hated to be **interrupt**ed when they were working.

"I'm Mrs. Jewls," he said.

"But you just said you weren't Mrs. Jewls," said the man.

"I changed my mind," said Louis.

The man got the package out of the back of the truck and gave it to Louis. "Here you go, Mrs. Jewls," he said.

"Uhh!" Louis **grunt**ed. It was a very heavy package. The word **FRAGILE** was **print**ed on every side. He had to be careful not to drop it.

The package was so big, Louis couldn't see where he was going. **Fortunate**ly, he knew the way to Mrs. Jewls's class **by heart**. It was straight up.

Wayside School was thirty **stories** high, with only one room on each story. Mrs. Jewls's class was at the very top. It was Louis's favorite class.

He pushed through the door to the school, then started up the stairs. There was no elevator.

There were stairs that led down to the **basement** too, but nobody ever went down there. There were dead rats living in the basement.

The box was **press**ed against Louis's face, **squash**ing his nose. Even so, when he reached the fifteenth floor, he could smell Miss Mush cooking in the **cafeteria**. It smelled like she was making **mushroom**s. Maybe on my way back I'll stop by Miss Mush's room and get some mushrooms, he thought. He didn't want to miss Miss Mush's mushrooms. They were her **specialty**.

He **huff**ed and **groan**ed and continued up the stairs. His arms and legs were very **sore**, but he didn't want to rest. This package might be important, he thought. I have to get it to Mrs. Jewls **right away**.

He stepped easily from the eighteenth story to the twentieth. There was no nineteenth story.

Miss Zarves taught the class on the nineteenth story. There was no Miss Zarves.

At last he **struggled** up the final step to the thirtieth story. He **knock**ed on Mrs. Jewls's door with his head.

Mrs. Jewls was in the middle of teaching her class about **gravity** when she heard the knock. "Come in," she called.

"I can't open the door," Louis gasped. "My hands are full. I have a package for you."

Mrs. Jewls faced the class. "Who wants to open the door for Louis?" she asked.

All the children raised their hands. They loved to be interrupted when they were working.

"Oh dear, how shall I choose?" asked Mrs. Jewls. "I have to be fair about this. I know! We'll have a spelling bee.[1] And the winner will get to open the door."

Louis knocked his head against the door again. "It's heavy," he complained. "And I'm very tired."

"Just a second," Mrs. Jewls called back. "Allison, the first word's for you. Heavy."

"Heavy," said Allison. "H-E-A-V-Y. Heavy."

"Very good. Jason, you're next. Tired."

"Tired," said Jason. "S-L-E-E-P-Y. Tired."

Louis felt the package slipping from his sweaty fingers. He shifted his weight to get a better grip. The corners of the box dug into the sides of his arms. He felt his hands go numb.

Actually, he *didn't* feel them go numb.

"Jenny, package."

"Package," said Jenny. "B-O-X. Package."

"Excellent!" said Mrs. Jewls.

---

1 spelling bee 단어를 듣고 철자를 맞추는 대회.

Louis felt like he was going to **faint**.

At last John opened the door. "I won the spelling bee, Louis!" he said.

"Very good, John," **mutter**ed Louis.

"Aren't you going to shake my hand?" asked John.

Louis shifted the box to one arm, quickly shook John's hand, then **grab**bed the box again and **stagger**ed into the room.

"Where do you want it, Mrs. Jewls?" he asked.

"I don't know," said Mrs. Jewls. "What is it?"

"I don't know," said Louis. "I'll have to put it down someplace so you can open it."

"But how can I tell you where to put it until I know what it is?" asked Mrs. Jewls. "You might put it in the wrong place."

So Louis held the box as Mrs. Jewls stood on a chair next to him and **tore** open the top. His legs **wobble**d beneath him.

"It's a computer!" **exclaim**ed Mrs. Jewls.

Everybody **boo**ed.

"What's the matter?" asked Louis. "I thought everyone loved computers."

"We don't want it, Louis," said Eric Bacon.

"Take it back, Jack," said Terrence.

"Get that piece of junk out of here," said Maurecia.

"Now, don't be that way," said Mrs. Jewls. "The computer will help us learn. It's a lot quicker than a pencil and paper."

"But the quicker we learn, the more work we have to do,"

complained Todd.

"You may set it over there on the **counter**, Louis," said Mrs. Jewls.

Louis set the computer on the counter next to Sharie's desk. Then he **collapse**d on the floor.

"Now watch closely," said Mrs. Jewls.

Everyone **gather**ed around the new computer. It had a full-color **monitor** and two disk drives.[2]

Mrs. Jewls pushed it out the window.

They all watched it fall and **smash** against the **sidewalk**.

"See?" said Mrs. Jewls. "That's gravity."

"Oh, now I **get it!**" said Joe.

"Thank you, Louis," said Mrs. Jewls. "I've been trying to teach them about gravity all morning. We had been using pencils and pieces of paper, but the computer was a lot quicker."

---

2 disk drive 컴퓨터의 디스크 드라이브. 디스크에 정보를 기록하고, 기록된 정보를 읽어 들이는 보조 기억 장치.

2. MARK MILLER

Mrs. Jewls rang her **cowbell**. "I would like you to meet Mark Miller," she said. "He and his family just moved here **all the way** from Magadonia!"

Everybody **stare**d at the new kid.

He stood at the front of the room. His knees were shaking.

He hated having to stand in front of the class. It was as if Mrs. Jewls had brought him in for show-and-tell.[1] He felt like some kind of **weirdo**. He just wanted to sit at a desk and be like

---

1 show-and-tell 학교 수업 활동의 하나로 학생들이 각자 물건을 가져 와서 발표하는 것을 말한다.

everybody else.

But worst of all, his name wasn't Mark Miller.

He was Benjamin Nushmutt. And he had moved from Hempleton, not Magadonia.

But he was too **scare**d to mention that to Mrs. Jewls. He was afraid to correct a teacher.

"Why don't you tell the class a little bit about yourself, Mark?" suggested Mrs. Jewls.

Benjamin didn't know what to say. He wished he really was Mark Miller. Mark Miller wouldn't be scared, he thought. He'd probably have lots to say. Everyone would like him. Nobody would think Mark Miller was **weird**.

"Well, I guess we'd better find you a place to sit," said Mrs. Jewls.

She put him at the empty desk between Todd and Bebe.

"Hi, Mark," said Todd. "I'm Todd. You'll like Mrs. Jewls. She's the nicest teacher in the school."

"Todd, no talking," said Mrs. Jewls. "Go write your name on the **blackboard** under the word **DISCIPLINE**."

"Hi, Mark," said Bebe. "I'm Bebe Gunn."

"Hi," Benjamin said quietly.

He decided he'd have to tell Mrs. Jewls his real name at **recess**. He **cringe**d. He didn't know why, but for some reason he had trouble saying his own name.

"And what's your name, little boy?" an adult would ask him.

12

"Benjamin Nushmutt," he'd answer.

"What?"

"BENjamin NUSHmutt."

"What?"

"Ben-Ja-Min Nush-Mutt."

"What?"

"BenjaMIN NushMUTT!"

"What?"

"Benjamin Nushmutt."

"Oh, nice to meet you, Benjamin."

He never knew what it was that made the person suddenly understand.

When the bell rang for recess, everyone **charge**d out of the room. Benjamin slowly walked to Mrs. Jewls's desk. Somehow, he had to tell her.

Mrs. Jewls was sorting papers. "Oh, hello, Mark," she said. "How are you enjoying the class so far?"

"Fine," said Benjamin.

"Good, I'm glad to hear that," said Mrs. Jewls.

Benjamin **shrug**ged, then walked out of the room. If I had told her my name, she would have thought I was weird for not telling her sooner, he realized.

He stood at the top of the stairs and looked down. Recess was only ten minutes long. It didn't seem **worth** it to go all the way down and then come all the way back up. He didn't have any friends down there anyway.

He had never been more unhappy in his whole life.

He sat on the top step. "Mark Miller," he said out loud. It was an easy name to say. Mark Miller probably would have made lots of friends by now, he thought.

Suddenly he heard a low **rumble**. Then the stairs began to shake. It felt like an **earthquake**! This whole stupid school is going to fall over, he thought. He put his head between his knees.

The rumbling got worse. I'm going to die and nobody will even know who I am, he worried. The new kid. Mark Miller. The weirdo!

But it wasn't an earthquake. It was just all the kids running back up the stairs.

"Hey, Mark, why are you sitting that way?" asked Deedee.

"You look funny," said Ron.

Benjamin looked up.

"How come you weren't at recess?" asked Jason. "We looked everywhere for you."

"Couldn't you find the **playground**?" asked Calvin.

"It's just straight down," said Bebe. "You can't miss it."

"But don't go in the **basement**," warned Sharie. "Whatever you do, don't go in the basement."

"We'll go down together at lunch," said Todd. "That way you won't get lost."

Benjamin smiled. He was glad everyone seemed to like him.

Or at least they liked Mark Miller. He wondered if they'd like Benjamin Nushmutt too.

"The bell has rung!" said Mrs. Jewls, standing in the **doorway**. "Now, everyone get inside." She made Todd put a check next to his name on the board for being late.

Mrs. Jewls handed a **stack** of **work sheet**s to Dameon and asked him to pass them out to the rest of the class.

Benjamin looked at his work sheet. At the top right corner there was a place to put his name. He didn't know which name to put there, Mark Miller or Benjamin Nushmutt.

He left it **blank** and started working on the first problem.

Louis, the **yard** teacher, entered the room carrying a white paper **sack**. "Benjamin forgot his lunch," he said. "His mother just brought it."

"Who?" asked Mrs. Jewls.

"Benjamin," said Louis.

"There's no Benjamin in my class," said Mrs. Jewls.

"Are you sure?" asked Louis. "It looks like a good lunch."

"I know the names of the children in my class!" Mrs. Jewls said **indignant**ly.

"Well, I'll just leave it here until I **figure** this **out**," said Louis. He left the lunch on Mrs. Jewls's desk and walked out of the room.

Benjamin **frown**ed. He looked at the white paper sack on Mrs. Jewls's desk. He couldn't tell Mrs. Jewls his real name now. She'd think he was making it up just to get a free lunch.

He wrote *Mark Miller* at the top of his work sheet.

But one of these days, he knew, he'd have to tell her his real name.

3. BEBE'S BABY BROTHER

Mrs. Jewls asked Dameon to pass back the homework.

Bebe Gunn waited nervously. Except for art, her grades had not been very good lately. If she didn't start bringing home better grades, her parents said they wouldn't let her **stay up** past midnight. She did her best **artwork** after midnight.

Dameon handed Calvin his homework, then Todd, then Joy.

"Where's yours?" asked Calvin.

"I don't know," said Bebe.

"Did you do it?" asked Calvin.

"Yes, I did it," said Bebe. "I worked extra hard on it! I hope

Mrs. Jewls didn't lose it."

Dameon finished passing out the homework. Bebe never got hers.

"Bebe, will you come here, please," said Mrs. Jewls.

She pushed out of her seat, stood up, and nervously walked to Mrs. Jewls's desk. "I did my homework, Mrs. Jewls," she said. "Really!"

"Yes, I know," said Mrs. Jewls. She held Bebe's homework in her hand.

"Whew!" Bebe **sigh**ed with **relief**. "I was afraid you lost it!"

"No, I didn't lose it," Mrs. Jewls said **stern**ly. She showed the back of the paper to Bebe. Someone had written:

MRS. JEWLS IS AS FAT AS A **HIPPOPOTAMUS!** (AND SHE SMELLS LIKE ONE, TOO.)

"I didn't write that!" **exclaim**ed Bebe. "I love the way you smell."

Mrs. Jewls smiled. "But if you didn't write it, who did?"

"Ray!" Bebe **instant**ly replied.

"Who's Ray?"

"He's my little brother. Ray Gunn. He must have **snuck** into my room after I was asleep. He's always playing mean **trick**s on me. He knew how hard I worked on my homework."

"Well, we'll show Ray," said Mrs. Jewls. She gave Bebe an A+. "There. I don't think he'll try that again."

"Thanks!" said Bebe.

"You may have a Tootsie Roll Pop,[1] too," said Mrs. Jewls.

Bebe took a Tootsie Roll Pop out of the coffee can on Mrs. Jewls's desk, then returned to her seat. She proudly showed Calvin her A+.

The next day Mrs. Jewls asked Dameon to hand back another **batch** of homework.

"How come Dameon always gets to do everything?" **griped** Kathy.

"I'm sorry, Kathy," said Mrs. Jewls. "Would you like to pass back the homework?"

"No!" **grump**ed Kathy. "I'm not your **slave**."

Dameon passed out the homework. Again Bebe didn't get hers.

Mrs. Jewls called her to her desk. On the back of her homework someone had written:

MRS. JEWLS HAS A HEAD FULL OF OATMEAL![2] (AND IT **LEAK**S OUT HER EARS.)

"I didn't write it," said Bebe.

"Ray?" asked Mrs. Jewls.

Bebe **nod**ded.

"Why don't you start checking the back of your homework?"

---

1 Tootsie Roll Pop 툿시 롤 팝. 초콜릿 캔디의 이름.
2 oatmeal 오트밀. 귀리 가루로 만든 죽으로 주로 아침식사로 먹는다.

suggested Mrs. Jewls.

"I did when I woke up!" said Bebe. "He must have done it after breakfast, while I was brushing my teeth. We had oatmeal for breakfast." She shook her head. "I won't brush my teeth anymore!"

"You have to brush your teeth," said Mrs. Jewls.

"My parents think he's such a little angel!" Bebe **complain**ed. "He's always **wreck**ing things, and then I'm always the one who gets in trouble. 'Why can't you be more like Ray?' they say. Yesterday he threw all my **underwear** out the window. Then my mother **yell**ed at me for it. She wouldn't believe that her little **darling** son would do something like that!"

Mrs. Jewls gave Bebe another A+ and another Tootsie Roll Pop.

For Friday everyone had to write a report and read it to the class. Bebe wrote her report about George Washington.[3] She stood at the front of the room and read it out loud.

". . . George Washington never told a lie. Not like Mrs. Jewls. She lies all the time. That's why her nose is so big. And she **snore**s when she sleeps, so Mister Jewls has to wear **ear plug**s."

Everyone was laughing.

Bebe stopped reading. "What's so funny?" she asked.

"Come here," said Mrs. Jewls.

Bebe **shrug**ged, then walked to Mrs. Jewls's desk.

Mrs. Jewls showed her what she had just read.

---

3 George Washington 조지 워싱턴. 미국의 초대 대통령으로 미국의 독립전쟁을 이끌고 연방헌법을 제정하여 미국 '건국의 아버지'라고 불린다.

"Did I just read that out loud?" Bebe asked.

Mrs. Jewls nodded.

"I was just reading it," Bebe explained. "I wasn't listening."

"It was Ray again, wasn't it?" asked Mrs. Jewls.

"Had to be," said Bebe. "Yesterday he put **toothpaste** in my socks. Then my mother got mad at me for making a **mess** and wasting toothpaste."

Bebe got an A+ on her report and another Tootsie Roll Pop.

After school Mrs. Jewls called Bebe's mother on the phone. "Hello, Mrs. Gunn. This is Mrs. Jewls from Wayside School."

"What's Bebe done now?" asked Mrs. Gunn.

"Bebe hasn't done anything wrong," said Mrs. Jewls. "She's a wonderful girl."

"Well, that's a surprise!" said Mrs. Gunn. "She's always causing trouble at home."

"I wanted to talk to you about that," said Mrs. Jewls. "I think you're being unfair to Bebe. I think she often gets into trouble when really Ray is to **blame**."

"Ray?" asked Mrs. Gunn.

"Yes. I know you think he's a perfect angel," said Mrs. Jewls, "but some children can be angels on the outside and **devil**s underneath."

"Yes, that sounds like Bebe," said Mrs. Gunn.

"I'm not talking about Bebe. I'm talking about Ray."

"Ray?" asked Bebe's mother. "Who's Ray?"

4. HOMEWORK

Mrs. Jewls was teaching the class about **fraction**s and **decimal**s. She explained that .5 was the same as 1/2.

Mac raised his hand.

Mrs. Jewls pretended not to see him.

"Oooh! Oooh!" Mac **groan**ed as he **stretch**ed his hand so high that it hurt.

Mrs. Jewls pretended not to hear him.

Jenny raised her hand.

"Yes, Jenny?" said Mrs. Jewls, glad to **call on** anyone **besides** Mac.

"Mac has his hand raised," said Jenny.

"Um, thank you, Jenny," muttered Mrs. Jewls. "Yes, Mac, what is it?"

"I couldn't find one of my socks this morning," said Mac. "Man, I looked everywhere! In my closet, in the bathroom, in the kitchen, but I just couldn't find it! I asked my mother, but she hadn't seen it either."

"That's very interesting, Mac," Mrs. Jewls said patiently, "but what does that have to do with decimals?"

"Because," said Mac, "I only could find *half* of my socks!"

"Oh. Right," said Mrs. Jewls. "Does anybody else have any questions about decimals? Yes, John?"

"Did you look under the bed?" asked John.

"That was one of the first places I looked," said Mac, "but it wasn't there."

"Did you check the dirty clothes?" asked Ron. "Maybe it was never washed."

"I checked," said Mac.

"Do you have a dog?" asked Bebe. "Maybe your dog took it."

"No, my dog doesn't wear socks," said Mac.

"Why didn't you just put on a different sock?" asked Allison. "Even if it didn't match?"

"I thought of that," said Mac. "See, but then if I wore a sock that didn't match, I'd be left with only one sock of that color for tomorrow. And then if I wore that sock, I'd have to wear a sock that didn't match with it. And so on for the rest of my life! I would never wear matching socks again."

"Well, **be that as it may**," said Mrs. Jewls, "we really need to get back to decimals. Yes, Stephen?"

"Once I had both my socks on," said Stephen, "but I wasn't wearing my shoes. My mom had just **waxed** the floor, too. I slid all around on it like I was skating. It was a lot of fun until I fell against the kitchen table and broke two dishes. Then I got in trouble."

"What's *that* got to do with *my* socks?" Mac asked **impatiently**.

Stephen shrugged.

"Did you ever find your other sock?" asked Leslie.

"Yep," said Mac, "but you'll never guess where. In the **refrigerator!**" He held out his arms in **bewilderment**. "How did it get there?"

No one knew.

"See, here it is," said Mac. He climbed on top of his desk so everyone could see his feet. He pointed to his left foot and said, "This is the sock I had from the beginning." He pointed to his right foot and said, "And this is the sock I couldn't find."

His socks were red with gold **lightning bolt**s down the side.

"Ooh, hot socks!" said Maurecia.

"No, it was cold after being in the refrigerator," said Mac, still standing on top of his desk. "I made it up a song, too, while I was looking for it. You want to hear it?"

He sang:

"I got one sock!

    Lookin' for the other

One sock!

    Lookin' for its brother.

When I find that sock!

    I'll tell you what I'll do.

I'll put it on my foot.

    and I'll stick it in my shoe!"

The bell rang for recess.

"Since we didn't finish the **arithmetic** lesson," said Mrs. Jewls, "you'll have to do the rest of it for homework."

All the kids groaned as they headed outside.

After recess was science. Mrs. Jewls was teaching the class about **dinosaur**s. She told the class that there were two types of dinosaurs; those that ate meat, and those that ate only vegetables.

"You mean like **broccoli**?" asked Rondi.

"I don't think they had broccoli back then," said Mrs. Jewls. "Just as there were different kinds of animals back then, there were also different kinds of vegetables."

Mac raised his hand.

Mrs. Jewls pretended not to see him.

"Ooh! Ooh!" Mac groaned. He looked like he was going to **explode**.

Mrs. Jewls pretended not to hear him. She called on Myron.

"Mac has his hand raised," said Myron.

"Um, thank you, Myron," muttered Mrs. Jewls. "Yes, Mac?"

"My uncle grew the biggest **watermelon** you ever saw in your whole life. Man, it was huge! It was so heavy I couldn't even lift it."

"Mac, what does this have to do with dinosaurs?" asked Mrs. Jewls.

"Because that must have been the kind of watermelon that dinosaurs ate," said Mac.

"Did you eat it?" asked D.J.

"Not all of it," said Mac, shaking his head. "Whew, it was too big for me, and I love watermelon!"

"What did it taste like?" asked Maurecia.

"Delicious!" said Mac. "But lots of **seed**s. You shouldn't eat the seeds. **Otherwise** a watermelon might grow inside your **stomach**. I once heard about a lady who was so fat that everyone thought she was going to have a baby. But she didn't have a baby. She had a watermelon!"

"Was it a boy or a girl?" asked Joy.

Everyone laughed.

Mrs. Jewls never finished her lesson about dinosaurs, so she had to **assign** it for homework.

After school Mac walked home with his girlfriend, Nancy. Nancy's class was on the twenty-third floor of Wayside.

Mac carried his arithmetic book, his science book, his reading book, his language book, and his **spell**ing book.

Nancy didn't have any books. "I'll carry your books for you, Mac," she offered.

Mac gave Nancy his books. "Don't you have any homework?" he asked.

She shook her head.

"Man, it's unfair," said Mac. "Mrs. Jewls assigns more homework than any other teacher in Wayside School."

5. ANOTHER STORY ABOUT SOCKS

Sharie brought a **hobo** to school for show-and-tell.

They stood **side by side** at the front of the room.

"This is a hobo," said Sharie. "I found him on the way to school."

"Ooh, how **neat**!" said Maurecia.

The hobo had long dirty hair and a **scraggly beard**. His shirt was covered with **stain**s. His pants had lots of colorful **patch**es. His coat was too big for him, but it wasn't as big as Sharie's coat.

Sharie was a little girl, but she wore the biggest coat in all of Wayside School.

The hobo wore old black shoes that also looked like they were too big for him, but that might have been because he wasn't wearing any socks.

"Tell the class something about your hobo," said Mrs. Jewls.

"His name is Bob," said Sharie. "I heard him ask a lady for **spare change**. The lady told him to take a bath. I tried to give him a **quarter**, but he said he never took money from kids. He said he likes kids a lot. He said he was once a kid himself."

"Does anybody have any questions they'd like to ask Hobo Bob?" asked Mrs. Jewls.

All the children raised their hands.

The hobo looked around the room. "Yes, you," he said, pointing at Jason.

"When's the last time you took a bath?" asked Jason.

"I never take baths," said the hobo.

"Oh, wow," said Jason. "You're lucky!"

"What about a shower?" asked Myron.

"I just walk outside in the rain," said the hobo.

"When it rains, I have to go inside!" complained Myron.

"Where do you live?" asked Joe.

"All over," said Bob. "In the winter I jump on a south**bound** train and ride until it's warm enough to jump off. In the summer I go north, where it's not too hot."

"How come you're not wearing any socks?" asked Leslie.

"I don't believe in socks," said Bob. "Yes, the boy in the green shirt."

"Were you really a kid once?" asked Todd.

"Yep," said Bob.

"Did you get in trouble a lot?" asked Todd.

"No, I never got in trouble," said Bob.

Todd smiled and **nod**ded his head.

"Did you like to pull girls' **pigtail**s?" asked Paul.

"Of course," said Bob. "Who doesn't?"

"Did you like ice cream?" asked Maurecia.

"I loved it," said Bob.

"What was your favorite subject?" asked Jenny.

"Spelling," said the hobo.

"Spelling!" exclaimed Jenny. "I hate spelling!"

"I once came in first place in a spelling bee, out of all the kids in my school," Bob said proudly.

"Well, how come you became a hobo?" asked Dameon. "I mean, if you're such a good speller?"

"I'm not sure," said Bob. "When you grow up, you're supposed to **turn into** something. Some kids turn into **dentist**s. Others turn into bank **president**s. I didn't turn into anything. So I became a hobo."

"Did you ever try to get a job?" asked Calvin.

"I tried," said Bob. "But nobody would **hire** me because I didn't wear socks."

"So why didn't you just wear socks?" asked Eric Fry.

"I told you. I don't believe in socks. Yes, the girl with the cute front teeth."

Rondi lowered her hand. She was missing her two front teeth. "What do you eat?" she asked.

"Mulligan stew,[1]" said Bob. "My friends and I collect **scrap**s of food all day, and then we cook it up in a big **pot** and share it. It's always different, but very **tasty**."

"Why is it called mulligan stew?" asked Stephen.

"There was once a hobo named Mulligan," said Bob. "He made the first mulligan stew."

"Was he a good cook?" asked Todd.

"No, he was eaten by **cannibal**s."

"**Yuck**!" everyone said together, except for Dana, who was very **confuse**d. She thought Bob had said he was eaten by **cannonball**s.

Allison raised her hand. "Can't you just wear socks, even if you don't believe in them?" she asked.

"Socks!" Bob shouted so loud it **scare**d everybody. "Is that all you kids ever talk about? Socks! Socks! Socks! Albert Einstein[2] didn't wear any socks! Why should I?"

"Who's Albert Einstein?" asked Eric Ovens.

Mrs. Jewls answered that question. She said, "Albert Einstein was the smartest man who ever lived."

"Was he also a hobo?" asked D.J.

"No, he was a great scientist," said Mrs. Jewls.

---

1 stew 스튜. 고기를 큼직하게 썰어서 버터로 볶다가, 양파, 감자, 당근 등을 차례로 넣고 물을 부어 푹 끓인 음식.

2 Albert Einstein 알버트 아인슈타인. 독일 태생의 이론물리학자로 상대성 이론을 발표했다. 1921년 노벨 물리학상을 수상했다.

"Why didn't Albert Einstein wear socks?" asked Joy.

"Because socks make you stupid," said Bob.

"That's not true," said Mrs. Jewls. "Albert Einstein was just too busy thinking about big important things to remember to put on his socks."

"Maybe," said Bob. "But remember I told you I won the school spelling bee? Well, the day I won it, I forgot to wear socks. Think about it."

Everyone thought about it.

"So after that I never wore socks again," said Bob.

Mac raised his hand. "Once I could only find one of my socks," he said. "Man, I looked everywhere for it! Under the bed, in the bathroom. You'll never guess where I finally found it."

"In the **refrigerator**," said Bob.

Mac's mouth dropped open. "How'd you know?"

Bob shrugged. "Where else?"

Everybody had lots more questions for Hobo Bob, but Mrs. Jewls rang her **cowbell**. "Show-and-tell is over," she **announce**d. "Let's all thank Bob."

"Thank you, Bob," everyone said together.

"You're welcome," he replied.

"Do you know the way out of the school?" asked Sharie.

"I'm not sure," said Bob.

"Just go straight down the stairs," said Sharie.

"Thank you," said Bob.

"But don't go in the basement," warned Sharie.

"I won't," said Bob. He shook Sharie's hand, then **wave**d good-bye to the rest of the class and headed out the door.

Everybody waved back. Sharie returned to her seat.

It was time for their weekly spelling test. "Everyone take out a piece of paper and a pencil," said Mrs. Jewls. "The first word is—"

"Wait a second!" called Calvin. "I'm not ready yet."

Mrs. Jewls waited while all the children took off their socks.

6. PIGTAILS

"Hi, Leslie," said Paul.

"Hi, Paul," said Leslie.

They were friends now. Paul hadn't pulled either of her **pigtails** for a long time.

Paul sat in the desk behind Leslie. Once, a long time ago, he had pulled Leslie's pigtails. It felt *great!*

That is—Paul thought it felt great. Leslie didn't think it felt too good.

But that was earlier in the year, when Paul was younger and **immature**. Now he **knew better**.

Still, her two long brown pigtails hung in front of his face, all day, every day.

The bell rang for **recess**.

"Leslie," said Paul. "Can I talk to you a second?"

"Sure, Paul," said Leslie.

They were alone in the room. All the other kids had **rush**ed down the stairs. Mrs. Jewls had run to the teachers' **lounge**.

"I've been good, right?" asked Paul. "I haven't pulled one of your pigtails in a long time, have I?"

"So what do you want, a medal?" asked Leslie.

Paul **chuckle**d. "No, well, can I ask you something?"

"Sure," said Leslie.

Paul took a breath. "May I pull just one of your pigtails?" he asked. "Please?"

"No!" said Leslie.

"Please?" Paul **begg**ed. "I won't pull it hard. No one will have to know. Please? Please? I wouldn't ask if it wasn't important! Please?"

"You're sick!" exclaimed Leslie.

Paul lowered his head. "I'm sorry," he said. "You're right. I don't know what **came over** me. I won't ask again."

"Good," said Leslie. She shook her head in **disgust**.

Paul watched her pigtails **waggle**. "Can I just touch one?" he asked. "I won't even pull it. I promise."

"No!"

"What's wrong with just touching one?" Paul asked.

"**Yuck**, you're **gross**!" said Leslie as she turned and **march**ed out of the room.

As Paul watched her go, her pigtails seemed to **wave** good-bye to him.

He **slap**ped himself in the face with both hands. What's wrong with me? he wondered.

He walked to the side of the room and **lean**ed over the **counter**. He stuck his head out the window to get some fresh air. Down below, he could see the kids playing on the **playground**. They looked like tiny toys.

Leslie stepped back into the classroom. "I'm getting my hair **trim**med tomorrow," she **announce**d. "If you want, I'll save the pieces for you. It'll just be some **split** ends."

Paul was so excited he forgot where he was. He quickly raised his head. It **bash**ed against the **window frame**, then he **bounce**d forward and **topple**d out the window.

Leslie **stare**d in **horror** at the open window, then rushed toward it. She leaned over the counter and looked down.

"Help!" **gasp**ed Paul.

There was one **brick** on the side of the building that stuck out a little farther than the others. Paul **desperate**ly held on to it with both hands.

"I'll go get Louis," said Leslie. "He'll save you."

"No, don't go!" cried Paul. "I can't hold on. My fingers are **slip**ping!"

Leslie reached down for him. "Try to **grab** my hand," she said.

Paul made a grab for it, but missed, then quickly **clutch**ed the brick. "I can't! Help, I'm scared."

"Just don't look down," said Leslie as she tried to stay calm. She pulled her head back in through the window.

"Where are you going!" cried Paul. "Help! Don't leave me."

Leslie looked around Mrs. Jewls's room for a rope or an **extension cord** or something for Paul to grab, but she couldn't find anything.

She returned to the window, sighed, then leaned out backward. Her hands tightly held the edge of the counter as she looked up at the sky. "Grab my pigtails," she said, then **winced**.

A big smile came across Paul's face. "Really?" he asked.

"Just do it!" said Leslie.

The pigtails hung about a foot above Paul's head. He let go of the brick with his right hand and grabbed her right pigtail.

"Yaaaaaaaaahhhhhhhhh!" Leslie **yelp**ed.

He grabbed her left pigtail with his left hand.

"Yaaaaaaaaaaaaaaaahhhhhhhhh!" she screamed.

"Okay, pull me in," said Paul. His legs **dangle**d beneath him.

Leslie's eyes **water**ed in pain as she tried to step away from the window. "I can't!" she groaned. "You're too heavy."

Paul **swung** his legs up against the side of the building. "Try now."

Leslie groaned, then took a small step away from the window as Paul took a small step up the wall. Then they each took another small step. At last Paul managed to get one foot on top of the brick that jutted out.

Leslie pulled her head inside the window. As she took another step, Paul let go of one pigtail and grabbed the **windowsill**. Leslie took another step, pulling Paul the rest of the way through.

They both **collapse**d on the floor, tired and **sore**.

"Ooh, my head hurts," said Leslie.

"Wow, you saved my life," said Paul. "Well, don't worry, some-day I'll save yours."

"You don't have to," said Leslie. "Just don't pull my pigtails anymore."

"I won't," said Paul. Suddenly he laughed.

"What's so funny?" asked Leslie.

"This time your pigtails pulled me."

7. FREEDOM

Myron **crumble**d a cracker[1] on the **windowsill** next to his desk, then looked away. He knew Oddly came only when nobody was looking.

A little while later a bird landed on the windowsill and ate the **crumb**s. Myron watched him **out of the corner of his eye.**

He was a black bird with a pink **breast**. Myron had named him "Oddly." Myron had named him **odd**ly.

"Is that your **dumb** bird again?" asked Kathy.

---

1 cracker 밀가루를 주재료로 하여 얇고 딱딱하게 구운 과자.

"No," said Myron. "Oddly is not *my* bird. I don't own him. He doesn't live in a **cage**. Oddly is free!"

"You're a birdbrain,[2]" said Kathy.

Myron watched Oddly fly away. It made him sad and glad at the same time. He wished he could fly away across the sky with Oddly.

Oddly probably thinks I live in a cage, he realized. Whenever he sees me, I'm sitting in this same desk. He probably thinks this desk is my cage!

So Myron got out of his chair and sat on the floor.

"Myron, what are you doing out of your seat?" asked Mrs. Jewls.

"I want to sit on the floor," said Myron.

Several kids laughed.

"Get back in your seat," ordered Mrs. Jewls.

Myron **reluctant**ly returned to his desk.

I *do* live in a cage, he thought. I'm not allowed out. I have to stay in my cage until the bell rings. Then I have to go down the stairs. Then when it rings again, I have to go up the stairs. Then when it rings again, I have to go down the stairs. Then when it rings again, I have to go up the stairs. I'm never free.

The bell rang.

Myron went down the stairs.

---

2 birdbrain '새대가리', '멍청이'라는 뜻의 속어.

It was so crowded with kids **rush**ing to recess that he couldn't stop if he wanted. It was as if someone had lifted his cage and was carrying him down the stairs.

The bell rang again.

Myron went up the stairs.

At lunch the bell rang again.

Myron went down the stairs.

After lunch the bell rang again.

Myron stood at the bottom of the **staircase** and looked up. "No!" he **declare**d. "I won't go. I have to be free!"

As all the other kids rushed past him, he **eased** his way around to the back of the stairs. As everybody else went up, Myron went down . . .

to

the

basement.

He nervously walked down the old **creaky** staircase. He didn't know what he'd find, or what would find him. He had heard that dead rats were living down there, or worse, maybe even Mrs. Gorf!

Mrs. Gorf was the meanest teacher Myron had ever had. She used to be the teacher on the thirtieth **story**, before Mrs. Jewls **took over**. But nobody believed that Mrs. Gorf was really gone. Everyone said she was still **lurk**ing somewhere inside Wayside School.

He stepped off the last step, at the very bottom of Wayside

School. It was too dark to see. Somewhere he heard a **drip** that **echo**ed all around the cold and **damp** room.

With his arms **outstretch**ed, he stepped across the **gritty** floor. His hand struck against a large, fat pipe above his head. The pipe felt like it was covered with a thousand **spiderweb**s. Still, Myron kept his finger on the pipe as he walked, so he wouldn't get lost. As long as he stayed with the pipe, he knew he'd be able to find his way back to the stairs.

Something **crawl**ed across his hand. He shook it off, then continued walking.

He thought he heard **footstep**s behind him. He stopped walking. The sound of the footsteps continued for a second, then stopped.

He started again, then stopped. The footsteps stopped a few seconds later.

He wasn't alone.

It was too dark for Myron to see who was following him, but he realized that meant that the person couldn't see him either. Whoever was coming after him had to have been following along the pipe, too.

So Myron left the safety of the pipe and headed **blind**ly across the basement.

The footsteps continued behind him.

He stopped.

The footsteps stopped, too.

He **bent** down, then **untie**d and took off his right **sneaker**. He threw it toward the other side of the basement. He heard it hit on the floor, then the footsteps started after it.

Very quietly, he took off his other sneaker and threw it in the same direction.

He never heard his shoe hit the ground.

The footsteps started after him again.

He started to run, but **slip**ped in his socked feet on a **spot** of **slime**. His hands hit loud and hard as he fell on the cold floor.

The footsteps came hurriedly toward him.

He **held his breath** and tried to be as quiet as possible.

A light turned on above his head.

He screamed.

"I believe this is yours," said a **bald** man. He was holding Myron's left sneaker.

Next to him were two men with black **mustache**s. One of the men held a black **attaché case**.

Myron shook his head. "That's not my shoe," he said. "I never saw it before."

The bald man **glance**d at Myron's shoeless feet.

"What's your name?" asked the man with the attaché case.

"Myron," said Myron. He regretted it as soon as he had said it. He wished he had **made up** a **fake** name.

The man opened his attaché case and took out a notebook. "Myron," he repeated, as he **thumb**ed **through** the notebook. "You're supposed to be in Mrs. Jewls's class, at the desk next to the window, in front of Sharie."

"What are you doing out of your cage—I mean, seat?" asked the other man with a mustache.

"I just wanted to be free," **chirp**ed Myron. "Please don't hurt me. If you let me go back to Mrs. Jewls's room, I'll never come down here again."

"Well, do you want to be free, or do you want to be safe?" asked the bald man.

"Huh?" asked Myron.

"You can't have it both ways," said the bald man.

"Do you want to be safe?" asked one of the men with a mustache. "Do you want to sit in the same chair every day, and go up and down the stairs every time the bell rings?"

"You'll have go to school five days a week," said the other man with a mustache. "And you'll have to go to bed at the same time every day."

"But first you'll have to brush your teeth," said the other man with a mustache.

"And you won't be allowed to watch TV until you finish your homework," said the other man with a mustache.

"You'll have to go inside when it rains," said the other man with a mustache.

"But first you'll have to **wipe** your feet," said the other man with a mustache.

"Or you can be free," said the bald man.

The man took a pencil and a piece of paper out of his attaché case. "So do you want to be safe, or do you want to be free?"

Myron looked at the three men. "I want to be free," he said bravely.

The man with the attaché case wrote something on the piece of paper and gave it to Myron. "Sign here," he said.

Myron couldn't read the piece of paper. It was written in some kind of **foreign** language. He signed his name.

The man took the paper and pencil from Myron and put them back into his attaché case. "Okay, you're free," he said.

"Good luck, Myron," said the bald man. "Here, I think you'll need this." He gave Myron his left sneaker, then reached up and pulled the chain. The light turned off.

Myron found himself alone in the darkness. He put his shoe back on, then **hop**ped across the basement floor. He had no idea how to get back.

At last his hand hit against a pipe. But he still didn't know which way to follow it, left or right. He didn't even know if it was the right pipe. He turned left and continued hopping, keeping his finger on the pipe.

He was just about ready to turn around and try the other way when he nearly fell over the bottom stair.

He hopped up the stairs, and continued hopping **all the way** up to Mrs. Jewls's room.

He was tired, **sore**, and dirty.

"You're late, Myron," said Mrs. Jewls. "Go write your name under

DISCIPLINE, then return to your seat for the **arithmetic** test."

But Myron didn't feel like taking an arithmetic test. And he **definite**ly didn't want to write his name on the board.

So he sat on the floor.

And there was nothing Mrs. Jewls could do about it.

He was free.

After school Mrs. Jewls found Myron's other sneaker in the teachers' **lounge**, in the refrigerator.

8. THE BEST PART

Todd brought a toy to school. It was a cute, **adorable** puppy dog. Everyone who saw it said, "Aw."

"Aw," said Jenny. "He has such a sweet face."

"Aw," said Stephen. "Look at her **darling** eyes."

"Aw," said Deedee. "Isn't he the cutest puppy you've ever seen?"

"Aw," said Calvin. "Isn't she adorable?"

Joy sat at the desk behind Todd. **Big deal**, she thought. It's just a **hunk** of plastic that happens to look like a dog.

But even though Joy didn't like Todd's toy, she decided to steal it.

"Wait," said Todd. "Let me show you the best part."

Before he could show them the best part, Mrs. Jewls rang her cowbell. "Take your seats!" she **command**ed. "The bell has rung!"

All the children returned to their desks.

"Todd, go write your name on the **blackboard**."

Todd was the only one who had been in his seat, yet he was the one who got in trouble. That was **typical**.

Mrs. Jewls had a system. The first time someone got in trouble, he had to write his name on the blackboard under the word DISCIPLINE. The second time he got in trouble, he had to put a check next to his name. And if he got in trouble a third time, he had to circle his name and then go home early, at twelve o'clock, on the **kindergarten** bus.

Todd went home on the kindergarten bus every day. Some of the other kids thought he was lucky, but he wished just once he could **make it** to twelve o'clock without getting into trouble three times.

He walked to the front of the room and wrote his name on the blackboard under the word DISCIPLINE.

While Todd was at the board, Joy reached over her desk and into Todd's. She **felt around** for the toy. But as she tried to lift it out, it caught on something and dropped to the floor.

Todd returned to his seat.

"Todd, is that your toy on the floor?" asked Mrs. Jewls.

"Hey, how'd that get there?" asked Todd.

"You know the rules, Todd," said Mrs. Jewls. "Toys must be kept inside your desk, or else I take them. Now bring it here."

Todd gave his toy to Mrs. Jewls.

"Awwww, how **precious**," **coo**ed Mrs. Jewls. "He's the most **lovable** puppy I've ever seen." She kissed Todd's plastic puppy on its plastic nose. "I guess I can **let** you **off** this time," she said. "But try to keep him in your desk." She kissed Todd's toy again, then handed it back to him. "You can **erase** your name from the board, too."

Todd could **hardly** believe it. For the first time ever, he erased his name from the board.

As he headed back to his seat, Mrs. Jewls said, "Here, take a Tootsie Roll Pop too, for the sweeeeeet puppy."

Todd was **amazed**.

So was Joy. Now, more than ever, she wanted that toy!

Out at recess everyone wanted to see Todd's toy.

"It's magic," said Bebe. "It kept you from getting into trouble."

"No, Mrs. Jewls is just a nice teacher," said Todd. "Here, let me show you the best part."

He grabbed hold of the dog's tail and turned it like a **crank**. Suddenly the cute **floppy** ears stood straight up. The mouth opened wide, and the teeth grew into sharp **fang**s.

"Wow," breathed Deedee.

Todd wasn't finished. He pulled the dog's nose and **stretch**ed out its face. The **cheek**s became thin and **bony**. The eyes were no longer sweet, but **grim** and **frighten**ing.

"What a great toy!" said Calvin.

The cute little puppy had **turned into** a mean, hungry, **man-eating** wolf.

"I still haven't shown you the best part," said Todd.

But before he could show them the best part, the bell rang, and everyone ran up the stairs to class.

I've got to get that puppy dog, thought Joy as she stared at the back of Todd's neck. Then I'll never get in trouble again! She didn't know Todd's toy had changed into a man-eating wolf.

Her lunch box was on her **lap**. She quietly opened it and took out a **carton** of cranberry juice and a tiny **straw**.

She stuck the straw into the carton and **suck**ed up some juice into it.

She waited for Mrs. Jewls to turn around, then blew the juice out of the straw. It **splatter**ed against Todd's neck.

He **slap**ped the back of his neck with his hand.

Joy laughed to herself. She sucked up some more juice, took careful **aim**, and **fired**.

Todd turned around, but Joy already had the straw out of her mouth and was looking down at her book.

Todd **rub**bed his neck and faced front.

Joy sucked up more juice and blew it onto Todd's neck.

"Hey!" he shouted, turning around.

"Leave me alone, Todd—I'm trying to work," said Joy.

"Todd, what's the matter with you?" asked Mrs. Jewls. "I try to be nice, but you just take **advantage**. Now go write your name on the blackboard."

Todd walked to the front of the room. He still thought Mrs. Jewls was the nicest teacher in the world. He looked up at the clock. It was almost eleven. I might just make it today, he thought. I just might make it. He started to write his name when he heard a loud scream.

He turned around and saw Joy jumping up and down and **waving** her hand in the air. His toy was **biting** her **pinky**, and she couldn't shake it off.

"Help!" screamed Joy as she **hop**ped around the room. "Todd, how do I get it off? Todd? Please?"

Todd smiled. "There," he said. "That's the best part."

9. MUSH

Miss Mush **wipe**d her hands on her **apron**. She smiled at the children who were lined up at the **cafeteria**. It warmed her heart to see how much they liked her food.

Maurecia was first in line.

"And what would you like today, Maurecia?" Miss Mush asked.

She knew the name of every child in Wayside School.

Maurecia looked at the sign.

SPECIAL TODAY:

MUSHROOM SURPRISE

"Just milk," said Maurecia. "I brought my lunch." Miss Mush smiled and gave Maurecia a **carton** of milk.

Joy was next in line.

"And what would you like, Joy?" asked Miss Mush.

"Milk," said Joy.

Miss Mush smiled and gave Joy a carton of milk. "And what would you like, Jason?"

"Milk, please," said Jason.

"Just milk," said Dameon.

"Milk," said D.J.

"Milk," said Leslie.

It was almost Ron's turn. He hadn't brought a lunch. He normally brought a peanut butter and jelly sandwich to school, but there hadn't been a single slice of bread in his house this morning.

"I know!" his mother had said. "I'll give you some money and you can buy a nice hot lunch from Miss Mush!" She thought it was a **brilliant** idea.

"Can't I just have a peanut butter and jelly sandwich without the bread?" Ron had asked.

Now he looked up at the sign.

SPECIAL TODAY:
MUSHROOM SURPRISE

He wished he weren't so hungry.

This was the eighteenth day **in a row** that the special was Mushroom Surprise. It was called Mushroom Surprise because it would have been a surprise if anybody had ever ordered it. No one ever did—except Louis, of course. That's why they'd had it for eighteen days. There **was** always plenty **left over**.

"Milk," said Terrence.

"Milk," said Sharie.

"Milk," said Calvin.

"Milk, please," said Bebe.

"And what would you like today, Ron?" asked Miss Mush.

Ron took a breath. "Mushroom Surprise," he **squeak**ed.

Tears of joy filled Miss Mush's eyes. She **blew her nose** on her apron, then said, "One Mushroom Surprise, coming right up!"

Tears came to Ron's eyes too, but for a different reason. He looked at the Mushroom Surprise. It was sort of green.

So was Ron.

Miss Mush proudly **dump**ed a hot **lump** of Mushroom Surprise on a paper **plate** and handed it to Ron. He put it on his **tray**, then pushed it over to the **cash register**, where he paid for it.

The news quickly spread around the cafeteria, then up and down the stairs and out to the playground.

"Ron ordered the Mushroom Surprise!"

"Ron ordered the Mushroom Surprise!"

Mrs. Jewls was sitting in the teachers' **lounge** on the twelfth floor when Bebe **burst** into the room.

All the teachers were shocked to see her.

"Bebe, you're not allowed in here," said Mrs. Jewls. "This is a secret place."

"Ron ordered the Mushroom Surprise!" Bebe shouted; then she ran back up to the cafeteria.

As Ron sat down at a table, eighty-seven kids crowded around him to watch him eat.

"I wonder what the surprise is," said Deedee. She had the best view. She was pushed right up **alongside** Ron's chair.

"Maybe it tastes good," said Leslie. "Maybe that's the surprise."

"No, I think it's called Mushroom Surprise because after you eat it, it's a surprise if you don't die," said Mac.

"Louis eats it. He's not dead," said Jason.

"Louis has been eating Miss Mush's food for so long, he's **immune** to it," said Allison.

Ron **dug** his plastic fork into the **goop**. He raised it to his mouth.

Dana covered her eyes. "I can't watch!" she **exclaim**ed.

Ron opened his mouth wide. The fork entered. He brought

the fork out again.

It was empty!

Ron **chew**ed twice, then **swallow**ed.

"He ate it!" Deedee announced for those who couldn't see.

Stephen screamed.

"Hmm," said Ron. "Not too bad. It sort of tastes like a **mixture** of bananas and **spinach**."

"What's the surprise?" asked Deedee.

Ron looked at Deedee. His face **flush**ed and his eyes changed color. His whole body began to shake, like a **washing machine** on the spin cycle.[1]

Deedee was afraid he was going to **throw up**. She tried to **get away**, but with everyone crowded around, there was no room for her to move.

But Ron didn't throw up. He stood up, put his arms around Deedee's neck, and kissed her **smack** on the lips.

He sat back down. His eyes returned to their normal color.

"Ylah!" said Deedee, wiping her mouth on her **sleeve**.

"What's the matter?" asked Ron.

"Don't you know what you just did?" asked Allison.

He **shrug**ged. "I ate some Mushroom Surprise. It wasn't bad. Sort of like a mixture of a hot dog and grape jelly. I wonder what the surprise is."

---

1 spin cycle 세탁기의 탈수 단계.

56

He dug his plastic fork back into the goop.

Everybody **ran away**.

When Mrs. Jewls entered the cafeteria, no one was there except for Ron. He was sitting alone at a table eating Mushroom Surprise.

Mrs. Jewls sat down next to him. "Hi, Ron," she said. "So how does it taste? And what's the surprise?"

Ron swallowed another **mouthful**. He looked at his teacher. His face flushed and his eyes changed color. . . .

10. MUSIC

Benjamin still hadn't told anybody he wasn't Mark Miller.

His grades had never been better. Mark Miller is a lot smarter than Benjamin Nushmutt, he thought.

When they chose up teams for **kickball**, he was always the first one picked. Mark Miller is a better kicker than Benjamin Nushmutt, he realized.

The girls in the class liked him too. Mark Miller is better looking than Benjamin Nushmutt, he decided.

But **unfortunate**ly, he knew he had to tell Mrs. Jewls his real name. He **sigh**ed, then slowly raised his hand.

Mrs. Jewls gave him a tambourine.

He had been so busy thinking about his problem, he hadn't noticed that Mrs. Jewls was passing out musical **instruments**. She had just asked, "Who would like the tambourine?" So when he raised his hand, she gave it to him.

"Who would like the triangle?" asked Mrs. Jewls. Joe raised his hand, and Mrs. Jewls gave it to him.

"Why is it called a triangle?" asked Joe.

"I don't know," said Mrs. Jewls.

"Maybe because it's shaped like a triangle," suggested John.

"No, that can't be it," said Mrs. Jewls. "Then the tambourine would have to be called a circle."

"Maybe it was **invent**ed by a person named Joe Triangle," said Rondi.

"That's probably it," said Mrs. Jewls. She held up the next instrument. It was a glockenspiel.[1] "Who would like the glockenspiel?" she asked.

Sharie raised her hand.

Nobody asked why it was called a glockenspiel. It was **obvious**.

Mrs. Jewls gave the bells to Stephen.

"Why are they called bells?" he asked.

Nobody knew.

Joy got the bongo drums.[2] Todd got the bass drum.[3] Jenny

---

1   glockenspiel 글로켄슈필. 조율된 금속 막대를 피아노 건반과 같은 방식으로 배열한 타악기.
2   bongo drums 봉고. 크고 작은 단면 드럼 두 개를 붙여 만든 타악기.

snared the snare drum.[4] And Leslie got the kettledrum.[5]

When they **bang**ed on them, it hurt everybody else's **eardrum**s.

Mrs. Jewls gave one cymbal[6] to Calvin and the other cymbal to Bebe.

D.J. got the gong.[7] The three Erics got kazoos.[8]

Mrs. Jewls shouted, "*Uno, dos, tres, cuatro!*[9]"

The children all played their instruments. They shook, **rattle**d, **rock**ed, and rolled.

Joy **bong**ed her bongos. D.J. **gong**ed his gong. Sharie glockened her glockenspiel. Stephen **jingle**d his bells. Calvin and Bebe slapped their cymbals together. And Joe's triangle went *ting*.

But something didn't sound right.

"What's wrong, Mark?" Mrs. Jewls shouted over the music. "Why aren't you playing the tambourine?"

"My name's not Mark," said Benjamin. "It's Benjamin Nushmutt. I'm sorry for not telling you before."

"What?" asked Mrs. Jewls. "I can't hear you."

---

3   bass drum 베이스 드럼. 낮은 음을 내는 커다란 드럼. 몸통 양쪽에 가죽을 대고, 머리가 공 모양을 한 북채로 한쪽 면의 가죽을 쳐서 소리를 낸다.
4   snare drum 스네어 드럼. 두 개의 막을 씌운 납작한 드럼. 아랫면 막에 스네어라고 하는 쇠 울림줄을 대어 달그락거리는 소리를 낸다.
5   kettledrum 케틀 드럼. 포물선 모양의 구리 통 위에 막을 팽팽하게 씌운 악기.
6   cymbal 심벌. 얇은 접시 모양의 금속으로 만든 타악기로 이 원판 두 개를 서로 맞부딪쳐서 소리를 낸다.
7   gong 공. 청동이나 놋쇠로 만든 원반 모양의 타악기. 악기 몸통을 채로 두드려서 소리를 낸다.
8   kazoos 커주. 관의 일부분에 양피지를 붙인 관악기.
9   uno, dos, tres, cuatro 스페인어로 1, 2, 3, 4.

"My name isn't Mark!" he said. "It's Benjamin."

"Louder!" said Mrs. Jewls.

So everyone played louder.

Todd **bash**ed his bass drum. Leslie cooked on her kettledrum. Calvin and Bebe **crash**ed their cymbals together. And Joe's triangle went *ting*.

"My name is Benjamin!" shouted Benjamin.

Mrs. Jewls put her hand to her ear. "Louder!" she said.

So everyone played louder.

D.J. kabonged his gong. Joy chongoed her bongos. Paul splacked his castanets.[10] Jenny spaghettied her snare drum. Calvin and Bebe wammered their cymbals. And Joe's triangle went *ting*.

"My name's Benjamin Nushmutt," **holler**ed Benjamin Nushmutt.

"Louder!" **yell**ed Mrs. Jewls.

So everyone played louder.

The three Erics screamed into their kazoos. Calvin and Bebe ran to opposite sides of the room with their cymbals, then **charged** toward each other.

Suddenly the door flew open, and a man entered. Benjamin had never seen him before.

The whole class became very quiet.

It was Mr. Kidswatter, the **principal**.

Calvin and Bebe **screech**ed to a **halt** just **in time**. Their cymbals

---

10 castanets 캐스터네츠. 조개 모양의 타악기. 상아 또는 단단한 나무로 만들며, 손가락에 끼고서 부딪쳐 소리를 낸다.

were less than an inch apart.

"Is something the matter, Mr. Kidswatter?" asked Mrs. Jewls.

"Several teachers have **complain**ed about your music," said Mr. Kidswatter. "Their students are having trouble hearing."

"I understand," said Mrs. Jewls.

"Good," said Mr. Kidswatter. He walked out of the room.

"Okay, you heard Mr. Kidswatter," said Mrs. Jewls. "We'll have to play louder so everyone can hear. *Uno, dos, tres, cuatro!*"

They shook, rattled, rocked, and rolled.

Benjamin frampled his tambourine.

"Excellent, Mark!" shouted Mrs. Jewls.

He smiled. He had never played so well before. Mark Miller is a better **musician** than Benjamin Nushmutt, he thought.

11. KATHY AND D.J.

Down on the **playground** Kathy was singing her favorite song.

> *"Wayside School is falling down,*
>   *falling down, falling down.*
> *Wayside School is falling down,*
>   *my fair lady.*
> *"Kids go* **splat** *as they hit the ground,*
>   *hit the ground, hit the ground.*
> *Kids go* splat *as they hit the ground,*
>   *my fair lady."*

D.J. was walking across the playground with his head down.

"Hi, Dr. **Jolly**," said Louis. Louis called D.J. "Doctor Jolly" because he was always smiling.

But now D.J.'s smile was **upside down**. He looked up at Louis.

Louis had never seen such a sad face. "What's wrong?" he asked.

D.J. just shook his head, then looked back down at the ground and sadly walked away.

Louis felt like crying.

"Hey, Louis, what's wrong with D.J.?" asked Ron.

"He's so sad!" said Deedee.

"I don't know," said Louis, shaking his head. "Hey, you guys want to play **kickball**?"

"No thanks," said Deedee. "I can't have fun when D.J. is unhappy."

"Me neither," said Ron.

Across the playground, all the children quit their games when they saw D.J. Nobody could have fun when D.J. looked so sad.

Except Kathy! She sang:

*"Broken bones and blood and **gore**,*
blood and gore, blood and gore.
Broken bones and blood and gore,
my fair lady.
"We don't have no school no more,
school no more, school no more.
We don't have no school no more,

64

my fair lady."

The bell rang. D.J. sadly looked up at the school and sighed.

"Hey, Deej, **snap out of it**," said Myron.

D.J. **stare**d through his friend.

"You want to walk up the stairs with us, Dojo?" asked Dameon.

D.J. shook his head. "I need to be alone," he **mumble**d.

Dameon and Myron looked at each other, then started up the stairs, leaving their sad friend behind.

D.J. headed on up, but stopped **halfway** between the ninth and tenth floors and sat down. He lowered his face into his hands and cried.

A moment later someone **burst** out laughing.

D.J. opened his eyes and saw Kathy **stand**ing **over** him.

"You shouldn't sit on the stairs, **Dumb Jerk**!" said Kathy with **glee**. "I almost kicked you in the head."

Kathy always called D.J. "Dumb Jerk."

She didn't like D.J. because he was always smiling. Now she was glad to see him so sad.

"Hi, Kathy," said D.J.

She **plop**ped down on the stair next to him. "What happened?" she asked. "Did your dog die?" She laughed.

D.J. shook his head.

"Are your parents getting **divorce**d?" she asked **hopeful**ly. "Did your house burn down?"

"No," said D.J. "My great-grandfather gave me a gold watch. It was over a hundred years old. I brought it to school today and—"

"You lost it!" Kathy exclaimed with **delight**.

D.J. sadly **nod**ded.

Kathy laughed. "Oh boy,[1] are you going to get in trouble!" She **rub**bed her hands together. "Your parents will **ground** you forever!"

"No, my parents never **punish** me," said D.J. "They know I learn from my mistakes."

"Oh," said Kathy, a little disappointed. "But your great-grandfather will *hate* you!" she said. "And he'll never give you another present for the rest of your life. Not even for your birthday!"

"No, he loves me **no matter** what I do," said D.J. "He likes people, not *things*."

Again Kathy was disappointed. "But the watch was **worth** a lot of money," she tried. "And *you'll* have to pay for it out of *your* **allowance**." She laughed **triumphant**ly, sure she had gotten him this time.

"I don't get an allowance," said D.J. "I don't like money."

Kathy **frown**ed. Still, she knew there had to be some reason why he was sad about losing the watch. "You'll never know what time it is!" she **squawk**ed.

"So?" asked D.J. "Time isn't real."

---

1 boy 소년이나 남자아이를 나타내는 명사가 아니라, 놀람이나 기쁨을 나타내는 감탄사로 '어머나' 혹은 '맙소사'라는 의미이다.

Kathy didn't know what D.J. meant by that, but she didn't care. "Well, if you don't know what time it is," she told him, "you'll miss all your favorite television shows."

"I don't have a favorite television show," said D.J. "I never watch television." He thought a moment. "I'm not sure if we have a TV in our house or not. Maybe there's one in a **closet** somewhere."

Kathy **glare**d at him. "Well, then how come you're so sad you lost that dumb watch?" she demanded.

"I'm afraid a bird might think it's food and **choke** on it," said D.J.

"Is that all?" **shriek**ed Kathy.

D.J. smiled. "I guess you're right," he said. "A bird probably wouldn't choke. In fact, maybe he could use it to make a **nest**. I hope so, don't you?" He hopped to his feet. "Thanks for talking to me, Kathy. I feel a lot better now. You're a good friend."

He hurried up to Mrs. Jewls's room, taking the stairs two and three at a time.

As D.J.'s smile turned up, Kathy's smile turned down. She followed up after him, **grumbling** to herself. "He doesn't like money. He doesn't worry about time. He never watches television. Why is he always so happy?"

Everyone in Mrs. Jewls's class cheered when they saw D.J. enter the room smiling.

Kathy walked in behind him frowning.

Mrs. Jewls was getting ready to show a movie. She gave D.J.

a piece of black construction paper.[2]

"Hey, look!" exclaimed Myron. "Oddly found a watch!"

Oddly, the bird, dropped the watch on the **windowsill**.

Kathy couldn't believe it! "It's D.J.'s," she **griped**.

Myron gave the watch to D.J.

"Here, you can have it, Kathy," said D.J. with a big smile. "It's worth a lot of money, and this way you won't miss any of your favorite television shows."

Kathy took the watch from him and put it around her **wrist**. "It'll probably make my skin turn green," she **groused**.

Mrs. Jewls started the movie **projector**. Stephen turned off the lights. Dameon pulled down the **shade**s. D.J. held the piece of black construction paper under his nose, because his smile was so bright.

---

2   construction paper 마분지.

12. PENCILS

Jason borrowed a pencil from Allison. When he gave it back to her, it was full of teeth **mark**s.

Allison held the pencil by its **point**. "**Yuck!**" she said. "You **chew**ed on it."

Jason felt **awful**. It is very **embarrass**ing to borrow somebody's pencil and then chew on it. "Sorry," he said. "I didn't do it **on purpose**."

"You can keep it," said Allison. She dropped the pencil on Jason's desk, then raised her hand. "Mrs. Jewls, can I go to the bathroom? I have to wash my hands. Jason **slobber**ed all over my pencil."

Everybody laughed.

Jason turned red. "I'm sorry, Allison," he said. "I know it's a **disgust**ing habit. I just can't help it."

"Don't let Jason touch any of my books," said Allison as she headed out of the room. "He might eat them!"

Everybody laughed again.

"Here, you can eat my book, Jason," said Todd. "I don't like it anyway."

Mrs. Jewls made Todd write his name on the **blackboard** under the word **DISCIPLINE**.

Jason was so mad at himself, he broke the chewed-up pencil to bits.

That wasn't a smart thing to do.

"Everybody take out a pencil and a piece of paper," said Mrs. Jewls. "It's time for our **spell**ing test."

Jason **slapp**ed himself on the **forehead**. I'm so stupid! he thought. "Rondi, may I borrow a pencil, please?" he asked.

Rondi **made a face**. "All my pencils are new," she said. "How do I know you won't eat it?"

"I won't," said Jason. "I promise."

"You better not," said Rondi. She gave him one of her pencils.

It was new and freshly **sharpen**ed. Jason liked the way it smelled.

"The first word is 'orchestra,'" said Mrs. Jewls.

Jason tried to remember how to spell *orchestra*. He stuck the back of the pencil in his mouth.

"Second word, 'garbanzo.[1]'"

Jason chewed on the **eraser**.

When the spelling test was over, Rondi's pencil was worse than Allison's.

Jason looked at it in **horror**. He didn't even remember chewing it. Oh, no! he thought. What am I going to do? He stuck it inside his desk.

"Jason, may I have my pencil back, please?" asked Rondi.

"What pencil?" asked Jason.

"The one I lent you," said Rondi.

Jason opened his desk and pretended to look for it. "I don't know where it is," he said.

"Mrs. Jewls, Jason stole my pencil!" called Rondi.

"Jason, give Rondi back her pencil," said Mrs. Jewls.

He gave it to her.

"You chewed on it!" exclaimed Rondi.

Everyone laughed.

"No I didn't," said Jason. "Those are your teeth marks."

"How can they be my teeth marks?" asked Rondi. She smiled. She was missing her two front teeth.

"So?" said Jason. "You don't chew pencils with your front teeth. You chew them with your back teeth."

"How do you know?" asked Rondi.

---

1   garbanzo 병아리콩. 노란빛이 도는 갈색의 작은 콩.

"Um, um, uh," said Jason.

Mrs. Jewls made Jason write his name on the board under the word DISCIPLINE because he chewed Rondi's pencil, then lied about it. "And try not to eat the **chalk**," she said.

Everyone laughed.

Rondi threw the chewed-up pencil out the window.

It hit Louis on the head.

Mrs. Jewls gave Dameon a **stack** of **work sheet**s and asked him to pass them out. They **contain**ed **arithmetic** problems.

Jason had to borrow another pencil.

"Allison, may I borrow another pencil, please?" he asked.

"Eat my socks," said Allison.

That wasn't such a bad idea, Jason realized. If he **stuff**ed a sock in his mouth, he wouldn't be able to chew a pencil.

Myron looked at his work sheet. "I don't feel like doing this stuff," he said. "Here, Jason, you can have my pencil."

"Thanks, Myron," said Jason. "I promise not to chew it." He hoped he'd be able to keep his promise.

He thought about asking Mrs. Jewls for a Tootsie Roll Pop. If I'm **suck**ing on that, I won't chew Myron's pencil. And a Tootsie Roll Pop would probably taste better than Allison's socks. He didn't know for sure because he had never tasted Allison's socks.

But before he could ask Mrs. Jewls, Mrs. Jewls called him. "Jason, will you come here for a moment," she said. "I think I know how to keep you from chewing pencils."

Jason smiled as he walked to her desk. "I like the purple ones," he told her.

But Mrs. Jewls didn't give him a Tootsie Roll Pop. Instead, she taped his mouth shut with **heavy-duty masking tape**. She had to use a lot of tape, because Jason had the second biggest mouth in the class. "There," she said.

Jason started back to his seat.

"Aren't you even going to say thank you?" asked Mrs. Jewls.

"Mhhmm hhm," said Jason.

"You're welcome," said Mrs. Jewls.

"Hey, Jason," **tease**d Allison. "You look like a **mummy**!"

"Don't **sneeze**," said Rondi. "You'll blow your head off!"

They both laughed.

"Mh mhhh mhrhhmmm!" Jason said back to them. It was a very bad thing to say. He wasn't supposed to use words like that.

"You better not pull the tape off," said Rondi. "You might **rip** off your lips!"

They both laughed again.

Jason had never been more embarrassed in his whole life. His ears burned as he set to work on the arithmetic problems.

They were tough problems. Several times the pencil **crash**ed against the tape, but the tape held firm.

Mrs. Jewls was very proud of herself. Not only did the tape **protect** Myron's pencil, but Mrs. Jewls also noticed that Jason was quieter than he'd ever been. I should tape all their mouths shut, she thought. Then they'd all be so nice and quiet.

It was such a good idea, she wondered why no other teacher had ever thought of it.

13. A GIGGLE BOX, A LEAKY FAUCET, AND A FOGHORN

Every day after lunch Mrs. Jewls read a story to the class.

Dana hated stories.

The last book Mrs. Jewls had read was a story about a pig and spider. The pig was real cute and the spider was very **wise**.

Dana thought it was a **horrible** book. It made her laugh too much. Everyone else laughed too, but the problem was that Dana always kept laughing long after everyone else in the class had stopped. It was very **embarrass**ing. And sometimes she **broke out** laughing at a part that wasn't even funny because she remembered something funny that had happened earlier.

John called her a **giggle** box.

That only made her laugh harder.

Once she broke up laughing in the middle of an **arithmetic** test because she remembered something funny the pig had said.

"There goes the giggle box," said John.

She hated John.

But that wasn't the worst part of the book. In the end, the spider died.

Dana couldn't stop crying. And she thought it was so **silly**, too, because in real life she didn't even like spiders! She **squash**ed them all the time.

John called her a **leaky faucet**. "Somebody better call a **plumber** to fix the leaky faucet," he said.

She laughed through her tears. She hated John.

Once in music, they had learned a song about a dragon. When the song begins the dragon is very brave, but then he loses his only friend, so he isn't brave anymore. He just goes back to his **cave**, where he is sad and lonely for the rest of his life.

The song always made Dana cry. Every **recess** John and Joe would **chase** after her, singing it. She'd run across the playground with her hands over her ears and tears **stream**ing down her face.

The bell rang. Lunch was over. Dana nervously walked up the stairs to Mrs. Jewls's room. Mrs. Jewls would start a new book today. She hoped it wouldn't be funny or sad. She hoped Mrs. Jewls would read a **boring** story with no jokes.

When she got to class, John and Joe were standing by her desk waiting for her.

"Happy Birthday, Dana," said John. He was holding a present. It was **wrap**ped in green paper and had a pink **bow**.

"But it's not my birthday," said Dana.

"Well, that's okay," said John. "You can have it anyway. Since I'm always **teasing** you." He and Joe **snicker**ed.

Dana eagerly **tore** off the wrapping paper. Maybe John wasn't so bad after all, she thought.

It was a box of tissues.

John and Joe laughed **hysterical**ly.

"That's not funny!" said Dana. She raised her **fist** and started to chase after them.

Mrs. Jewls rang her **cowbell**, and all the children settled quietly in their seats.

"We are ready to begin a new story," said Mrs. Jewls. She held up the book. "It's called 'Stinky.'"

Dana laughed at the title, then quickly covered her mouth.

"It's about a cute and **playful skunk**," said Mrs. Jewls.

"Oh, no!" **gasp**ed Dana. She knew animal stories always made her cry. The animal's mother would get shot by human **hunter**s. Or else humans would build a shopping center and destroy the animal's home.

She hated humans. But she knew that was silly, because she was a human, and so were all her friends. The only human she really hated was John, and she didn't think he was even human!

Mrs. Jewls read:

"It was such a beautiful day, Stinky and his mother went for a walk across the forest. 'Hi, Stinky,' said Charlie the **chipmunk**. 'Hi, Charlie,' said Stinky. '**Come along**, Stinky,' called his mother. Stinky hurried after her. They came to a road. Suddenly Stinky heard a noise he had never heard before. It was very loud, like **thunder**. A car, driven by humans, was **speed**ing toward him! '**Look out!**' shouted his mother. Stinky stopped in the middle of the road and stared at the **onrushing** car. He had never seen a car before. His mother pushed him out of the way just **in time**. He was safe, but **unfortunate**ly, the car **ran over** his mother. 'Mama, Mama,' he **sob**bed over and over again, but his mother didn't answer. She was dead."

Dana cried.

"Uh-oh, there goes the leaky faucet," said John. He and Joe laughed.

Dana **sniffle**d and **wipe**d her eyes, but the tears wouldn't stop. She just kept thinking about poor Stinky. What would he do without his mother? she wondered. Maybe he could go live with Charlie the chipmunk, she hoped.

She pulled a tissue out of the box John had given her and loudly **blew her nose**.

"There goes the foghorn,[1]" said John.

Dana laughed into her tissue. She blew her nose again, even

louder.

"It must be a very **foggy** day," said John.

The next day after lunch Dana hurried up the thirty **flights of stairs** before the bell rang, so she could talk to Mrs. Jewls before class started.

"Yes, Dana?" said Mrs. Jewls.

"Can I leave the room when you read today?" asked Dana.

"Why?" asked Mrs. Jewls.

"Because I hate stories," said Dana. "They make me laugh and cry too much."

"You don't hate stories, Dana," Mrs. Jewls told her. "You love stories. I wish everybody laughed and cried as much as you."

"Really?" asked Dana. She couldn't believe it. All this time she thought she hated stories when really she loved them. She was glad she really loved stories.

Suddenly she **made a face**. "Oh, yuck!" she said.

"What is it?" asked Mrs. Jewls.

"What if I really love John, too?"

---

1 foghorn 무적(霧笛). 항해 중인 배에게 안개를 조심하라는 뜻에서 울리는 고동. 다른 선박과의 충돌을 피하거나 자신의 위치를 나타내기 위해 울린다.

14. CALVIN'S BIG DECISION

It was Calvin's birthday. His mother had made chocolate cupcakes with jelly beans[1] on top. Mrs. Jewls passed them out to the class.

"Hey, Dana," said Leslie. "I'll **trade** you my black jelly bean for your red one."

"Okay," said Dana.

Everyone traded jelly beans. That was the most fun part of the party.

Bebe was very excited. "Tell everybody what you're getting

---

1 jelly bean 젤리 빈. 콩 모양의 젤리로 다양한 맛이 있다.

for your birthday, Calvin!" she said.

"I don't know," Calvin **mumble**d as he stared at his yellow jelly bean.

"He's getting the best present!" said Bebe.

"What are you getting, Calvin?" asked Mrs. Jewls.

Calvin frowned. "I don't know!" he griped. "I mean, I know what it is, but I don't know what it is."

"Huh?" asked Jason.

"See, I usually get toys," Calvin tried to explain. "But they always break, or get lost, or something happens to them. But this year I'm getting something I'll never lose. I'll have it for the rest of my life."

"What is it?" asked Terrence.

"A **tattoo**," said Calvin.

"Oooh, how **neat**!" **exclaim**ed Maurecia.

Everyone thought it was a great present.

"You're so lucky, Calvin," said Rondi. "I wish I could get a tattoo too! Instead I got a tutu.[2]"

"I got a tutu too," said Dana.

"My parents won't let me get a tattoo," **complain**ed John.

"My parents wouldn't let me get one either," said Calvin. "Then, for my birthday, they said I could get one. But now I can't decide what to get. My dad's taking me to the tattoo **parlor** after school today! I just can't make up my mind."

---

2 tutu 발레리나가 착용하는 스커트.

"Get a snake," said Stephen.

"No, get an eagle," said Deedee. "They're the best!"

"A dead rat!" suggested Kathy.

"I just don't know," said Calvin. "I've never had to make such a tough decision. Nothing else I do matters very much. It's not like choosing jelly beans! If you pick the wrong color jelly bean, **big deal**, you can always **spit** it out. But once you get a tattoo, you can't change your mind. You can't erase tattoos. Whatever I get I'll have for the rest of my life!"

"Get a **naked** lady," said Jason.

Calvin shook his head. "I just don't know. I just don't know."

"Where are you going to put your tattoo?" asked Allison.

Calvin threw up his hands. "I don't know!"

"You should put it on your arm," said Myron. "That's the best place for tattoos."

"You're crazy, Myron," said Todd. "Put it on your **chest**, Calvin."

"I know where you should put it," said Dana. "But I can't say." She **giggle**d like a **maniac**. Then she whispered it in Jenny's ear. Jenny giggled too.

All day everyone had lots of suggestions for Calvin. they told him what kind of tattoo he should get, and where he should put it. A rainbow on his **forehead**. A flower on his **cheek**. An **anchor** on his arm.

It was easy for the others to make suggestions. They wouldn't have to live with it for the rest of their lives.

"I just don't know," Calvin repeated over and over again.

Bebe drew a lot of pictures for him, in case he wanted to choose one of those. She drew lions, tigers, **buffalo**es, and butterflies.

"If you like one, I can draw it on your skin for you," said Bebe. "Then the tattoo man can **trace** over it."

"I just don't know," **mutter**ed Calvin. "I just don't know."

After school Calvin's father **pick**ed him **up** and drove him to the tattoo parlor.

The next day when he walked into class, everybody stared at him. They couldn't see a tattoo.

"Did you get one?" asked Maurecia.

Calvin smiled. "Yep," he said.

"Where is it?" asked Jason.

Dana gasped. "I know where!" she exclaimed.

She and Jenny giggled.

"Well, what'd you get?" asked Todd.

"It was a real tough decision," said Calvin. "I almost got a **leopard** fighting a snake. But then my dad told me to think about it. He said it was sort of like getting a second nose. You may think you want another nose, because that way if one nose gets **stuff**ed up, you can breathe through the other nose. But then he asked me, 'Calvin, do you really want two noses?'"

"Your father is very **wise**," said Mrs. Jewls.

Calvin nodded. "That made me think," he said. "I decided I didn't want a snake and a leopard fighting on my body for the rest of my life. I suddenly knew **exact**ly what I wanted."

He pulled up his left pant leg. There was a small tattoo just above his **ankle**.

Everyone crowded around to look at it.

"A potato!" exclaimed Leslie. "How stupid!"

"That's the worst tattoo in the world!" said Mac.

They all thought it was a **dumb** tattoo.

"Anything is better than a potato!" said Jason.

"It's a pretty potato," said Bebe, trying to be nice. "I wish I could draw potatoes that good." But even Bebe thought it was a dumb tattoo.

"I like potatoes," said Calvin.

"I would hope so," said Mrs. Jewls.

Calvin could tell Mrs. Jewls didn't like his tattoo either.

"I would have gotten an eagle," said Deedee, "**soar**ing across the sky!"

"Not me," said Terrence. "I would have gotten a lion!"

"I would have gotten a kangaroo," said Leslie.

All day everyone told Calvin what they would have gotten: a fire-breathing dragon, a **lightning bolt**, a **creature** from **outer space**.

None of them said they would have gotten a potato.

But Calvin **knew better**. He knew it was easy for his friends to say what they would have gotten, because they really hadn't had to choose. He was the only one who really knew what it was like to pick a tattoo. Even Mrs. Jewls didn't know that.

He looked at his potato. He smiled. It made him happy.

He was sure he had made the right choice.

At least he was pretty sure.

15. SHE'S BACK!

Deedee ran across the **playground** screaming.

At first Louis thought she was just having fun, but then he realized something was wrong. He hurried after her and **grab**bed her arm.

"Deedee, are you all right?" he asked.

She **stare**d at him **wide-eyed** as she continued to scream.

Several other kids **gather**ed around. "What's wrong with Deedee?" asked Myron.

"I don't know," said Louis.

Deedee **hiccup**ped three times, then gasped, "I saw her!"

"Who?" asked Louis.

Deedee didn't answer—she just stared right through him.

But everyone else knew whom Deedee had seen. Most of them had seen her too, during the last two weeks.

"Where was she?" asked Todd.

"On the monkey bars,[1]" said Deedee, still **trembling** and breathing hard. "I was hanging **upside down**, and suddenly she was hanging upside down right next to me!"

"Did she **wiggle** her ears?" asked Jenny.

"Only one," said Deedee. "I jumped off and **ran away** before she could wiggle the other one."

"That's good," said Rondi.

"Who is she?" asked Louis. "A **hippopotamus**?"

"No!" said Myron with a laugh. "Why do you say that?"

"Because when a hippopotamus gets mad, it wiggles its ears."

"She's worse than a hippopotamus," said Allison.

"I saw her last week, at the water **fountain**," said Todd. "I **bent** down to get a drink, and then there she was, drinking at the **faucet** next to me."

"I saw her on the stairs," said Rondi. "I was going up the stairs, and she went right past me, sliding down on the **banister**."

"Who?" asked Louis.

"Mrs. Gorf!" said Deedee. Just saying the name sent a **shiver**

---

1   **monkey bars** 정글짐. 아이들이 오르내리며 놀도록 만든 운동 기구. 철봉을 가로세로로 엮어서 만든다.

of fear through her body.

"Oh, your old teacher," said Louis with a **shrug**. "Is she back? I always wondered what happened to her."

The children looked at each other. Mrs. Gorf was the teacher they had had before Mrs. Jewls **took over**. They had never told anyone how they had **gotten rid of** her. They especially couldn't tell Louis.

She was the meanest teacher in the history of Wayside School. Of course there are other teachers at other schools who are meaner.

Louis looked toward the monkey bars. "I don't see her," he said.

"Well, she was there," Deedee **insist**ed. "I saw her!"

"You just imagined you saw her, Deedee," said Louis. "If you hate somebody, or if you love somebody, you often think you see that person when she isn't there. It's very common. It's just like Mrs. Drazil."

"Who's Mrs. Drazil?" asked Todd.

"She was the worst teacher I ever had," said Louis. He shivered just thinking about her. "She was my teacher when I was your age. I sometimes think I see her, too. And I still have **nightmare**s about her."

"Was she mean?" asked Rondi.

"She was *horrible!*" said Louis. "Every morning she used to check our **fingernail**s. If they were dirty, she'd tell the whole class. 'Louis has dirty fingernails this morning,' she'd say in a really **nasty** voice. And if you talked in class, she would pick up the **wastepaper** basket and put it over your head. You had to leave it on your head until the bell rang."

"Did she ever put it over your head?" asked Todd.

"Lots of times," said Louis.

Everybody laughed.

"It wasn't funny," said Louis. "My mother always knew when I got in trouble, because I'd have bits of trash stuck in my hair."

"Did it get stuck in your **mustache**, too?" asked Rondi.

"Louis didn't have a mustache when he was our age!" said Allison. "Did you, Louis?" she asked.

Suddenly, Louis screamed.

Everyone stared at him.

"She's back!" he shouted, as he shook with fear. Then he **slap**ped himself in the face. "Excuse me," he said. "Sorry. For a second I thought I saw Mrs. Drazil."

He turned to Deedee. "C'mon, let's go to the monkey bars."

"No!" **declare**d Deedee. "I'm not going back. I'm never getting on the monkey bars again!"

Louis took hold of her hand. "Mrs. Gorf isn't there," he said. "You just imagined her."

They headed to the monkey bars. No one else **dare**d to follow.

"If she starts to wiggle her ears, run away as fast as you can," warned Deedee. She held tightly on to Louis's hand.

When they reached the monkey bars, no one was there. "Where were you when you saw her?" Louis asked.

"I was hanging upside down over there," said Deedee, pointing.

"Okay, go hang upside down," said Louis.

"No!" exclaimed Deedee.

"Don't worry, I'll be right here in case anything happens."

It had rained during the night, so the sand under the monkey bars was wet and **somewhat** hard.

Deedee walked across the sand and pulled herself up on the bar. She **hook**ed her legs over, then hung from her knees.

"Well, do you see her?" Louis asked.

"No, it's safe now," said Deedee. "Thanks, Louis. I guess you're right. I must have seen my shadow or something."

Deedee pulled herself right side up, then **hop**ped down from the monkey bars. She and Louis walked away **hand in hand**. She held Louis's hand not because she was **scare**d but because she liked him.

"Mrs. Drazil sounds almost as bad as Mrs. Gorf," said Deedee.

"She was," said Louis. "She once made me put gum on my nose, because I was **chew**ing it in class."

"How can you chew your nose?" asked Deedee.

Behind them, Deedee's **footprint**s could be seen in the wet sand under the monkey bars. There was also another set of footprints, made by a person who had much bigger feet.

16. LOVE AND A DEAD RAT

Dameon was in love with one of the girls in his class. Can you guess which one?

He thought about her all the time.

Myron threw a red ball to Dameon. It **bounced** off his face.

"Huh?" said Dameon.

"Why didn't you catch the ball?" asked Myron.

"What ball?" asked Dameon.

"The one that hit you in the face," said Myron.

"Did a ball hit me in the face?" asked Dameon.

"Yes," said Myron.

"Oh, good," said Dameon. "I was wondering why my nose hurt."

He had been thinking about the girl he loved.

He was in love with Mrs. Jewls.

That was why he was always doing things for her, like passing out papers. He thought she was very pretty and nice. He thought she was smart, too. In fact, he thought she was one of the smartest people in the class.

After recess he hurried back up the stairs.

"Hello, Dameon," said Mrs. Jewls.

"Hello, Mrs. Jewls," he said.

"You're always the first one here, aren't you?" asked Mrs. Jewls.

Dameon **blush**ed and shrugged his shoulders. "Do you need any papers passed out or anything?" he asked.

"It's so nice of you to ask," said Mrs. Jewls.

"I think you're nice too," said Dameon.

Mrs. Jewls gave him a **stack** of **workbook**s to hand out. Then she gave him a Tootsie Roll Pop from the coffee can on her desk for being so helpful. "But don't eat it until after lunch," she said.

"I won't," he **assured** her.

He ate lunch with Myron and D.J. He saved his Tootsie Roll Pop for last.

Joy and Maurecia came up behind him.

"Hi, Dameon," said Joy. "How's your *girlfriend?*"

"What?" asked Dameon. He turned red. "Who are you talking

about? I don't have a girlfriend!"

"You're in love with Mrs. Jewls!" **accused** Maurecia.

"You better **watch out**," said Joy. "Mister Jewls might come after you."

The two girls laughed.

"I don't know what you're talking about," said Dameon. "I'm not in love with Mrs. Jewls!" He looked to his friends for support.

Myron shrugged.

D.J. smiled.

"**Prove** it!" said Joy. "Prove you're not in love with her."

"That's stupid," said Dameon. "How can I prove I'm not in love with Mrs. Jewls?"

"Give her this," said Joy. She handed Dameon a paper bag.

"Your lunch?" asked Dameon.

"Look inside," said Maurecia.

Inside the paper bag was a dead rat.

Dameon knew Mrs. Jewls hated dead rats more than anything in the world.

"Put it in her desk," said Joy.

"If you don't, it means you love her," said Maurecia.

"I'm not in love with her," said Dameon.

"Prove it," said Joy.

"Okay, I will!" said Dameon.

The girls left.

"You don't have to put the dead rat in her desk," said D.J.

"We don't care," said Myron.

"You think I'm in love with her too, don't you?" asked Dameon.

Myron shrugged.

D.J. smiled.

"Some friends you are!" said Dameon. "I'll show you!"

After lunch he was the first one back in class. He carried Joy's paper **sack**.

"Hello, Dameon," said Mrs. Jewls. "Did you have a nice lunch?"

"It was all right," he **mutter**ed.

"Oh, would you mind getting the construction paper from the **closet** and putting it on my desk?" asked Mrs. Jewls. "Thank you."

Dameon went to the closet and got the construction paper. He put it on her desk. Then, when she wasn't looking he opened her desk **drawer** and **dump**ed the dead rat into it. He shut the drawer.

"Thank you, Dameon," said Mrs. Jewls. "You're always so helpful. It's such a pleasure to have you in my class."

Dameon felt **awful**.

Mrs. Jewls read a story to the class.

Dameon couldn't **pay attention**. He kept wondering when she'd open her drawer.

After the story they had art. Everyone was supposed to make **snowflake**s.

Dameon folded his piece of construction paper in half.

Mrs. Jewls screamed.

"What's wrong, Mrs. Jewls?" asked Joy.

"Somebody put a dead rat in my desk," said Mrs. Jewls.

"I did!" declared Dameon.

"Dameon?" Mrs. Jewls said with great surprise. "Why?"

"Because I hate you!" said Dameon. "You're always making me do things for you."

"Oh, I see," said Mrs. Jewls.

"Should I write my name on the board under **DISCIPLINE?**" he asked.

"No, that won't be **necessary**," said Mrs. Jewls.

That made him feel even worse. Why did I have to prove myself to Joy? he wondered. I don't like Joy. I like Mrs. Jewls. He felt **rotten**.

When the bell rang, Dameon waited for all the other kids to leave. Then he walked to Mrs. Jewls's desk.

She was **grading** papers. "Yes, Dameon?"

"Do you want me to **erase** the board for you?" he asked.

"That's all right," said Mrs. Jewls. "I'll do it myself."

Dameon sadly walked out of the room and down the stairs. When he reached the bottom, he turned and ran **all the way** back up to Mrs. Jewls's room.

She was just putting on her coat.

"I love you, Mrs. Jewls!" Dameon declared. "I'm sorry I put the dead rat in your desk. I did it because I didn't want everyone to know I loved you. I'm sorry."

"I love you, too, Dameon," said Mrs. Jewls.

"You do? But what about Mister Jewls?"

"Just because I love Mister Jewls, it doesn't mean I can't also love you. Love is different from most things." She picked up a piece of **chalk**. "If I gave my piece of chalk to someone, then I wouldn't have it anymore. But when I give my love to someone, I **end up** with more love than I started with. The more love you **give away**, the more you have left."

Dameon smiled. "I love you, Mrs. Jewls," he said. He felt his heart fill up with more love.

"I love you, Dameon," said Mrs. Jewls.

"This is getting **disgust**ing!" said the dead rat. It climbed out of Mrs. Jewls's desk and walked out of the room.

17. WHAT?

It was purple.

So Jenny read the story backward. When she finished, she **threw up**.

"Okay," said Jenny.

"So read the story backward," suggested Mrs. Jewls. "That way the beginning will be a surprise."

"But I already know how the story ends!" Jenny complained. "I only like stories with surprise endings."

"Good point," said Mrs. Jewls. "Here, you can read the story yourself. It's very funny." She gave the book to Jenny.

"All I heard was the last sentence," said Jenny. "It isn't funny unless you know what happened first."

"Why aren't you laughing, Jenny?" asked Mrs. Jewls. "Didn't you think it was a funny story?"

That made Dana laugh harder.

"There goes the giggle box," said Myron.

Everybody laughed, except for Jenny. Dana laughed **hysterical**ly.

Mrs. Jewls looked back at the story she had been reading before Jenny's **interrupt**ion. There was only one sentence left for her to read. She read it to the class.

Jenny **made a face**. She could still taste the **awful** stuff.

"And next time you'll drink your **prune** juice more quickly," said Mrs. Jewls.

Jenny sat down.

Mrs. Jewls waited for Jenny to sit down.

Jenny wrote her name on the **blackboard** under the word DISCIPLINE.

"Well, that's no excuse," said Mrs. Jewls. "Now go write your name on the blackboard under the word DISCIPLINE."

"I couldn't leave the table until I finished it," explained Jenny. "And then I missed the bus."

"What does prune juice have to do with anything?" asked Mrs. Jewls.

"Because I hate prune juice!" Jenny **grip**ed.

"Why are you late?" asked Mrs. Jewls.

"I can't hear you," said Jenny. "I better take off my helmet." She took off her helmet.

"Take off your helmet," said Mrs. Jewls.

"What?" asked Jenny.

"Why are you late?" asked Mrs. Jewls.

Jenny **caught her breath**. "What?" she asked. She couldn't hear too well because she was still wearing the **motorcycle** helmet.

Mrs. Jewls looked up from the story she had been reading to the class. "You're late," she said.

She hopped off the bike in front of Wayside School and **charged** up the stairs. Her **stomach** was still going up and down as she opened the door to Mrs. Jewls's room.

She put on her helmet; then her father drove her to school on the back of his motorcycle. It was a very **bumpy** ride.

"Put on your helmet," said her father. "I'll drive you to school on the back of my motorcycle."

"I missed the bus," Jenny **grumble**d.

"What are you doing home?" asked her mother.

She finally got it all down, then hurried as fast as she could to the bus stop. When she got there, the bus was just **pull**ing **away**. She **sigh**ed, then turned around and ran all the way back home.

Her mother wouldn't let her leave the breakfast table until she finished her prune juice. It took her forever. She hated prune juice more than anything in the world.

One day Jenny was late for school.

18. THE SUBSTITUTE

Benjamin couldn't **take it** any longer. Today was the day he would finally tell Mrs. Jewls his real name. So what if nobody likes me? he thought. So what if I stop getting high **mark**s?

"Hi, Mark," said Jason.

"Hi, Mark," said Stephen.

"Hi, hi," he **glum**ly replied, then started up the stairs.

"Hi, Mark," said Bebe as he took his seat next to her. "Guess what? We have a **substitute**!"

"Yahoooo!" shouted Maurecia.

Everyone in Mrs. Jewls's class loved it when they had substitute teachers. They loved playing mean and horrible **trick**s on them.

Benjamin **frown**ed. He finally had the courage to tell Mrs. Jewls his real name. "Rats!¹" he said.

"That's a good idea!" said Terrence. "We'll put dead rats in her desk!"

"Let's trick her into going outside," said Joy, "then **lock** her out of the room."

"But what if she tells Mr. Kidswatter?" asked Eric Fry.

"So what?" said Joy. "She'll have to go all the way down to the office, and then all the way back up. By then we'll unlock the door. Mr. Kidswatter will think she's **bonkers**!"

Benjamin looked at the substitute teacher sitting at Mrs. Jewls's desk. She looked like a nice lady.

She wore tiny **spectacles** and had long gray hair tied in a **ponytail**. He felt sorry for her, and he felt sorry for himself. I was going to tell Mrs. Jewls my name, he thought. I really was!

The substitute stood up and walked to the center of the room. "Good morning," she said. "My name is Mrs. Franklin."

Nobody said "Good morning" back to her.

Calvin handed Benjamin a note: *At ten o'clock drop your book on the floor. Pass it on.*

Benjamin read it, then passed it on to Todd.

"Okay, who can tell me what page we're on?" asked Mrs. Franklin.

---

1 rats '쥐'가 아니라 '제기랄'이라는 뜻으로 사용하였다.

"Page seventeen," called Myron.

"A hundred and twelve," said Maurecia.

"Ninety-eight," said Eric Ovens.

"Three thousand," said Joe.

Mrs. Franklin smiled. "I guess we'll have to study all those pages," she said.

Benjamin raised his hand.

"Yes, the handsome young man in the red shirt," said the substitute.

He told her the correct page. "We're on page one hundred and two," he said.

"Thank you," said the substitute. "And what is your name, please?"

Benjamin thought a moment. He looked around the room, then **bold**ly told the truth. "My name is Benjamin!" he stated proudly.

Several kids **snicker**ed.

"Thank you, Benjamin," said the substitute.

There were more snickers.

"You're welcome," said Benjamin. He felt good, even if the other kids were laughing at him.

Mrs. Franklin asked a question from page 102.

Jason answered it correctly.

"Very good," said the substitute. "And what is your name, please?"

Jason looked around. "Benjamin!" he **assert**ed.

Half the class **giggle**d.

"Thank you, Benjamin," said Mrs. Franklin.

The other half giggled.

Dana answered the next question.

"And what's your name?" Mrs. Franklin asked Dana.

"Benjamin!" Dana **blurt**ed, then fell giggling onto the floor.

"Thank you, Benjamin," said the substitute.

Everyone was **hysterical**.

"My,[2] it is certainly a pleasure to teach such happy students," said the substitute. "Who knows the answer to question four?"

They all raised their hands. They all wanted to tell the substitute their names were Benjamin.

They were having so much fun, they forgot to drop their books at ten o'clock.

At **recess** everyone **congratulate**d Benjamin on his great trick.

"You're a **genius**, Mark," said Todd.

"Benjamin is such a funny name," said Jason. "How'd you ever think of it?"

"But my name really is Benjamin," said Benjamin.

"So is mine," said Stephen.

"Mine too," said Leslie.

They all laughed.

---

2 my 이런, 어머나. 놀라움이나 낭패를 나타내는 표현.

"Do you think she really believes we're all named Benjamin?" asked Eric Ovens.

"Probably," said Joy. "She's so stupid!"

"If she thought we were lying, she would have gotten mad," said Eric Bacon.

The bell rang, and they all hurried back to class.

After recess was **social studies**.

"Who would like to read?" asked Mrs. Franklin.

Every hand went up.

"Okay, Benjamin," said Mrs. Franklin as she pointed at Dana.

Everyone laughed.

Dana giggled a few seconds, then got control of herself and read from the book.

"Thank you, Benjamin," said the substitute when Dana finished reading. "Okay, Benjamin, you may read next," she said, pointing at Terrence.

Everyone laughed.

It was the first time all year Terrence had **volunteer**ed to read.

All day, everyone **paid** very close **attention**. They all wanted the teacher to **call on** them. Because as funny as it was when Mrs. Franklin called somebody else Benjamin, it was even funnier when she called you Benjamin.

So everyone worked hard and listened closely. As a result, they learned more from the substitute in a day than they usually learned from Mrs. Jewls in a month.

When the final bell rang, everyone crowded around her desk.

"Are you coming back tomorrow, Mrs. Franklin?" asked Eric Bacon.

"Please, Mrs. Franklin, say you will," **plead**ed Kathy.

"You're the best substitute teacher we've ever had!" said Jason.

The substitute smiled. "School is over," she said. "You don't have to call me Mrs. Franklin anymore. That sounds so formal. Since we're friends now, you may call me by my first name."

"What is your first name?" asked Maurecia.

The substitute **gather**ed up her things and put them in a **straw** bag. "Benjamin," she said, then walked out of the room.

Everyone stared silently after her.

"Do you think that's really her name?" asked Joy.

19. A BAD CASE OF THE SILLIES

Allison started up the stairs five minutes before the bell rang for school to start. The stairs were completely empty. Allison liked it that way. When the bell rang, the stairs would be **cram**med with a thousand screaming kids **scurry**ing to their rooms, but now it was nice and **peaceful**.

She walked up past the eighteenth **story** and toward the twentieth. There was no nineteenth story in Wayside School. Miss Zarves taught the class on the nineteenth story. There was no Miss Zarves.

Allison didn't understand it. If there was no nineteenth story, then wasn't her class really on the twenty-ninth?

Suddenly she heard **footsteps charging** up behind her. She turned around to see Ron and Deedee **racing**.

She **lean**ed against the wall to get out of their way, but Deedee **stamp**ed on her foot; then Ron's **elbow jam**med her in the stomach.

"Umph!" she **grunt**ed, as she fell and rolled down three steps.

Deedee and Ron didn't even stop to say they were sorry.

Allison slowly stood up. **Fortunate**ly she wasn't hurt, but her **windbreaker** was **torn**.

She thought Ron and Deedee were **silly**. They race up the stairs, and then when they get to Mrs. Jewls's room they're too **pooped** to learn anything.

Allison thought all the kids in Mrs. Jewls's class were silly, even Rondi, and Rondi was her best friend. Then there was Jason, who was always **pester**ing her. That was because Jason hated her. Or else he loved her. Allison wasn't sure which.

When she got to class, Deedee and Ron were sitting with their heads flat on their desks and their tongues hanging out.

"You could have said you were sorry," Allison said as she walked past them. She sat up straight in her chair, folded her hands on her desk, and waited as everyone else **wander**ed in.

Jason entered the room carrying a glass bowl with a **goldfish** swimming inside it. "Look what I brought!" he said.

"What's the name of your goldfish?" asked Mrs. Jewls.

"Shark!" said Jason.

Everyone laughed. Allison **roll**ed **her eyes**.

"It makes him feel important," Jason explained. "Where should I put him?"

"How about on top of the coat closet?" suggested Mrs. Jewls.

Jason had to stand on a chair on his **tiptoe**s. He held the bowl at the very bottom as he tried to **nudge** it over the edge of the closet.

Suddenly the chair **topple**d over. "Aaaaaahh-**gulp!**" **yell**ed Jason as he fell on the floor. He was holding the bowl **upside down** above his wet face.

Mrs. Jewls hurried to the back of the room. "Quick, somebody fill the bowl with water," she said. "Where's Shark?"

Jason **made a face**. "I **swallow**ed him."

The class went crazy.

What a **show-off**, thought Allison.

Mrs. Jewls rang her **cowbell** and told everyone to settle down. "You have a bad case of the sillies this morning," she said.

She took **roll**. "Who's **absent**?" she asked.

"Allison," said Rondi.

"Very funny, Rondi," said Allison.

"Anybody **besides** Allison?" asked Mrs. Jewls.

"I'm here, Mrs. Jewls," said Allison. She sat behind Eric Fry, so she thought Mrs. Jewls couldn't see her. Eric Fry was the biggest kid in the class.

"Just Allison," said Mrs. Jewls. She **mark**ed it on her green roll card. "Dameon, will you please take the roll card to the office."

108

Allison stood up. "I'm not absent," she said.

Dameon took the roll card and walked out the door.

"Mrs. Jewls, did you just mark me absent?" asked Allison.

Mrs. Jewls didn't answer her.

Allison **march**ed to her desk. "Mrs. Jewls, did you mark me absent?" she asked again.

Mrs. Jewls looked up. "Terrence, what are you whispering about?"

"Nothing," **mumble**d Terrence.

"If you can say it to Jenny, you can say it to me," said Mrs. Jewls.

"**Get off my case**, Buzzard[1] Face!" said Terrence.

"Terrence!" **exclaim**ed Mrs. Jewls. "Go write your name on the blackboard under the word DISCIPLINE."

"But that's what I said to Jenny," Terrence **protest**ed.

"Mrs. Jewls, what about me?" Allison demanded.

Mrs. Jewls **ignore**d her.

Allison screamed as loud as she could.

Mrs. Jewls didn't hear her.

Allison faced the class. "Can't anybody see me?" she asked.

Nobody answered her.

"Rondi?" shouted Allison. "Dana? Jason?

"This isn't funny," said Allison. "I know you're all just pretending."

---

1   buzzard 말똥가리. 수리목 수리과에 속하는 갈색 계통의 새.

She stood right in front of Jason, leaned over his desk, and **stared** him straight in the eye. "I know you can see me," she said. "You're trying not to laugh."

He stared right through her.

She stuck out her tongue at him.

He leaned forward, causing Allison's tongue to **lick** his nose.

"**Yuck**!" she exclaimed, then **wiped** her tongue on her **sleeve**.

Mrs. Jewls began the morning lesson.

"Have you gone crazy?" shouted Allison. She ran out of the room and down to the class on the twenty-ninth story. "Come quick," she said. "There's something wrong with Mrs. Jewls's class."

No one heard her.

She **slam**med the door, then continued down the stairs to the class on the twenty-eighth floor. No one saw her there, either.

Tears **stream**ed down her **cheek**s. Is the whole school playing a joke on me? she wondered. "It's not funny!" she shouted as loud as she could.

She continued down the stairs, screaming anything that came to her head, hoping that someone, somewhere, would notice her.

"Fish for sale! Fresh fish! Fat fish! Get your fresh, fat fish!"

A tall, skinny lady with very short hair stepped out of one of the classrooms. "Sh!" she whispered.

"This is a school, not a fish market!"

"You can hear me?" asked Allison. She was so happy, she wanted to hug her.

"Yes, I can hear you," the woman said **stern**ly. "My whole class can hear you. You're making it impossible for us to get any work done."

"I'm sorry," said Allison. "But something's wrong in Mrs. Jewls's class."

"You'd better come in here," said the teacher.

Allison followed the teacher into her classroom.

"What's your name?" the teacher asked her.

"Allison."

"Boys and girls, this is Allison," the teacher **announce**d to her students. "She'll be joining our class."

"What?" said Allison. "But—"

"My name is Miss Zarves," said the teacher. "Welcome to the nineteenth story."

19. A WONDERFUL TEACHER

Allison was still on the nineteenth story.

The desks were **arranged** in **cluster**s of four. Allison sat at a cluster with a girl named Virginia, a boy named Nick, and a boy named Ray.

But Virginia looked old enough to be her mother. And Nick looked like he should be in high school. Ray was a couple of years younger than Allison.

"Miss Zarves is a wonderful teacher," said Virginia in a **singsong** voice. "She's the nicest teacher I ever had."

"She's the *only* teacher you ever had," said Nick.

"So? She's still nice," said Virginia. "I've always gotten all A's."

"Aren't you a little old to be going to school?" Allison asked her.

"You're never too old to learn," said Virginia.

"No one ever leaves Miss Zarves's class," said Nick. "How long have you been here, Virginia?"

Virginia thought a moment. "Thirty-two wonderful years."

"I've been here nine years," said Nick.

"But she always gives us good grades," said Virginia.

"That's true," Nick agreed. "I've gotten all A's since I've been here too."

"Me too," said Ray. "And sometimes I answer all the problems wrong **on purpose**!"

"Where were you before you came here?" Allison asked him.

"I went to, um, I was . . . " Ray shook his head. "That's funny—I don't remember."

"I don't remember where I came from either," said Virginia.

"Well, I do!" said Allison. "I was in . . ." But suddenly she couldn't remember either. Then it came to her. "Mrs. Jewls's class! And Rondi was in the class, and Jason, and Dana, and Todd . . ."

She named every member of the class, **including** all three Erics. She didn't want to forget where she came from. If I forget where I came from, I might never get back, she thought.

"Did you say there was a girl named Bebe Gunn?" asked Ray.

"Yes," said Allison. "Bebe's a very good artist."

"My last name is Gunn, too," said Ray. "I wonder if we're **related**."

"Ray, no talking please," said Miss Zarves. "Now, everyone please take out a pencil and some paper. I want you to write all the numbers from zero to a million in **alphabetical order**."

"From zero to a million?" asked Allison. She couldn't believe it.

"Don't worry," said Virginia. "If you **run out of** paper, Miss Zarves has more in the **closet**."

Allison stared at her in **horror**. "But it will take over a hundred years," she said.

"So?" asked Virginia. "What's your hurry?"

Allison started to work. It was bad enough having to write down all the numbers from zero to a million, but she couldn't imagine how she'd ever put them in alphabetical order.

One came before two.

Three came after one, but before two.

Four came before one.

Five came before four.

Six came after one, but before three.

"Don't worry," said Virginia. "Even if you miss a few, Miss Zarves will give you an A when you finish."

Seven came after one and before six.

Eight came first. Allison couldn't think of any number that would come before eight, so she wrote it down. She also knew zero would come last, if she ever got that far. By then she'd be older than Virginia.

I'll talk to Louis at recess, she thought. He'll save me.

"When's recess?" she asked.

"There is no recess," said Ray. "We're not allowed out of the classroom."

"What about if you have to go to the bathroom?"

"What's a bathroom?" asked Virginia.

"We don't eat, either," said Nick. "We just work all the time."

"But we never have homework," Virginia said **cheerful**ly.

"That's because we never go home," said Nick. "We get a two-minute **break** every eleven hours."

"But don't worry," said Virginia. "Miss Zarves always gives us good grades."

Miss Zarves walked around the room checking everybody's work. "Excellent, Ray!" she said. "Very good, Virginia. You're doing wonderfully, Allison. You get an A for the day."

Big deal! thought Allison. She had to **figure out** some way out of there. It was clear that Virginia, Nick, and Ray were all too far gone to help her.

"Are there any other new kids in the class?" she asked.

"Ben's new," said Nick. He pointed Ben out to her.

Ben appeared to be about Allison's age. She was glad about that. When the two-minute break came, she went over and talked to him.

"Are you Ben?" she asked.

"No," he said.

"Oh," said Allison. "I was looking for Ben."

"That's me," said the boy.

"But you just said—"

"My name's Mark Miller," said the boy. "But for some reason everybody calls me Benjamin Nushmutt."

"There's a Mark Miller in my class!" exclaimed Allison.

"I know, that's me," said Mark. "I'm Mark Miller."

"No, I mean my other class," said Allison.

"What other class?"

Allison thought a moment. "I don't remember . . ." she said.

After putting numbers in alphabetical order for eleven hours, her brain had **turn**ed **into** spaghetti.

"Time's up,[1]" said Miss Zarves. "Everyone back to work."

---

1 **time's up** 시간이 다 되었다.

19. FOREVER IS NEVER

Allison was still stuck on the nineteenth story.

Fourteen two-minute breaks had passed.

"It's **dictionary** time," said Miss Zarves.

Everybody got out a dictionary. Allison found a dictionary in her desk, too.

"What are we supposed to do with it?" she asked.

"**Memorize** it," said Nick.

"But that's impossible!" said Allison.

"No, it's easy," Virginia **assure**d her. "You memorize one word at a time, until you get a whole page. Then you go on to the next page."

"How many words have you memorized?" asked Allison.

"I'm almost finished with the B's," Virginia said proudly. "And I've only been doing it for thirty-two years!"

Allison opened her dictionary. *Mrs. Jewls's class!* she suddenly remembered. She **sigh**ed with **relief**. For the last six days she'd been trying to remember where she came from.

In her mind she went through everybody in her former class. She didn't want to forget again. As she thought about each person, tears filled her eyes. She missed them very much. Even Jason. They were all so wonderful in their own special ways.

When the two-minute **break** came, she talked to Mark again. He was the only person in the class who still seemed to have a brain.

"How did we get here?" she asked.

"Maybe we're dead," said Mark. "Maybe we died and went to—"

"This isn't Heaven!" said Allison.

"That wasn't what I was going to say," said Mark.

Allison felt a **chill** run up her **spine**. She looked at Miss Zarves. Miss Zarves smiled back at her.

"But she seems so nice," said Allison. "Could someone as nice as her really be the **devil**?"

"I don't know," said Mark. "She always gives good grades."

"What would happen if we didn't do our work?" asked Allison.

118

"We have to do our work," said Mark.

"Why?" asked Allison. "What's Miss Zarves going to do to us—keep us after school?"

"I don't know," said Mark. "Teachers can always find new ways to **punish** you. They're **expert**s at it."

"Your two minutes are up, boys and girls," announced Miss Zarves. "Everyone back to work."

Allison returned to her seat. She tried to figure it all out, but she had so much busy work to do, she didn't have time to think.

That's her plan! Allison suddenly realized. She **shiver**ed as it all came together for her. Miss Zarves **assign**s us lots of busy work so we don't have time to think. She makes us memorize stupid things so that we don't think about the important things. And then she gives us good grades to keep us happy.

Miss Zarves walked around the room. "Very good, Virginia," she said. "You are doing so well. Excellent, Ray! Good job, Nick." She stopped when she got to Allison. "Allison, why aren't you working?"

Allison looked at her. She knew Mark was right. Teachers are experts at finding ways to punish you. And if Miss Zarves was the devil, who knew what she might have up her **sleeve**? Still, Allison had to **take a chance**. If she wanted to get back to Mrs. Jewls's class, she had to act as if she were in Mrs. Jewls's class.

She took off her shoes and socks, sat on the floor, and **suck**ed her toes.

"Allison, what are you doing?" asked Miss Zarves.

Allison took her toe out of her mouth. "**Get off my case**, Buzzard Face," she said.

Miss Zarves was **furious**. "Return to your desk, young lady!" she ordered.

Allison returned to her desk. But instead of sitting at it, she climbed on top of it and sang a song.

> *"I got one sock!*
> > *Lookin' for the other.*
>
> *One sock!*
> > *Lookin' for its brother.*
>
> *When I find that sock!*
> > *I'll tell you what I'll do.*
>
> *I'll put it on my foot,*
> > *and I'll stick it in my shoe!"*

Mark Miller smiled at her and silently **clap**ped his hands. Everyone else looked at her like she was crazy.

"Your socks are on the floor, next to your shoes," Miss Zarves said coldly. "I'll give you ten seconds to put them on your feet. Ten . . . nine . . . eight . . . seven . . ."

Allison climbed down from her desk. She picked up her socks and put them on her ears. "How's this?" she asked.

"Six . . . five . . . four . . ."

"Albert Einstein didn't wear socks," said Allison. "Why should I?"

"Three . . . two . . ."

Allison closed her eyes.

"One!"

She felt something **slam** down on her foot. Something else **jam**med into her **stomach**. "Umph!" she **grunt**ed as she fell and rolled down three steps.

"Are you all right?" asked Deedee.

"Huh?" said Allison. She was on the stairs, somewhere between the eighteenth and twentieth stories.

"Sorry," said Ron. "I didn't see you. Deedee and I were **racing** up the stairs, and then you suddenly appeared."

"You **knock**ed off her shoes and socks!" exclaimed Deedee.

"Oh, I **rip**ped your **windbreaker**, too," said Ron. "I'm sorry."

"That's okay," said Allison. She picked up her shoes and socks. "Race you up the stairs!"

All three ran up to Mrs. Jewls's room. When they got there, they were so **pooped**, they sat with their heads flat on their desks and their tongues hanging out.

"Hi, Allison," said Rondi.

Allison raised her head. "Hi, Rondi," she said happily. "What did I miss while I was **absent**?"

"When were you absent?" asked Rondi. "Hey, how come you're not wearing your shoes and socks?"

Allison hung her socks from her ears. "What do you think?"

she asked. "It's the new look!"

Rondi laughed.

"Allison," said Mrs. Jewls, "you seem to have a bad case of the sillies this morning."

Allison **giggle**d.

Jason entered the room carrying a glass bowl with a **goldfish** swimming inside it. "Look what I brought!" he said.

"What's the name of your goldfish?" asked Mrs. Jewls.

"Shark!" said Jason.

Everyone laughed.

"It makes him feel important," Jason explained. "Where should I put him?"

"How about on top of the coat **closet**?" suggested Mrs. Jewls.

Jason had to stand on a chair on his **tiptoe**s. He held the bowl at the very bottom as he tried to **nudge** it over the edge of the closet.

Allison turned around to watch. She didn't want to miss this!

20, 21, & 22. ERIC, ERIC, & ERIC

Mr. Kidswatter's voice **crackled** over the **loudspeaker**. "MRS. JEWLS, SEND ERIC TO MY OFFICE, **AT ONCE**!" He sounded mad.

Mrs. Jewls was **confused**. "When did we get a loudspeaker?" she asked.

"Louis put it in yesterday," said Jenny.

Mrs. Jewls was still confused. There were three Erics in her class. She didn't know which one Mr. Kidswatter meant.

Eric Fry was fat, but not short.

Eric Bacon was short, but not fat.

Eric Ovens was short and fat.

Mrs. Jewls chose the biggest Eric. "Eric Fry, Mr. Kidswatter wants to see you."

Eric Fry **trembl**ed as he slowly stood up.

The other two Erics smiled.

The **principal**'s office was on the first floor. It's not fair, Eric thought as he headed down to his doom. Anytime any Eric does something wrong, I'm the one who gets in trouble.

He stood in front of the principal's door. His heart beat very fast. He took a couple of breaths, then **knock**ed lightly.

"Enter!" **boom**ed Mr. Kidswatter.

Eric turned the **doorknob**. He took one step inside, then stood with his back against the wall, as far away from Mr. Kidswatter as he could get.

Mr. Kidswatter sat behind an **enormous** desk. He wore mirrored sunglasses[1] so Eric couldn't tell where he was looking. "Sit down, Eric," he said.

Eric moved to the small metal chair in front of the desk. A **bare light bulb** hung above his head.

Mr. Kidswatter **crack**ed his **knuckle**s. "We can do this the easy way, or we can do this the hard way," he said. "It's your choice."

"I don't know what you're talking about," said Eric. "I didn't do anything."

---

1 **mirrored sunglasses** 눈이 보이지 않게 렌즈에 편광 필터가 부착된 선글라스.

"So it's the hard way, is it?" asked Mr. Kidswatter. "Very well. You'll talk. **One way or another**, you'll tell me everything I want to know."

"But—"

Mr. Kidswatter **pound**ed his **fist** on his desk. "When was the last time you **sharpen**ed your pencil?"

Eric tried to remember, but he was too nervous to think. "Um, wait, let me think," he **stammer**ed.

"We had a **spell**ing test on Friday, but I borrowed—"

"Where were you yesterday afternoon, at a quarter past twelve?" asked Mr. Kidswatter.

"Yesterday?" asked Eric. "I was here, at Wayside School. I remember I ate lunch and then I played **kickball**."

Mr. Kidswatter smiled. "Do you kick with your left foot?" he asked.

"No, I'm right-footed," said Eric Fry.

"Hmph!" **grumble**d Mr. Kidswatter. "Have you ever gotten your hair cut at Charley's **Barber** Shop?"

"Yes," said Eric. "Two weeks ago."

"Aha!" said Mr. Kidswatter. "So you admit it! Do you know what a Mugworm Griblick is?"

Eric Fry turned **pale**. "No, please!" he **beg**ged. "I didn't do it! I'm **innocent**! You've got the wrong Eric. There are two other Erics in my class."

Mr. Kidswatter **scowl**ed. "So that's the way you're going to play it, is it? Well, that's fine with me. I've got all the time in the world."

He **flick**ed on the microphone. "MRS. JEWLS! SEND ME ANOTHER ERIC!"

Twenty-nine floors above them, Mrs. Jewls looked at the two remaining Erics.

"Okay, Eric Ovens," she said.

Eric Ovens **shiver**ed. His eyes filled with tears.

Why me? he asked himself over and over again as he walked down the stairs. It's my parents' fault! Why did they have to name me Eric? Why couldn't they name me Osgood?

He **tap**ped on the door to the principal's office.

"Come in!" **bellow**ed Mr. Kidswatter.

Eric Ovens **gulp**ed, then walked inside. He sat in the little chair in front of Mr. Kidswatter's enormous desk.

Eric Fry was nowhere to be seen.

"Wh-what ha-happened to Eric Fry?" he asked.

"I'll ask the questions!" barked Mr. Kidswatter. "But don't worry, Eric," he said gently. "You have nothing to fear. **So long as** you tell the truth." He cracked his knuckles.

Eric Ovens was very **scare**d. Mrs. Jewls always said that there was more than one answer to every question. He hoped he gave Mr. Kidswatter the right ones.

"Did you have a spelling test last Friday?" Mr. Kidswatter asked.

"Yes," said Eric Ovens. "How did you know that?"

"I have my ways," Mr. Kidswatter said **sly**ly, behind his mirrored glasses. "When was the last time you sharpened your pencil?"

"This morning," said Eric Ovens. "Maurecia **accidental**ly stepped on it and—"

"Did you play kickball yesterday at a quarter after twelve?"

"No, I played tetherball.[2]"

"Right- or left-handed?"

"Right."

Mr. Kidswatter **toss**ed a **stapler** at him.

Eric caught it with his right hand.

Mr. Kidswatter scowled. "Okay, Eric, tell me this. Have you ever gotten your hair cut at Charley's Barber Shop?"

"No, but I will. I'll go right now if you want."

"You're not going anywhere!" shouted Mr. Kidswatter. "Have you ever heard of a Mugworm Griblick?"

Eric Ovens screamed.

Upstairs, Mrs. Jewls heard Mr. Kidswatter's voice **resound** over the loudspeaker. "MRS. JEWLS, SEND ME THE LAST ERIC!"

"On my way!" said Eric Bacon. He **hop**ped out of his chair and **bounce**d down the stairs.

He didn't **bother** knocking on Mr. Kidswatter's door. He just walked right in. "What can I do for you?" he asked.

There was no sign of Eric Ovens.

"Have a seat," said Mr. Kidswatter. "I just want to ask you a few

---

2   tetherball 테더 볼. 기둥에 매단 공을 치고 받는 게임. 이 게임에 쓰이는 공을 가리키기도 한다.

questions."

"Sure thing," said Eric Bacon. He sat in the little chair. He **lean**ed back with his hands behind his head and his feet up on Mr. Kidswatter's desk.

He looked at himself in Mr. Kidswatter's mirrored glasses, took a **comb** out of his back pocket, and combed his hair. His hair was very **neat** and **trim**. He had gotten it cut yesterday, at 12:15, at Charley's Barber Shop.

Mr. Kidswatter cracked his knuckles. "When's the last time you sharpened your pencil?" he asked.

"November eleventh," Eric Bacon answered **right away**. "It was three minutes before five o'clock in the afternoon. I remember because my watch stopped."

"Where were you yesterday at twelve-fifteen?"

"I was in the garden, having tea."

"Did Maurecia step on somebody's pencil this morning?" asked Mr. Kidswatter.

"Yes."

"Whose?"

"She stepped on everybody's pencil," said Eric Bacon.

"Are you left-handed or right-footed?" demanded Mr. Kidswatter.

"I write with my left foot, and I kick with my right hand," replied Eric Bacon.

Mr. Kidswatter scowled. "Have you ever gotten your hair cut at Charley's Barber Shop?"

"No, I never get my hair cut," said Eric Bacon. "I'm **bald**. This is a **wig**."

Mr. Kidswatter took off his glasses and **glare**d at him. "Do the words 'Mugworm Griblick' mean anything to you?"

Eric Bacon shook his head. "I can look it up in the **dictionary** if you want."

Mr. Kidswatter shook his head. "I tried that," he said. "It's not there." He **rub**bed his **chin**. "Okay, boys, you can come out now."

Eric Ovens and Eric Fry **crawl**ed out from under the desk.

Mr. Kidswatter looked at each Eric. "One of you is lying," he said. "I don't know who it is, but I'll find out. And when I do, whoever it is will be very sorry. Now I'll give you one last chance to **come clean**."

Eric Fry trembled.

Eric Ovens shivered.

"C'mon, let's blow this Popsicle **stand**,[3]" said Eric Bacon. He walked out of the room. The other two Erics followed.

Mr. Kidswatter rubbed the back of his neck. He looked at the white card on top of his desk. On one side it said:

CHARLEY'S BARBER SHOP

---

3 let's blow this Popsicle stand (= Let's get out of here.) 이곳에서 나가자. Popsicle은 막대 아이스크림의 상표명이며, 이것을 판매하는 가판대(Popsicle stand)는 어디에서나 흔히 볼 수 있다. 보통 '지루하고 따분한 곳을 얼른 떠나자'라는 의미로 사용한다.

Under that, in blue ink, it said:

Eric, Tuesday, 12:15

He turned the card over. On the other side, a left-handed person had written with a sharp pencil:

Mr. Kidswatter is a Mugworm Griblick.

23. TEETH

Something **terrible** happened. Rondi grew two new front teeth.

Rondi was afraid nobody would think she was cute anymore.

Mrs. Jewls was giving a health lesson. "Always brush your teeth," she said, "and remember to **scrub** behind your ears."

"But I'll get **toothpaste** in my ear!" **exclaim**ed Todd.

Everyone laughed. Except Rondi. She didn't want anybody to see her teeth. She hadn't smiled for a week.

Mrs. Jewls made Todd write his name on the board under the word **DISCIPLINE**.

At **recess** Rondi decided to tell Louis her problem.

Louis was talking to Deedee.

"Do you have any green balls left?" asked Deedee.

"I'm sorry, I've already given them all away," said Louis.

"That's not fair!" said Deedee. "Why don't you ever save one for me?"

"You know I can't do that," said Louis. "If I save a ball for you, then all the other kids will want me to save balls for them, too."

"Thanks for nothing, Louis!" said Deedee. She **storm**ed away.

It was Rondi's turn. She made sure nobody else was listening. "Louis, will you help me?" she whispered.

"Sure, Rondi, what's the problem?" asked Louis. Rondi smiled, showing Louis her teeth.

"Very nice," said Louis.

"And listen to this," said Rondi. "She sells **seashell**s by the **seashore**."

"Very good," said Louis.

"No it isn't!" **complain**ed Rondi. "I used to whistle when I said words with s's in them. Now nobody will think I'm cute."

"I think you're cute," said Louis.

"You don't **count**," said Rondi.

"Well, thanks a lot," said Louis.

"I didn't mean it bad," said Rondi. "You think everybody's cute, even Miss Mush! That's why I like you."

"Thank you, Rondi. I like you, too."

"Thank you," said Rondi. "Will you please kick me in the teeth?"

132

"No," said Louis.

"Why not?" asked Rondi. "You said you liked me. If you liked me, you'd kick me in the teeth."

"You know I can't," said Louis. "If I kick you in the teeth, then all the other kids will want me to kick them in the teeth, too."

Rondi **scowl**ed. "Thanks for nothing, Louis!" she said. She crawled into the **bush**es where nobody would be able to see her mouth.

"Louis! Louis!" shouted Stephen and Jason as they ran toward him.

"Terrence stole our ball!" said Jason.

"I wish you children would learn to share," said Louis.

"Make him give it back!" said Stephen.

Louis started to say something, then stopped. He **twirl**ed his **multicolored mustache**. "Hey, Rondi," he called. "Will you help me?"

Rondi crawled out of the bushes. "You wouldn't help me," she said. "Why should I help you?"

"Terrence stole their ball," said Louis. "Make him give it back."

"Her?" asked Stephen and Jason.

"Me?" asked Rondi.

Louis **wink**ed at her.

Rondi's eyes **lit up**. "Okay, Louis," she said. "That's a good idea. That's a wonderful idea!"

She hurried across the **playground**. Stephen and Jason ran after her.

Terrence kicked a red ball up into the air, then ran under it and caught it.

"Hey, Terrence!" said Rondi. "That's not your ball. You stole it!"

"**Drop dead**, Ketchup Head," said Terrence.

Rondi walked up to him, **stared** him straight in the eye, and said, "In your hat, Muskrat![1]"

That surprised Terrence. He took a step back. Then he **collected** **himself** and said, "**Dig** a hole, Milly **Mole!**"

Rondi took another step toward him. "Kiss a **goose**, Dr. Seuss![2]" she replied.

Terrence looked around. A group of kids had formed a circle around them. "Go to **jail**, **Garbage Pail!**" he said.

Rondi **held her ground**. "Go to the zoo, Mr. Jagoo!" she **retort**ed.

Everyone was very **impress**ed by how brave Rondi was.

"Now, give me the ball!" she demanded.

"You want it?" asked Terrence. "I'll give it to you all right!" He raised his fist in the air.

"Good, let me have it!" said Rondi. She smiled, showing him her two new teeth.

Terrence shook his fist at her. "You're asking for it," he said.

"That's right!" said Rondi. "I am." Her teeth **gleam**ed at him.

Terrence brought his fist way back behind him.

---

1 muskrat 머스크랫. 물가에 서식하며 사향을 분비하기 때문에 사향쥐라고 불린다.

2 Dr. Seuss 닥터 수스. 미국의 어린이 문학 작가이자 만화가이다. 운율에 맞춘 재미있는 이야기를 담고 있는 작품으로 유명하다.

Rondi closed her eyes.

"Hey, look!" exclaimed Bebe. "Rondi's got new teeth!"

"They're cute," said Jenny.

Rondi opened her eyes. "You think so?" she asked.

"No, you were cuter before," said Paul.

"I think she's cuter now," said Todd.

They took a **vote**. Twelve kids thought she looked cuter with her two new teeth and twelve thought she looked cuter before. Three thought she should keep just one tooth.

So Rondi decided to keep her teeth. They were good for **biting carrot**s.

"Uh-oh!" She suddenly remembered.

She **duck**ed just **in time**.

24. ANOTHER STORY ABOUT POTATOES

Joe was next in line. He had forgotten his lunch.

"And what would you like, Joe?" asked Miss Mush.

"What do you have?" Joe asked.

"Potato salad," said Miss Mush.

"Anything else?" asked Joe.

"No, just potato salad," said Miss Mush.

Mrs. Jewls had made Miss Mush throw away the rest of the **Mushroom** Surprise, and she made Miss Mush promise never to make it again.

"Okay, I'll have potato salad," said Joe.

Miss Mush smiled. She **scoop**ed a large **glop** of potato salad out of the **vat** and **plop**ped it on Joe's paper **plate**.

Sharie was next in line. She had also forgotten her lunch.

"And what would you like, Sharie?" asked Miss Mush.

"What do you have?" asked Sharie.

"Potato salad."

"What else is there?" asked Sharie.

"Nothing," said Miss Mush.

"Okay," said Sharie. "I'll have that."

"Potato salad?" asked Miss Mush.

"No, nothing," said Sharie.

Joe was the only one who ordered the potato salad. Everyone else ordered nothing.

He slid his paper plate over to the **cash register** and paid for his lunch. Then he went to the ketchup and mustard table.

He looked at the **grayish**-white **mound** on his plate. He thought it needed more color. He **squirt**ed **squiggly** lines of mustard all over it. Then he added several **dollop**s of red ketchup.

"That's very pretty, Joe," said Bebe. "I didn't know you were such a good artist."

"Thanks," said Joe. He looked for a place to sit.

"Hey, Joe! Over here!" called John.

Joe sat next to him. "Hi, **pal**," he said.

"Hi, good **buddy**," replied John.

They were best friends.

John had brought his lunch. He looked at Joe's potato salad covered with yellow squiggles and red **polka dot**s. "That's very colorful," he said.

"Thanks," said Joe.

They both stared at it.

"I wonder what it tastes like," said John.

"Who knows?" said Joe.

"There's plenty more potato salad!" called Miss Mush. "Who wants **second**s?"

Nobody wanted seconds of potato salad. Several kids went back for seconds of nothing, but soon Miss Mush **ran out of** nothing.

Finally Joe picked up his plastic fork and stuck it into the glop.

"What does it feel like?" asked John.

"**Lump**y and **gooey**," said Joe. He **drag**ged his fork over the mound, **swirl**ing the mustard and ketchup together. "Kind of **spongy**, too." The colors mixed with the potato salad. It turned a **pale** orange.

"It looks like a face," said John.

Joe laughed. He shaped it so it would look even more like a face. He **pile**d up some potato salad in the center, giving it a nose.

John had a plastic spoon. He **dug** out two holes for the eyes, then made **eyebrow**s.

"That's good," said Joe. He gave it a big smiling mouth.

John made long, **pointy** ears.

138

They both laughed at their **creation**.

"I wonder what it tastes like," said John.

"Who knows?" said Joe.

They stared at it.

"It kind of looks familiar," said John. "Like somebody I know."

"Who?" asked Joe.

"I'm not sure," said John.

Joe noticed it, too. "It does look familiar," he agreed.

"I've seen that face somewhere before," said John.

"Me too," said Joe.

The smile on the potato salad **abrupt**ly **turn**ed **into** a **frown**.

"Wow, did you see that?" asked Joe.

John's eyes filled with **terror**. "I—I just **figure**d **out** who it looks like," he whispered.

"Who?" asked Joe.

"Mrs. Gorf."

The potato salad laughed.

"Ha! Ha! Ha!" said Mrs. Gorf. "Now I'll get you! You think you're so cute, don't you! Well, you won't **get away** from me this time!"

She **wiggle**d her ears, first her right one, then her left.

"Quick, Joe!" said John. "Eat her!"

The two boys dug their plastic **utensil**s into the potato salad and **shovel**ed it into their mouths as fast as they could.

Joe **swallow**ed the final **mouthful**.

"Whew!" said John. "That was close."

Joe **rub**bed his **belly** and **sigh**ed.

They both stared at the empty plate.

"You know, Joe," said John, "that didn't taste too bad."

"It was pretty good," Joe agreed.

They went back for seconds.

25. A STORY THAT ISN'T ABOUT SOCKS

It was class picture day. The children were all **dress**ed **up** in their best clothes.

Stephen came to school wearing a three-piece **suit**: gray **trouser**s, a gray **vest**, and a gray jacket. Underneath his vest was a white shirt and a red-and-gold-**striped** tie. On his feet were hard, black, shiny shoes.

He was very handsome.

The other kids laughed when they saw him.

"You've worn lots of **silly costume**s," said Bebe, "but this is the silliest one yet!"

Bebe was wearing yellow shorts, a red shirt with white **polka dot**s, and a **floppy** green hat.

Mrs. Jewls rang her cowbell. "Settle down!" she said.

The children settled in their seats. Stephen remained standing.

"Look at Stephen," said Maurecia. "His jacket is the same color as his pants."

"They're supposed to be the same color," Stephen tried to explain. "It's a suit. And they're not called pants, they're called *trousers*."

"Ooooooh," said Maurecia. "Can you go swimming in your suit?"

"No," said Stephen.

"I can go swimming in my suit," said Maurecia.

Maurecia had on a black-and-white-striped bikini.

"I'm sure Stephen's suit is good for other things," said Mrs. Jewls.

"It is," said Stephen.

"Like what?" asked Todd.

"**Stand**ing **around** and looking important," said Stephen.

"What about sitting?" asked Todd.

"No, I'm not supposed to sit," said Stephen. "The suit might get **wrinkle**d. I'm just supposed to stand around and look important."

"Oh," said Todd.

Todd was wearing white shorts, a Hawaiian shirt,[1] and sunglasses.

Deedee crawled across the floor to Stephen so she could get a better look at his shoes. "They're so shiny!" she said. "I can see

---

1 Hawaiian shirt 하와이를 원산지로 하는 화려한 무늬의 셔츠. 알로하 셔츠라고도 부른다.

myself." She **knock**ed on one of his shoes with her **fist**. "They're hard, too!"

"Deedee, get up," said Mrs. Jewls.

Deedee stood up. She had on a black T-shirt that came down to her knees. In the middle of the shirt was a red heart. Above the heart in **sparkling** silver and gold letters it said LOVE **GODDESS**.

"I **bet** they're good for **kickball**, huh, Stephen?" she asked. "Since they're so hard."

"No," said Stephen. "I can't run in them. And they hurt my feet."

"Then why do you wear them?" asked Deedee.

"Because they're uncomfortable," Stephen explained. "You have to wear uncomfortable shoes if you want to look important."

"Oh," said Deedee.

"What's that thing around your neck?" asked Paul.

"It's a tie," said Stephen.

"Does it keep your neck warm?" asked Paul.

"No," said Stephen.

"Does it hold your shirt on?" asked Paul.

"No," said Stephen.

"Well, what's it for?" asked Paul.

"It **choke**s me," said Stephen.

"Oh," said Paul.

"The more it chokes me, the better I look," Stephen explained. "See?" He **tighten**ed his tie.

"Oh, yeah," said Paul. "You look real handsome."

Paul was wearing cowboy-and-Indian pajamas.

Stephen pulled his tie tighter. "Now how do I look?" he asked.

"Wow, you look great!" said D.J. "Pull it tighter!"

Stephen pulled his tie even tighter. "How's this?" he **gasp**ed.

"You look great and very important," said D.J.

D.J. was wearing a toga² made out of his **bed sheet**.

"Pull it tighter!" said Bebe.

Stephen pulled on his tie. He could no longer breathe.

"Tighter!" everyone **yell**ed.

Stephen pulled it even tighter. His eyes **bulge**d and his nose turned blue. He had never been more handsome.

"Tighter!" they all shouted.

Stephen pulled his tie so hard that he **rip**ped it in half.

"Ohhhhhhhhh," the whole class **groan**ed.

"Darn!" said Stephen. "Now I'm not great and important anymore."

"Yes you are, Stephen," said Mrs. Jewls. "You're just as great and important as you ever were."

"I am?" Stephen asked.

"Certainly," said Mrs. Jewls. "The tie didn't make you important. It doesn't matter what you wear on the outside. It's what's underneath that **count**s."

"Underneath?" asked Stephen.

---

2 **toga** 토가. 고대의 로마 시민이 입던 겉옷. 긴 천을 여러 가지 방법으로 몸에 걸친다.

"Yes," said Mrs. Jewls. "If you want to be great and important, you have to wear expensive **underpant**s."

"Oh," said Stephen.

Mrs. Jewls had on a **flowered** tank top[3] and a grass skirt.[4]

---

3 **tank top** 러닝 셔츠처럼 소매가 없는 상의.
4 **grass skirt** 하와이의 훌라춤을 추는 무용수들이 입는 풀잎을 엮어 만든 치마. 훌라 스커트라고도 부른다.

26. THE MEAN MRS. JEWLS

Everybody in Mrs. Jewls's class thought she was a very nice teacher.

They were wrong. There is no such thing as a nice teacher.

If you think you have a nice teacher, then you are wrong too.

Inside every nice teacher there is a mean and **rotten** teacher **burst**ing to get out. The nicer the teacher is on the outside, the meaner the teacher inside is.

As Mrs. Jewls was changing the **bulletin board** before class, a mean and rotten voice whispered inside her brain. "Give the children lots of busy work today," it said. "And then make them do it over again if their **handwriting** isn't perfect."

146

Mrs. Jewls tried very hard to **ignore** the voice. She didn't like giving busy work. Instead she tried to teach the children three new things every day. She believed that if they learned three new things every day, they would **eventually** learn everything there is to know.

There are some classes where the teachers give so much busy work that the children never learn anything.

"What do you care if the children learn anything?" asked the mean and rotten voice. "It's not your job to teach them. It's your job to **punish** them. Keep them in at recess. Hit them with your **yardstick**!"

The bell rang and all the kids **scurried** to their desks.

"We are going to learn three new things today," Mrs. Jewls **announce**d. "How to make pickles,[1] seven plus four, and the **capital** of England."

All the children **paid** close **attention**.

"The capital of England is London," said Mrs. Jewls. "Seven plus four **equal**s eleven. And pickles are made by sticking **cucumber**s in **brine**."

On her desk she had a box of cucumbers and a **vat** of brine for a **demonstration**.

"Okay, Joe," said Mrs. Jewls. "How much is seven plus four?"

Joe **shrug**ged.

"But I just told you, Joe," said Mrs. Jewls. "Weren't you listening?"

---

1 pickle 피클. 오이와 양파 등의 채소를 식초, 설탕, 소금, 향신료를 섞어 만든 액체에 담아 절여서 만든다.

"I don't know," said Joe.

"Okay, who can tell me how pickles are made? Yes, Jason."

"Eleven!" Jason **declare**d.

Mrs. Jewls **frown**ed. "That's a correct answer," she said, "but **unfortunate**ly I didn't ask the right question. Can anyone tell me how pickles are made? Yes, Bebe."

"In London," said Bebe.

"I suppose they make some pickles in London," said Mrs. Jewls. "Okay, let's start again. Calvin, what's the capital of England?"

"Could you write England on the board?" asked Calvin. "I can do a lot better when I can see the question."

Mrs. Jewls wrote *England* on the board.

"Oh, okay," said Calvin, now that he saw the question. "The capital of England is E."

"Yes, that's one capital of England," Mrs. Jewls had to admit. "Okay, I will say it one more time. The capital of England is London."

"Isn't that where they make all the pickles?" asked Jenny.

"No, they don't make all the pickles in London," explained Allison. "Just eleven."

"Well, where do they make the rest of the pickles?" asked Stephen.

"Shut up!" shouted Mrs. Jewls. "Well, **that does it**. You're all staying inside for recess!"

Everyone stared at her. Mrs. Jewls had never told anyone to shut up. It was against the class rules for anyone to use that expression. If you did, you had to write your name on the **blackboard** under the word **DISCIPLINE**.

Mrs. Jewls put her hand over her mouth, then took it away. "Oh dear, I'm very sorry," she said. "I don't know what **came over** me."

She wrote her own name on the blackboard under the word DISCIPLINE.

"Perhaps you'll learn the lesson better if you write it down," she suggested. "Everyone please take out a piece of paper and a pickle."

Everybody laughed.

"Pencil!" **snap**ped Mrs. Jewls. "I meant to say pencil. It just came out pickle."

"I didn't know pickles came from pencils," said Jenny. "I thought they came from cucumbers."

"I thought they came from London," said Todd.

Mrs. Jewls **made a**n ugly **face**. "Todd, didn't I just tell you to shut up?" she asked. She picked up her yardstick and held it over Todd's head. "Well, answer me!" she demanded. "Didn't I tell you to shut up?"

"Yes," said Todd.

"How **dare** you **talk back** to me!" snapped Mrs. Jewls. "Didn't I just tell you to shut up?"

Todd kept his mouth shut.

"Well, answer me!" she demanded.

Todd didn't know what to do. He **nod**ded his head.

"Keep still!" ordered Mrs. Jewls. "Now I don't want you to

say another word, is that clear?"

Todd stared at her.

"Is that clear?" she asked again.

"Yes," Todd said **meek**ly.

Mrs. Jewls **slam**med down the yardstick. Todd quickly moved out of the way. The yardstick **bang**ed against his desk and broke in half.

Mrs. Jewls stared at the eighteen inches she held in her hand. "Oh my **goodness**," she said. "I'm sorry, Todd. I don't know what's the matter with me today. I must have gotten up on the wrong side of the bed this morning.[2]"

She put a check next to her name under the word DISCIPLINE.

"Okay, let me try to make this very simple," she said. "If I have seven cucumbers. And then I get four more cucumbers. And then I drop all the cucumbers in brine and take them to the capital of England. What do I have? How many? And where am I?"

"Huh?" said D.J.

"What?" asked John.

"Could you write the question on the board, please?" asked Rondi.

"Shut up!" Mrs. Jewls yelled a third time. In a **mock**ing voice she said, "'Could you write the question on the board, please?' You kids think you are so cute! Well, we'll see just how cute you really

---

2 get up on the wrong side of the bed '꿈자리가 사납다' 또는 '기분 나쁘게 하루를 시작하다'라는 의미의 표현.

are." She picked up the vat of brine from her desk. "How would you like it if I **pour**ed this on your heads? You won't be so cute when you're all **shrivel**ed up and covered with **wart**s, like pickles!"

She walked up and down the **aisle**s carrying the pickle juice and **glaring** at the children.

No one dared make a sound.

She stopped next to Leslie. "How about you, Leslie?" she asked. "How would you like pickled **pigtail**s?"

Leslie **trembled**. Her pigtails **wiggled**.

"Well, I'm going to ask you three questions, Leslie," said Mrs. Jewls. "And if you don't answer them all correctly, I'm going to **dump** this on your head."

Leslie **gulp**ed.

"Question one," said Mrs. Jewls. "How much is seven plus four?"

Leslie quickly tried to count on her fingers but she didn't have enough. "Eleven?" she guessed.

A look of disappointment came over Mrs. Jewls's face. "Okay, question two: What is the capital of England?"

"L-London," Leslie said nervously.

"Rats!" said Mrs. Jewls. "Okay, question three." She looked down at the vat of brine she was holding and shook her head. She thought a moment, then smiled. "What is the name of my cousin who lives in Vermont?"

Leslie had no idea, so she just had to **take a wild guess**. She closed her eyes and said, "Fred Jewls?"

"Wrong!" exclaimed Mrs. Jewls. She raised the vat of brine high above Leslie's head and started to **tip** it over.

Paul jumped out of his seat. Those pigtails had once saved his life. Now it was his turn to return the **favor**!

He pushed the vat of brine back the other way. He was just trying to push it up straight, but he pushed too hard. It poured all over Mrs. Jewls, **drench**ing her.

Paul **froze** in **terror**.

Mrs. Jewls **blink**ed her eyes. Pickle juice **drip**ped down her face. "Thanks, Paul," she said. "I needed that."

The brine had **cure**d her.

She circled her name on the blackboard and sent herself home early on the **kindergarten** bus.

27. LOST AND FOUND

Joy and Maurecia were best friends. They sat down on the grass to eat their lunches, but then Maurecia remembered she needed chocolate milk. She went to get some from Miss Mush.

When she returned, she couldn't find her lunch.

"What happened to my lunch?" she asked.

Joy looked up at her, then shrugged her shoulders.

"I set my lunch down right here!" said Maurecia. "You saw me, didn't you?"

Joy shook her head.

"I put it here, then I went to Miss Mush's room to get some

chocolate milk. I had a peanut butter and banana sandwich! And there's **no way** I can eat a peanut butter and banana sandwich without chocolate milk."

Joy shrugged her shoulders.

Maurecia didn't know what to do.

"Ca' I haf a thip uff your milk?[1]" asked Joy.

It was hard for Joy to talk, because her mouth was full of peanut butter and bananas.

Maurecia handed Joy the **carton** of chocolate milk.

Joy took a big drink, then **swallow**ed.

Maurecia looked all around for her lunch. She **crawl**ed in the **dirt** as she searched through the **bush**es.

"Any luck?" asked Joy as she finished Maurecia's chocolate milk.

"I found it!" Maurecia **exclaim**ed.

Joy **cough**ed on the chocolate milk. "You did?" she asked, then coughed again.

Maurecia crawled out of the bushes holding a paper **sack**. She sat back down next to Joy and opened it.

"Is it your lunch?" asked Joy.

"No," said Maurecia.

"Too bad," said Joy.

"It's money!" exclaimed Maurecia.

Joy's eyes nearly **pop**ped out of her head as she looked at the

---

1   Can I have a sip of your milk? 네 우유를 한 모금 마셔도 되겠니?

154

paper bag. It was **stuff**ed with dollar **bill**s. And they weren't just one-dollar bills. There were a few five-dollar bills, some ten-dollar bills, but mostly twenty-dollar bills.

"We found a million dollars!" Joy whispered.

"*We?*" asked Maurecia.

They **count**ed the money. It wasn't a million dollars. It was twenty thousand six hundred and fifty-five dollars.

"Let's **split** it," said Joy. "You take half and I'll take half."

"Maybe I should show it to Louis," said Maurecia.

"Louis!" exclaimed Joy. "Are you crazy? Let's spend it. We can buy a skateboard, or a bicycle, or a horse, or a **fancy** car, or an airplane!"

"I like taking the bus," said Maurecia.

"You could buy ice cream!" said Joy. "All the ice cream you ever want for the rest of your life."

She knew Maurecia loved ice cream more than anything else in the world.

Maurecia smiled as she thought about it. "No, I better show it to Louis. He'll know what to do."

"You'll just get in trouble," warned Joy. "Louis will think you **rob**bed a bank. You'll go to **jail** for the rest of your life."

"Louis knows I'm not a bank **robber**," said Maurecia.

"But what if the real bank robbers find out you have their money?" asked Joy. "They'll come after you and **murder** you."

"Oh, I didn't think of that," said Maurecia.

"You better give it to me," said Joy.

"Louis will **protect** me," said Maurecia. She walked across the playground.

Louis was talking to Terrence. He said, "If you ever tie Leslie's pigtails to the tetherball **pole** again, I'll—"

"Louis, look!" said Maurecia. She held the paper sack up to his face.

"No thank you, Maurecia, I'm not hungry," said Louis.

"It's not my lunch," said Maurecia. "Look inside!"

Louis took the bag from her and looked inside.

"Very nice," he said, then gave it back to her. "Now I want you to go **untie** Leslie and tell her—"

He suddenly stopped talking and **blink**ed his eyes. He looked at Terrence, then at Maurecia, then at Terrence, then at Maurecia, and then at the paper sack. "Let me see that again," he said.

Maurecia gave him the bag.

"Hey, what about me?" asked Terrence.

"**Get lost**, Jack Frost,[2]" said Louis.

Terrence **ran away**.

"Did you rob a bank?" asked Louis.

"No, I found it in the bushes," said Maurecia.

"I believe you," said Louis. "We'll have to put it in the **lost and found**."

---

2 Jack Frost 잭 프로스트. 서리, 눈, 얼음 등을 의인화한 추위의 요정. 눈과 얼음으로 만들어졌고 장난을 좋아한다.

"I know," said Maurecia. "Whoever lost it is probably very sad."

"But if no one **claim**s it in two weeks, you can have it," said Louis. He took the bag of money and headed to the office.

Joy was waiting for Louis at the door. "Hey, Louis," she said. "I lost a bag full of money. Have you seen it?"

"Help!" Leslie screamed from the tetherball **court**.

A week later, Maurecia was eating lunch alone. She was eating a piece of **sweet potato** pie. Joy was crawling around in the dirt looking for more bags of money.

"Maurecia," said Louis, "I'd like you to meet someone. This is Mr. Finch."

Mr. Finch was an old man with white hair and a long white **beard**. He shook Maurecia's hand with both of his hands.

"It's your money, isn't it?" asked Maurecia.

Mr. Finch **nod**ded. "It was my life's **savings**," he said. "For fifty years I made pencils. I got a penny for every pencil I made. I hate pencils! But finally I saved enough money to quit my job and do what I always wanted to do."

"What's that?" asked Maurecia.

"I'm going to open my own ice cream **parlor**," he said, then started to cry. "When I lost that money, I thought I'd have to start making pencils again."

Maurecia cried too.

"Here, I want you to have this," **blubber**ed Mr. Finch. He gave her an envelope **contain**ing five hundred dollars.

It was the second largest amount of money Maurecia had ever had.

"And I will give you free ice cream for the rest of your life at my ice cream parlor," he promised.

"Thank you!" said Maurecia.

"No, thank *you*," said Mr. Finch. "I'm so glad someone as kind and as honest as you found it. There are so many dishonest people in the world. It's good to know there are still good people too."

They hugged each other.

Joy crawled out of the bushes. "Hey. Who's that?" she asked.

"This is Mr. Finch," said Maurecia. "It's his money. Look, he gave me a **reward** of five hundred dollars. And I'll get free ice cream for the rest of my life!"

"Well, what about me?" Joy demanded. "Don't I get anything?"

"Oh, dear me," said Mr. Finch. "I didn't realize there was someone else **involv**ed."

"Maurecia would never have found the money if it wasn't for me," said Joy.

"Why, what'd you do?" asked Louis.

"I stole her lunch!" Joy said proudly.

Mr. Finch gave her a pencil.

28. VALOOOSH

Mrs. Jewls rang her cowbell. "I have some wonderful news," she said.

The children stopped what they were doing and looked up. They waited for Mrs. Jewls to tell them the wonderful news.

"You are a very lucky class indeed," said Mrs. Jewls. "Mrs. Waloosh, the world famous dancer, will be coming here to Wayside School! She will teach you how to dance!"

Everyone was still waiting for the wonderful news.

"Isn't that exciting?" asked Mrs. Jewls. "You will see her every Wednesday instead of going to P.E.[1]"

"Will girls have to dance with *boys?*" asked Jenny.

"I suppose," said Mrs. Jewls.

"**Gross**!" exclaimed Leslie.

"**Yuck**!" said Dana.

"Will boys have to dance with *girls?*" asked Ron.

"**Obviously**," said Mrs. Jewls.

"**No way!**" said Eric Fry.

"I'd rather dance with a dead rat!" said Terrence.

Everybody started talking **at once**—about **cootie**s, and **wart**s, and other **horrible disease**s you get from touching girls or boys.

Mrs. Jewls rang her cowbell again and told them to settle down.

"Mrs. Jewls, I don't need to take dancing lessons," said Eric Bacon. "I already know how to dance!"

"Yes, Eric, I've seen you 'dance,'" Mrs. Jewls said **sarcastic**ally.

Eric Bacon was a great breakdancer.[2] But breakdancing was no longer allowed at Wayside School. That was because every time Eric danced, he broke something.

"Mrs. Waloosh will teach you the **grace** and beauty of **classical ballroom** dancing,[3]" said Mrs. Jewls.

Everybody **groan**ed.

On Wednesday they all headed down to their first dancing

---

1   P.E. (= Physical Education) 체육 수업.

2   **breakdancer** 브레이크댄스를 추는 사람. 브레이크댄스는 1980년대부터 유행한 미국의 힙합댄스의 하나로 '비보잉'이라고도 부른다.

3   **ballroom dance** 사교댄스. 사교적인 즐거움을 위해 두 사람 또는 그 이상이 함께 추는 모든 종류의 춤을 말한다. 왈츠, 탱고, 블루스 등이 여기에 포함된다.

lesson. Except Myron. Myron went to P.E.

"How come Myron never has to do anything?" asked Jason.

"I don't know!" said Calvin. "I've been wondering about that too."

"Myron's father must be friends with the **president**," said Bebe.

"I think Myron gave Mr. Kidswatter a thousand dollars," said Todd.

"No, I **bet** he's **blackmail**ing Mrs. Jewls," said Jenny.

"How could he do that?" asked Benjamin.

"Maybe Mrs. Jewls got drunk!" said Jenny. "And then she danced on top of her desk with a **lampshade** on her head. And Myron took her picture. And so now Mrs. Jewls has to let Myron do anything he wants, or else he'll show the picture to Mr. Kidswatter!"

"That **makes sense**," said Mac.

"Except if she had a lampshade on her head, how would Mr. Kidswatter know it was Mrs. Jewls?" asked Todd.

No one knew the answer to that.

They entered the room on the second floor.

"Velcome!" said Mrs. Waloosh, a strange-looking woman with bright red hair. It looked like her head was on fire. "My name eez Meez Valoosh. It's so vonderful to be here at Vayside School."

She wore pink tights and a **sparkling** pink top. "I hope ve vill be friends, yes?" she asked.

Nobody said a word.

All around were red and green balls. There was also one yellow ball. This was the room where Louis kept the balls for lunch and **recess**. It was also the room that was always used for school dances. It was the ballroom.

"So!" exclaimed Mrs. Waloosh. "Who vill be first?"

Everyone tried to hide behind someone else.

Mrs. Waloosh put her hands on Ron's face. "Vhat eez your name?" she asked.

"Ron," he **squeak**ed.

"RONALDO!" **bellow**ed Mrs. Waloosh. "King of the Gypsies!⁴"

"I don't know how to dance," said Ron.

"Da*h*nce?" asked Mrs. Waloosh. She looked very surprised. "Ve are not going to da*h*nce," she said.

"We're not?" asked Ron.

"No, Ronaldo," whispered Mrs. Waloosh. "Ve are going to *tango!*⁵"

She put her left arm around Ron's **waist**. Then she **grab**bed his left hand with her right and stuck it way out in front of them. Suddenly the music started.

Mrs. Waloosh **dragg**ed poor Ron across the room as she **stomp**ed her feet **in time** to the music.

Domp. Domp-domp. Domp-domp. Da-da-domp. Domp! Domp! Domp! Domp! Domp-domp-domp-domp-domp, "HEY!"

---

4   Gypsy 인도 북부에서 이동을 시작해 현재 거의 전 세계에 흩어져 살고 있는 유랑 민족을 말한다.

5   tango 탱고. 남아메리카의 아르헨티나에서 시작되어 유럽으로 전해진 사교 댄스. 4분의 2박자, 8분의 4박자의 느린 곡에 맞춰 춤을 춘다.

When she yelled "HEY!" she threw Ron up in the air and **clap**ped her hands. Ron turned a **somersault** in **midair**; then Mrs. Waloosh caught him. They tangoed back to where they started. Ron's eyes were spinning in opposite directions.

"Hey, that looked like fun," said Maurecia. "Do me."

"Very vell," said Mrs. Waloosh. She grabbed Maurecia and tangoed with her across the room. Domp. Domp-domp. Domp-domp. Da-da-domp. Domp! Domp! Domp! Domp! Domp-domp-domp-domp-domp, "HEY!" She threw Maurecia up in the air and clapped her hands.

Maurecia turned a double somersault before Mrs. Waloosh caught her. They tangoed back to the front.

"My turn," said Terrance.

As Mrs. Waloosh tangoed with Terrence, the other kids **stamp**ed their feet along with Mrs. Waloosh. They all yelled "HEY!" at the same time and clapped their hands.

One by one, Mrs. Waloosh tangoed with every kid in the class. The other kids danced with each other. Boys danced with girls, and girls danced with boys. They didn't care. Paul danced with Leslie. Dana danced with John. Terrence danced with Rondi. Allison danced with Jason. D.J. danced with Kathy. Todd danced with Joy.

"HEY!" they all shouted together.

Of course, they weren't strong enough to throw each other up in the air. Instead, they tried to **trip** each other and throw each other to the ground. "HEY!"

Even Kathy was having fun. "HEY!" she shouted as she kicked D.J. in the rear end.

They also threw the balls at each other. "HEY!"

Mrs. Waloosh began to get tired. Sometimes she didn't catch the children after she **toss**ed them in the air.

Deedee **crash**ed to the floor. "Wow," she said, "this is more fun than **murder**-the-man-with-the-ball! HEY!"

At last the music stopped. Domp! Domp! Domp! Domp! Domp-domp-domp-domp-domp. And everyone shouted "HEY!" one last time.

Mrs. Waloosh clapped her hands. "Vonderful!" she exclaimed. "Fahntasteek!"

They all **stagger**ed out of the ballroom, **cut up**, **bruise**d, and **bleed**ing.

"Next veek, ve valtz!" Mrs. Waloosh called after them.

"So how did everyone like dancing?" asked Mrs. Jewls when they returned.

"Da*h*nce?" asked Ronaldo, King of the Gypsies. "Ve didn't da*h*nce."

"You didn't?" asked Mrs. Jewls.

"No," said Ronaldo. "Ve *tangoed!*"

Everyone cheered.

"It vas vonderful!" exclaimed Kathy.

"Fahntasteek!" said Terrence.

164

Myron was sorry he had missed it.

"I can't vait till next Vednesday," said Todd.

29. THE LOST EAR

Mrs. Jewls was teaching the class about **mammal**s. "All mammals have hair," she said.

Bebe raised her hand. "Is my father a mammal?" she asked.

"Yes, all people are mammals," said Mrs. Jewls.

"But my father doesn't have any hair," said Bebe. "He's **bald**!"

Everybody laughed.

Benjamin **stared** down at his desk top. He was very **determined**. Mrs Jewls would be handing out report cards at the end of the week. He had to tell her his real name before then.

He raised his hand.

But Mac also had his hand raised.

"Yes, Mac," said Mrs. Jewls.

"I heard about a man who was getting his hair cut," said Mac. "And the **barber** cut off one of the man's ears! See, the man had very long hair. I think he was a hippie.[1] So the barber couldn't see his ear until it fell on the floor."

"Thank you, Mac," said Mrs. Jewls. "That was a very interesting story."

"I'm not finished," said Mac. "When the barber saw the ear on the floor, he said, 'Is that your ear on the floor?' And then the hippie said 'What? I can't hear you.' So the barber showed him his ear; then he called an **ambulance** to take the hippie to the hospital."

"Were they able to put his ear back on?" asked Todd.

"Well, see," said Mac, "the doctors were all set to **sew** it to his head. They were in the **operating** room and everything. But suddenly they couldn't find the ear. Man, they looked everywhere for it!"

"Did they look under the operating table?" asked Joy.

"Yep," said Mac. "It wasn't there."

"How about in the bathroom?" asked Eric Bacon. "Maybe they lost it when they washed their hands."

"They looked, but it wasn't there," said Mac.

"Did they leave it at the barber shop?" asked Jenny.

---

1 hippie 히피. 1960년대부터 미국을 중심으로 생겨난 평화주의를 주장하는 집단을 말한다. 이들은 기성의 사회통념, 제도, 가치관을 부정하고 반사회적인 행동을 하는 것으로 유명하다.

"Nope."

"Did they ever find it?" asked Allison.

"Yes," said Mac, "but you'll never guess where!"

"In the **refrigerator**," **grumble**d Mrs. Jewls.

"No, how would it get there?" asked Mac.

"Well, we really need to get back to mammals," said Mrs. Jewls. "Yes, Mark."

Benjamin lowered his hand. "My name's not Mark," he said. "My name really is Benjamin. Benjamin Nushmutt! And I came from Hempleton, not Magadonia."

"Fine," said Mrs. Jewls. "But we were talking about mammals. Now the whale is the largest mammal. Even though it lives in the ocean, it is still a mammal, not a fish."

"Do whales have hair?" asked John.

"Yes," said Mrs. Jewls.

Dana laughed. "A whale with **pigtail**s!" she exclaimed.

"Boy, I'd love to pull one of those!" said Paul.

Benjamin couldn't believe it. "Didn't you hear what I just said?" he asked.

"Yes, Benjamin," said Mrs. Jewls.

"Well, don't you think I'm strange?" asked Benjamin. "All this time you've been calling me by the wrong name, and I never told you? Don't you think I'm crazy?"

"No," said Mrs. Jewls.

Benjamin was getting upset. "Well, don't you think it's a stupid name? Benjamin Nush-mutt!" He looked around at his **classmate**s. "Doesn't anybody think I'm **weird**?"

"No, you're not weird!" said Sharie. "I'll tell you what's weird. What's weird is bringing a **hobo** to school for show-and-tell. I'm the one who's weird."

"That's not weird!" said Bebe. "What's weird is telling everyone you have a brother when you don't. I'm the **weirdo**!"

"You call that weird?" exclaimed Stephen. "*I'm* weird. Who else would **choke** himself just to look nice?"

"That's not weird," said Jenny. "That's normal. Try reading a story backward. That's weird. I'm the weird one in this class."

"That's a laugh!" said Rondi. "If you're so weird, then how come you never asked Louis to kick you in the teeth? I'm the one who's crazy!"

"No, that's not crazy," said Todd. "I'll tell you what's crazy. What's crazy is that we all go to school on the thirtieth floor, and the bathrooms are way down on the first!"

Everyone agreed with that, even Mrs. Jewls.

Benjamin shook his head. What a **bunch** of weirdos! he thought. Then he smiled. He felt proud to be in a class where nobody was strange because nobody was normal.

"Oh, this must be your lunch," said Mrs. Jewls. She gave Benjamin the white paper **sack** that had been sitting on her desk since Benjamin's first day of school.

At lunch Allison headed down the stairs. "Mark!" she exclaimed.

"Hi, Allison," said Mark Miller. "Long time no see." He carried a white paper sack just like Benjamin's.

Allison was afraid she was back on the nineteenth **story**.

"Don't worry," said Mark. "Suddenly everyone realized my name was Mark Miller and not Benjamin Nushmutt. And then Miss Zarves gave me this bag and told me to take it to the hospital."

"Is it your lunch?" asked Allison.

"Look inside," said Mark. He handed her the bag.

Allison looked inside.

There was an ear.

Allison's eyes **lit up**. "Oh, now I **get it**!" she exclaimed. "I understand everything! There is no Miss Zarves! See, Mac was talking about the ear, then Mark Miller, I mean Benjamin Nushmutt, said his name wasn't Mark Miller, so that means you—"

"What?" asked Mark.

Allison suddenly looked very **confused**. "**Never mind**," she **mumbled**.

For just a second Allison had understood everything, but then she lost it.

30. WAYSIDE SCHOOL IS FALLING DOWN

A strong wind **whoosh**ed around the **playground** in the early morning before school, blowing **dirt** and leaves in the faces of the children.

When the bell rang, they could **hardly make it** from the playground to the school. The wind was blowing directly at them, pushing their hair straight back.

With every **gust** of wind the school building **teeter**ed one way, then **totter**ed back the other.

As they headed up the stairs, they could feel the building **sway back and forth**. The higher they got, the more it swayed.

"**Hooray!**" **yell**ed Kathy. "Wayside School is falling down!"

"What are you so happy about?" asked Joe. "We'll all die."

"Yes, but we won't have to do our homework," said Kathy.

They entered the room on the thirtieth **story**.

Mrs. Jewls rang her **cowbell**. "Find your seats," she said.

That wasn't easy. All the desks were **cram**med together on one side of the room. The building swayed, and the desks slid to the other side of the room.

Finally the children all found their seats and **plant**ed their feet firmly on the floor.

"We are going to have a fire **drill** today," Mrs. Jewls told them. "So let's be prepared. Who is our door **monitor** this week?"

"I am," said Maurecia.

"Good," said Mrs. Jewls. "Who is our help monitor?"

"I am," said Jason.

"Very good," said Mrs. Jewls. "You have a big mouth."

Stephen raised his hand. "What if there really is a fire?" he asked.

"There's not going to be a real fire," said Mrs. Jewls. "It's just a drill."

"I know, but what if there really is a fire?" asked Stephen. "And then the **firemen** won't come because they'll think it's a drill! The school will burn down!"

"Don't worry," said Kathy. "The school is not going to burn down. It's going to fall down!"

BLEEP! BLEEP! BLEEP! . . . BLEEP! BLEEP! BLEEP! . . . BLEEP! BLEEP! BLEEP!

It was the fire drill.

Maurecia, the door monitor, held open the door.

Jason, the help monitor, ran to the window. "Help!" he screamed. "Save us! We're up here. Help! Help!"

Mrs. Jewls led the children out of the room. If there was a real fire, the children might not be able to see her because of the smoke, so she **constant**ly rang her cowbell. There wouldn't be time to go **all the way** down the stairs, either. Mrs. Jewls led them up the **ladder** and through the **trapdoor** to the **roof**. If there was a real fire, helicopters would **rescue** them.

The wind was even worse on the roof than it was on the playground. Mrs. Jewls stood in the center and held the cowbell high above her head. She looked just like the **Statue** of **Liberty**.[1]

"Everyone stay away from the edge!" she warned.

Kathy sang: "Wayside School is falling down, falling down . . ."

"It's not falling down," said Stephen. "It's burning down! And no one will rescue us because they think it's a drill."

Jenny noticed a dark, **funnel**-shaped cloud off in the **distance**. "Tornado!²" she screamed. "We're all going to get **suck**ed off the roof!"

A **flash** of **lightning** lit the sky, followed by a loud **crack** of **thunder**.

---

1   Statue of Liberty 자유의 여신상. 미국 뉴욕항의 리버티섬에 세워진 거대한 여신상.
2   tornado 토네이도. 바다나 넓은 평지에서 발생하는 매우 강하게 돌아가는 깔때기 모양
    의 회오리바람.

"We're going to be struck by lightning!" shouted Todd.

"No we won't," said Stephen. "We'll burn in the fire."

"No, we'll be sucked up in the tornado," said Jenny.

"No, the school is going to fall down," said Kathy.

Mrs. Jewls continued to ring her cowbell. *Klabonk! Klabonk! Klabonk!* The strong wind carried the sound for miles.

Suddenly, screams came from down below. Then the whole building began to shake **violent**ly.

"**Earthquake!**" yelled Benjamin.

"Fire," corrected Stephen.

"The school must have been struck by lightning," said Todd.

"Tornado," said Jenny.

"All fall down," said Kathy.

The building continued to **rumble** and shake. There were more screams.

"Listen!" said Myron. "They're trying to warn us about something."

Down below, over five hundred kids and teachers were shouting together: "STAR BRINGING PURPLE!"

"What are they saying?" asked Mrs. Jewls.

"I don't know," said Myron.

Mrs. Jewls **rattle**d her cowbell.

"STAR BRINGING PURPLE!" they shouted again.

"It sounds like 'Star bringing purple,'" said Myron.

"What does that mean?" asked Mrs. Jewls.

Myron **shrug**ged.

Mrs. Jewls rang her bell even louder.

"STAR BRINGING YORBEL!"

"Wait," said Myron. "They're not saying, 'Star bringing purple.' They're saying, 'Star bringing yorbel.'"

"What's a yorbel?" asked Mrs. Jewls. She rang her bell even louder.

The school shook and rumbled.

"STOP BRINGING YORBEL!"

"Stop something," said Myron.

Mrs. Jewls rang her cowbell.

"STOP RINGING YOUR BELL!"

"Stop ringing your bell," said Myron.

"Oh," said Mrs. Jewls. She stopped ringing her bell.

Down below, all the students and teachers **clap**ped their hands.

But it was too late.

Rondi opened the trapdoor. "Cows!" she **exclaim**ed.

The school was filled with cows.

From all over the **countryside**, cows had heard Mrs. Jewls's cowbell and **heed**ed the call. There were thousands of them. They filled the stairs and all the classrooms.

There was **no way** for the children to get down. Helicopters finally came and took them one at a time off the roof.

Wayside School didn't blow down. It didn't burn down. It wasn't struck by lightning, sucked up in a tornado, or destroyed by an earthquake.

It was cowed.

No one knew how to **get rid of** the cows. Cows are strange animals. They don't mind walking upstairs, but nothing can make them walk downstairs.

Someone suggested **starving** the cows, but the farmers wouldn't allow that. Thousands of **bale**s of **hay** were sent in. Several cows had **calves**.

The newspapers thought it was funny and made jokes about smart cows learning to read and write.

And so Wayside School was closed. The kids and teachers were **temporarily** sent to different schools.

Only one person stayed behind. He was there all day and all night trying to get the cows to go home.

"C'mon," **plead**ed Louis, the **yard** teacher, as he pushed and pulled on the cows. "Go home. Please? Pretty please?[3]"

Everybody **moo**ed.

---

3 pretty please 귀여운 표정을 짓고 애교 가득한 목소리로 부탁을 할 때 사용하는 표현.

WORKBOOK

WAYSIDE SCHOOL
IS FALLING DOWN

LOUIS SACHAR
ILLUSTRATED BY TIM HEITZ

Contents

'아동 도서계의 노벨상!' 미국 최고 권위의 아동 문학상

뉴베리 상(Newbery Award)은 미국 도서관 협회에서 해마다 미국 아동 문학 발전에 가장 크게 이바지한 작가에게 수여하는 아동 문학상입니다. 1922년에 시작된 이 상은 미국에서 가장 오랜 역사를 지닌 아동 문학상이자, '아동 도서계의 노벨상'이라 불릴 만큼 높은 권위를 자랑하는 상입니다.

뉴베리 상은 그 역사와 권위만큼이나 심사 기준이 까다롭기로 유명한데, 심사단은 책의 주제 의식은 물론 정보의 깊이와 스토리의 정교함, 캐릭터와 문체의 적정성 등을 꼼꼼히 평가하여 수상작을 결정합니다.

그해 최고의 작품으로 선정된 도서에게는 '뉴베리 메달(Newbery Medal)'이라고 부르는 금색 메달을 수여하며, 최종 후보에 올랐던 주목할 만한 작품들에게는 '뉴베리 아너(Newbery Honor)'라는 이름의 은색 마크를 수여합니다.

뉴베리 상을 받은 도서는 미국의 모든 도서관에 비치되어 더 많은 독자들을 만나게 되며, 대부분 수십에서 수백만 부가 판매되는 베스트셀러가 됩니다. 뉴베리 상을 수상한 작가는 그만큼 필력과 작품성을 인정받게 되어, 수상 작가의 다른 작품들 또한 수상작 못지않게 커다란 주목과 사랑을 받습니다.

왜 뉴베리 수상작인가?
쉬운 어휘로 쓰인 '검증된' 영어원서!

뉴베리 수상작들은 '검증된 원서'로 국내 영어 학습자들에게 큰 사랑을 받고 있습니다. 뉴베리 수상작이 원서 읽기에 좋은 교재인 이유는 무엇일까요?

1. 아동 문학인 만큼 어휘가 어렵지 않습니다.
2. 어렵지 않은 어휘를 사용하면서도 '문학상'을 수상한 만큼 문장의 깊이가 상당합니다.
3. 적당한 난이도의 어휘와 깊이 있는 문장으로 구성되어 있기 때문에 초등 고학년부터 성인까지, 영어 초보자부터 실력자까지 모든 영어 학습자들이 읽기에 좋습니다.

실제로 뉴베리 수상작은 국제중·특목고에서는 입시 필독서로, 대학교에서는 영어 강독 교재로 다양하고 폭넓게 활용되고 있습니다. 이런 이유로 뉴베리 수상작은 한국어 번역서보다 오히려 원서가 훨씬 많이 판매되는 기현상을 보이고 있습니다.

'베스트 오브 베스트'만을 엄선한 「뉴베리 컬렉션」

「뉴베리 컬렉션」은 뉴베리 메달 및 아너 수상작, 그리고 뉴베리 수상 작가의 유명 작품들을 엄선하여 한국 영어 학습자들을 위한 최적의 교재로 재탄생시킨 영어원서 시리즈입니다.

1. 어휘 수준과 문장의 난이도, 분량 등 국내 영어 학습자들에게 적합한 정도를 종합적으로 검토하여 선정하였습니다.
2. 기존 원서 독자층 사이의 인기도까지 감안하여 최적의 작품들을 선별하였습니다.
3. 판형이 좁고 글씨가 작아 읽기 힘들었던 원서 디자인을 대폭 수정하여, 판형을 시원하게 키우고 읽기에 최적화된 영문 서체를 사용하여 가독성을 극대화하였습니다.
4. 함께 제공되는 워크북은 어려운 어휘를 완벽하게 정리하고 이해력을 점검하는 퀴즈를 덧붙여 독자들이 원서를 보다 쉽고 재미있게 읽을 수 있도록 구성하였습니다.
5. 기존에 높은 가격에 판매되어 구입이 부담스러웠던 오디오북을 부록으로 제공하여 리스닝과 소리 내어 읽기에까지 원서를 두루 활용할 수 있도록 했습니다.

루이스 새커(Louis Sachar)는 현재 미국에서 가장 인기 있는 아동 문학 작가 중 한 사람입니다. 그는 1954년 미국 뉴욕에서 태어났으며 초등학교 보조 교사로 일한 경험을 바탕으로 쓴 「웨이사이드 스쿨(Wayside School)」 시리즈로 잘 알려져 있습니다. 그 외에도 그는 「마빈 레드포스트(Marvin Redpost)」 시리즈, 『There's a Boy in the Girls' Bathroom(여자화장실에 남자가 있다고?)』, 『The Boy Who Lost His Face(얼굴을 잃어버린 소년)』 등 20여 권의 어린이책을 썼습니다. 그가 1998년에 발표한 『Holes』는 독자들의 큰 사랑을 받으며 National Book Award 등 많은 상을 수상하였고, 마침내 1999년에는 뉴베리 메달을 수상하였습니다. 2006년에는 『Holes』의 후속편 『Small Steps』를 출간하였습니다.

「Wayside School」 시리즈는 저자 루이스 새커가 학점 이수를 위해 힐사이드 초등학교(Hillside Elementary School)에서 보조 교사로 일한 경험을 바탕으로 쓴 책입니다. 그곳의 학생들은 루이스를 운동장 선생님(Louis the Yard Teacher)이라고 불렀다고 합니다. 이 시리즈의 주인공들은 힐사이드 초등학교에서 루이스가 만난 아이들의 이름에서 따왔고, 저자 자신을 반영한 인물인 운동장 선생님 루이스도 등장합니다.

웨이사이드 스쿨은 원래는 1층 건물에 30개의 교실을 지을 예정이었지만, 1층에 1개의 교실이 있는 30층 건물로 지어졌습니다. (학교를 지은 건설업자는 매우 미안하다고 했습니다.) 책의 주인공들은 30층에 있는 학급의 아이들 30명이고, 이들은 모두 별나고 이상합니다.

각 장마다 별나고 이상하며 때로는 초현실적인 일이 일어나는 웨이사이드 스쿨 시리즈는 미국 어린이들의 마음을 사로잡았습니다. 어린이들이 직접 선정하는 IRA-CBC Children's Choice에 선정되었고, 1,500만 부 이상의 판매를 올렸습니다. 또한 TV 애니메이션 시리즈로도 제작되어 큰 사랑을 받고 있습니다.

원서 본문

<u>내용이 담긴 원서 본문입니다.</u>
원어민이 읽는 일반 원서와 같은 텍스트지만, 암기해야 할 중요 어휘들은 볼드체로 표시되어 있습니다. 이 어휘들은 지금 들고 계신 워크북에 챕터별로 정리되어 있습니다.

학습 심리학 연구 결과에 따르면, 한 단어씩 따로 외우는 단어 암기는 거의 효과가 없다고 합니다. 단어를 제대로 외우기 위해서는 문맥(context) 속에서 단어를 암기해야 하며, 한 단어당 문맥 속에서 15번 이상 마주칠 때 완벽하게 암기할 수 있다고 합니다.

이 책의 본문에서는 중요 어휘를 볼드체로 강조하여, 문맥 속의 단어들을 더 확실히 인지(word cognition in context)하도록 돕고 있습니다. 또한 대부분의 중요 단어들은 다른 챕터에서도 반복해서 등장하기 때문에 이 책을 읽는 것만으로도 자연스럽게 어휘력을 향상시킬 수 있습니다.

또한 본문 하단에는 내용 이해를 돕기 위한 '각주'가 첨가되어 있습니다. 각주는 굳이 암기할 필요는 없지만, 알아 두면 도움이 될 만한 정보를 설명하고 있습니다. 각주를 참고하면 스토리를 더 깊이 있게 이해할 수 있어 원서를 읽는 재미가 배가됩니다.

워크북(Workbook)

Check Your Reading Speed

해당 챕터의 단어 수가 기록되어 있어, 리딩 속도를 측정할 수 있습니다. 특히 리딩 속도를 중시하는 독자들이 유용하게 사용할 수 있습니다.

Build Your Vocabulary

본문에 볼드 표시되어 있는 단어들이 정리되어 있습니다. 리딩 전·후에 반복해서 보면 원서를 더욱 쉽게 읽을 수 있고, 어휘력도 빠르게 향상될 것입니다.

단어는 〈스펠링 – 빈도 – 발음기호 – 품사 – 한글 뜻 – 영문 뜻〉 순서로 표기되어 있으며 빈도 표시(★)가 많을수록 필수 어휘입니다. 반복해서 등장하는 단어는 빈도 대신 '복습'으로 표기되어 있습니다. 품사는 아래와 같이 표기했습니다.

n. 명사 | a. 형용사 | ad. 부사 | v. 동사

conj. 접속사 | prep. 전치사 | int. 감탄사 | idiom 숙어 및 관용구

Comprehension Quiz

간단한 퀴즈를 통해 읽은 내용에 대한 이해력을 점검해 볼 수 있습니다.

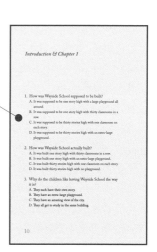

「뉴베리 컬렉션」 이렇게 읽어 보세요!

아래와 같이 프리뷰(Preview) → 리딩(Reading) → 리뷰(Review) 세 단계를 거치면서 읽으면, 더욱 효과적으로 영어 실력을 향상할 수 있습니다.

1. 프리뷰(Preview) : 오늘 읽을 내용을 먼저 점검하자!

- 워크북을 통해 오늘 읽을 챕터에 나와 있는 단어들을 쭉 훑어봅니다. 어떤 단어들이 나오는지, 내가 아는 단어와 모르는 단어는 어떤 것들이 있는지 가벼운 마음으로 살펴봅니다.
- 평소처럼 하나하나 쓰면서 암기하려고 하지는 마세요! 익숙하지 않은 단어들을 주의 깊게 보되, 어차피 리딩을 하면서 점차 익숙해질 단어라는 것을 기억하며 빠르게 훑어봅니다.
- 뒤 챕터로 갈수록 '복습'이라고 표시된 단어들이 늘어나는 것을 알 수 있습니다. '복습' 단어인데도 여전히 익숙하지 않다면 더욱 신경을 써서 봐야겠죠? 매일매일 꾸준히 읽는다면, 익숙한 단어들이 점점 많아진다는 것을 몸으로 느낄 수 있습니다.

2. 리딩(Reading) : 내용에 집중하며 빠르게 읽어 나가자!

- 프리뷰를 마친 후 바로 리딩을 시작합니다. 방금 살펴봤던 어휘들을 문장 속에서 다시 만나게 되는데, 이 과정에서 단어의 쓰임새와 어감을 자연스럽게 익히게 됩니다.
- 모르는 단어나 이해되지 않는 문장이 나오더라도 멈추지 말고 전체적인 맥락을 파악하면서 속도감 있게 읽어 나가세요. 이해되지 않는 문장들은 따로 표시를 하되, 일단 넘어가고 계속 읽는 것이 좋습니다. 뒷부분을 읽다 보면 자연히 이해가 되는 경우도 있고, 정 이해가 되지 않는 부분은 리딩을 마친 이후에 따로 리뷰하는 시간을 가지면 됩니다. 문제집을 풀듯이 모든 문장을 분석하면서 원서를 읽는 것이 아니라, 리딩을 할 때는 리딩에만, 리뷰를 할 때는 리뷰에만 집중하는 것이 필요합니다.
- 볼드 처리된 단어의 의미가 궁금하더라도 워크북을 바로 펼치지 마세요. 정 궁금하다면 한 번씩 참고하는 것도 나쁘진 않지만, 워크북과 원서를 번갈아 보면서 읽는 것은 리딩의 흐름을 끊고 단어 하나하나에 집착하는 좋지 않은 리딩 습관을 심어 줄 수 있습니다.
- 같은 맥락에서 번역서를 구해 원서와 동시에 번갈아 보는 것도 좋은 방법이 아닙니다. 한글 번역을 가지고 있다고 해도 일단 영어로 읽을 때는 영어에만 집중하고 어느 정도 분량을 읽은 후에 번역서와 비교하도록 하세요.

모든 문장을 일일이 번역해서 완벽하게 이해하려는 것은 오히려 좋지 않은 리딩 습관을 심어 주어 장기적으로는 바람직하지 않은 결과를 얻을 수 있습니다. 처음부터 완벽하게 이해하려고 하는 것보다는 빠른 속도로 2~3회 반복해서 읽는 방식이 실력 향상에 더 도움이 됩니다. 만일 반복해서 읽어도 내용이 전혀 이해되지 않아 곤란하다면 책 선정에 문제가 있다고 할 수 있습니다. 그럴 때는 좀 더 쉬운 책을 골라 실력을 다진 뒤 다시 도전하는 것이 좋습니다.

- 초보자라면 분당 150단어의 리딩 속도를 목표로 잡고 리딩을 합니다. 분당 150단어는 원어민이 말하는 속도로, 영어 학습자들이 리스닝과 스피킹으로 넘어가기 위해 가장 기초적으로 달성해야 하는 단계입니다. 분당 50~80단어 정도의 낮은 리딩 속도를 가지고 있는 경우는 대부분 영어 실력이 부족해서라기보다 '잘못된 리딩 습관'을 가지고 있어서 그렇습니다. 이해력이 조금 떨어진다고 하더라도 분당 150단어까지는 속도에 대한 긴장감을 놓치지 말고 속도감 있게 읽어 나가도록 하세요.

3. 리뷰(Review) : 이해력을 점검하고 꼼꼼하게 다시 살펴보자!

- 해당 챕터의 Comprehension Quiz를 통해 이해력을 점검해 봅니다.
- 오늘 만난 어휘들을 다시 한번 복습합니다. 이때는 읽으면서 중요하다고 생각했던 단어를 연습장에 써 보면서 꼼꼼하게 외우는 것도 좋습니다.
- 이해가 되지 않는다고 표시해 두었던 부분도 주의 깊게 분석해 봅니다. 다시 한번 문장을 꼼꼼히 읽고, 어떤 이유에서 이해가 되지 않았는지 생각해 봅니다. 따로 메모를 남기거나 노트를 작성하는 것도 좋은 방법입니다.
- 사실 꼼꼼히 리뷰하는 것은 매우 고된 과정입니다. 원서를 읽고 리뷰하는 시간을 가지는 것이 영어 실력 향상에 많은 도움이 되기는 하지만, 이 과정을 철저히 지키려다가 원서 읽기의 재미를 반감시키는 것은 바람직하지 않습니다. 그럴 때는 차라리 리뷰를 가볍게 하는 것이 좋을 수 있습니다. '내용에 빠져서 재미있게', 문제집에서는 상상도 못할 '많은 양'을 읽으면서, 매일매일 조금씩 꾸준히 실력을 키워 가는 것이 원서를 활용하는 기본적인 방법이며, 영어 공부의 왕도입니다. 문제집 풀듯이 원서 읽기를 시도하고 접근해서는 실패할 수밖에 없습니다.
- 이런 방식으로 원서를 끝까지 다 읽었다면, 다시 반복해서 읽거나 오디오북을 활용하는 등 다양한 방식으로 원서 읽기를 확장해 나갈 수 있습니다. 이에 대한 자세한 안내가 워크북 말미에 실려 있습니다.

Chapters 1 & 2

1. Which of the following was NOT one of Louis's jobs?
   A. Passing out the balls during lunch
   B. Passing out the balls during recess
   C. Picking up garbage on the school yard
   D. Making sure the kids didn't kill each other

2. Why did Louis tell the man in the truck that he was Mrs. Jewls?
   A. Louis wanted to be a teacher at Wayside School.
   B. Louis didn't want the man disturbing the children.
   C. Louis wanted to surprise Mrs. Jewls with a present.
   D. Louis didn't want the man to carry the heavy package and hurt himself.

3. How did Mrs. Jewls choose who would open the door for Louis?
   A. She chose the winner of a spelling bee.
   B. She chose the winner of a kickball game.
   C. She chose the student who was closest to the door.
   D. She chose the student who raised his or her hand first.

4. How did Mrs. Jewls say that the computer would help her class learn?
   A. She said that it would make learning more fun.
   B. She said that it would make learning quicker.
   C. She said that it would make learning more interesting.
   D. She said that it would make learning more interactive.

5. Why did Benjamin not mention his real name to Mrs. Jewls when she introduced him to the class?
   A. He was afraid to correct a teacher.
   B. He thought that she was just joking with him.
   C. He thought his name was hard to pronounce.
   D. There was already another Benjamin in the class.

6. How did Benjamin feel about the name Mark Miller?
   A. He thought that Mark Miller would get in trouble.
   B. He thought that there might already be a Mark Miller in the school.
   C. He thought that Mark Miller was a boring name.
   D. He wished he really was named Mark Miller.

7. Why did Benjamin not tell Mrs. Jewls his name after recess?
   A. He thought that he would cause a lot of trouble for her.
   B. He thought that she would be angry for not telling her earlier.
   C. He thought that she would think he was trying to get a free lunch.
   D. He thought that she would think he was weird for not telling her earlier.

$$\frac{1,072 \text{ words}}{\text{reading time (} \quad \text{) sec}} \times 60 = (\quad) \text{ WPM}$$

Build Your Vocabulary

yard**
[jɑːrd]

n. (학교의) 운동장; 마당, 뜰; 정원
A yard is a flat area of concrete or stone that is next to a building and often has a wall around it.

frown*
[fraun]

v. 얼굴을 찌푸리다; n. 찡그림, 찌푸림
When someone frowns, their eyebrows become drawn together, because they are annoyed or puzzled.

mess*
[mes]

n. (지저분하고) 엉망(진창)인 상태; (많은 문제로) 엉망인 상황; v. 엉망으로 만들다
If you say that something is a mess or in a mess, you think that it is in an untidy state.

junk*
[dʒʌŋk]

n. 쓸모없는 물건, 쓰레기
Junk is old and used goods that have little value and that you do not want any more.

garbage*
[gáːrbidʒ]

n. 쓰레기(통)
Garbage is rubbish, especially waste from a kitchen.

recess*
[risés]

n. (학교의) 쉬는 시간; (의회·위원회 등의) 휴회 기간
A recess is a break between classes at a school.

sigh*
[sai]

v. 한숨을 쉬다, 한숨짓다; n. 한숨
When you sigh, you let out a deep breath, as a way of expressing feelings such as disappointment, tiredness, or pleasure.

playground*
[pléigràund]

n. (학교의) 운동장; 놀이터
A playground is a piece of land, at school or in a public area, where children can play.

parking lot
[páːrkiŋ lat]

n. 주차장
A parking lot is an area of ground where people can leave their cars.

honk
[haŋk]

v. (자동차 경적을) 울리다; n. 빵빵(자동차 경적 소리)
If you honk the horn of a vehicle or if the horn honks, you make the horn produce a short loud sound.

horn*
[hɔːrn]

n. (차량의) 경적; (양·소 등의) 뿔
On a vehicle such as a car, the horn is the device that makes a loud noise as a signal or warning.

bushy
[búʃi]

a. 숱이 많은; 무성한, 우거진
Bushy hair or fur is very thick.

disturb★★
[distə́:rb]

v. (작업·수면 등을) 방해하다; (제자리에 있는 것을) 건드리다
If you disturb someone, you interrupt what they are doing and upset them.

interrupt★★
[intərʌ́pt]

v. (말·행동을) 방해하다, 중단시키다
If you interrupt someone who is speaking, you say or do something that causes them to stop.

grunt★
[grʌnt]

v. 끙 앓는 소리를 내다; (돼지가) 꿀꿀거리다; n. 꿀꿀거리는 소리; 끙 하는 소리
If you grunt, you make a low sound, especially because you are annoyed or not interested in something.

fragile★
[frǽdʒəl]

a. 부서지기 쉬운, 손상되기 쉬운; 취약한, 허술한
Something that is fragile is easily broken or damaged.

print★★★
[print]

v. 인쇄하다; (책·신문 등을) 찍다; (사진을) 인화하다; n. 활자; 출판(업)
If numbers, letters, or designs are printed on a surface, they are put on it in ink or dye using a machine.

fortunate★★
[fɔ́:rtʃənət]

a. 운 좋은, 다행한 (fortunately ad. 다행스럽게도, 운이 좋게도)
If you say that someone is fortunate, you mean that they are lucky.

by heart

idiom 외워서, 암기하여
If you know something such as a poem by heart, you have learned it so well that you can remember it without having to read it.

story★★
[stɔ́:ri]

① n. (건물의) 층 ② n. 이야기, 소설; 설명
A story of a building is one of its different levels, which is situated above or below other levels.

basement★★
[béismənt]

n. (건물의) 지하층
The basement of a building is a floor built partly or completely below ground level.

press★★
[pres]

v. (무엇에) 바짝 대다; (버튼 등을) 누르다; n. 언론; 인쇄
If you press something somewhere, you push it firmly against something else.

squash★
[skwaʃ]

v. 짓누르다, 으깨다, 찌부러뜨리다; n. 스쿼시; 호박
If someone or something is squashed, they are pressed or crushed with such force that they become injured or lose their shape.

cafeteria★
[kæfətíəriə]

n. 카페테리아, 구내식당
A cafeteria is a restaurant where you choose your food from a counter and take it to your table after paying for it.

mushroom★
[mʌ́ʃru:m]

n. 버섯
Mushrooms are fungi that you can eat.

specialty
[spéʃəlti]

n. (식당의) 전문 음식; 전문 (분야)
A specialty of a particular place is a special food or product that is always very good there.

huff
[hʌf]

v. (화가 나서) 씩씩거리다
If you huff, you indicate that you are annoyed or offended about something.

groan*
[groun]

v. (고통·짜증으로) 신음 소리를 내다; (기뻐서) 낮게 탄성을 지르다;
n. 신음, 끙 하는 소리
If you groan, you make a long, low sound because you are in pain, or because you are upset or unhappy about something.

sore**
[sɔ:r]

a. 아픈, 따가운; n. 상처
If part of your body is sore, it causes you pain and discomfort.

right away

idiom 즉시, 곧바로
If you do something right away, you do it immediately.

struggle**
[strʌgl]

v. 몸부림치다, 허우적거리다; 힘겹게 나아가다; n. 싸움, 몸부림; 투쟁
If you struggle to do something, you try hard to do it, even though other people or things may be making it difficult for you to succeed.

knock**
[nak]

v. (문 등을) 두드리다; 치다, 부딪치다; (때리거나 타격을 가해) ~한 상태가 되게 만들다;
n. 문 두드리는 소리
If you knock on something such as a door or window, you hit it, usually several times, to attract someone's attention.

gravity**
[grǽvəti]

n. (지구) 중력
Gravity is the force which causes things to drop to the ground.

gasp*
[gæsp]

v. 숨이 턱 막히다, 헉 하고 숨을 쉬다; n. (숨이 막히는 듯) 헉 하는 소리를 냄
When you gasp, you take a short quick breath through your mouth, especially when you are surprised, shocked, or in pain.

spell**
[spel]

v. 철자를 맞게 쓰다, 맞춤법에 맞게 글을 쓰다; (어떤 단어의) 철자를 말하다
(spelling n. 철자법, 맞춤법)
When you spell a word, you write or speak each letter in the word in the correct order.

complain**
[kəmpléin]

v. 불평하다, 항의하다
If you complain about a situation, you say that you are not satisfied with it.

slip*
[slip]

v. 미끄러지다; 슬며시 가다; (재빨리·슬며시) 놓다; n. (작은) 실수; 미끄러짐
If something slips, it slides out of place or out of your hand.

sweaty
[swéti]

a. 땀투성이의, 땀에 젖은; 땀나게 하는
If parts of your body or your clothes are sweaty, they are soaked or covered with sweat.

shift*
[ʃift]

v. 옮기다, 이동하다; 바꾸다; n. (위치·입장·방향의) 변화; 교대 근무 (시간)
If you shift something or if it shifts, it moves slightly.

weight**
[weit]

n. 무게, 체중
If you move your weight, you change position so that most of the pressure of your body is on a particular part of your body.

grip**
[grip]

n. 꽉 붙잡음, 움켜쥠; 통제, 지배; v. 꽉 잡다, 움켜잡다; (마음·흥미·시선을) 끌다
A grip is a firm, strong hold on something.

dig**
[dig]

v. (dug-dug) ~을 찌르다; (구멍 등을) 파다; n. 쿡 찌르기; 발굴
If you dig one thing into another or if one thing digs into another, the first thing is pushed hard into the second, or presses hard into it.

numb*
[nʌm]

a. (신체 부위가) 감각이 없는; 멍한; v. 감각이 없게 만들다
If a part of your body is numb, you cannot feel anything there.

14

faint*
[feint]

v. 실신하다; a. (빛·소리·냄새 등이) 희미한
If you faint, you lose consciousness for a short time, especially because you are hungry, or because of pain, heat, or shock.

mutter*
[mʌ́tər]

v. 중얼거리다; 투덜거리다; n. 중얼거림
If you mutter, you speak very quietly so that you cannot easily be heard, often because you are complaining about something.

grab*
[græb]

v. (와락·단단히) 붙잡다; ~을 잡아채려고 하다; n. 와락 잡아채려고 함
If you grab something, you take it or pick it up suddenly and roughly.

stagger*
[stǽgər]

v. 비틀거리다, 휘청거리며 가다; 큰 충격을 주다, 깜짝 놀라게 하다
If you stagger, you walk very unsteadily, for example because you are ill or drunk.

tear**
[tɛər]

① v. (tore-torn) 찢다, 뜯다; 구멍을 뚫다; n. 찢어진 곳, 구멍 ② n. 눈물
If you tear paper, cloth, or another material, or if it tears, you pull it into two pieces or you pull it so that a hole appears in it.

wobble
[wabl]

v. (불안하게) 뒤뚱거리며 가다; 흔들리다; 주저하다; n. 흔들림, 떨림; 동요
If something or someone wobbles, they make small movements from side to side, for example because they are unsteady.

exclaim*
[ikskléim]

v. 소리치다, 외치다
If you exclaim, you cry out suddenly in surprise, strong emotion, or pain.

boo
[buː]

v. (우우하고) 야유하다; n. 야유 (소리)
If you boo a speaker or performer, you shout 'boo' or make other loud sounds to indicate that you do not like them, their opinions, or their performance.

counter*
[káuntər]

n. (식당·바 등의) 카운터, 스탠드; (은행·상점 등의) 계산대
In a place such as a shop or café a counter is a long narrow table or flat surface at which customers are served.

collapse*
[kəlǽps]

v. (의식을 잃고) 쓰러지다; 붕괴되다, 무너지다; n. 실패, 붕괴
If you collapse, you suddenly faint or fall down because you are very ill or weak.

gather**
[gǽðər]

v. (사람들이) 모이다; 모으다, 챙기다
If people gather somewhere or if someone gathers people somewhere, they come together in a group.

monitor*
[mánətər]

n. 화면, 모니터; 감시 요원; v. 추적 관찰하다
A monitor is a screen which is used to display certain kinds of information.

smash*
[smæʃ]

v. (단단한 것에 세게) 부딪치다, 충돌하다; 박살내다; 박살나다; n. 박살내기
If something smashes or is smashed against something solid, it moves very fast and with great force against it.

sidewalk*
[sáidwɔːk]

n. (포장한) 보도, 인도
A sidewalk is a path with a hard surface by the side of a road.

get it

idiom 알다, 이해하다
You can say get it when you understand something or get the right answer.

1분에 몇 단어를 읽는지 리딩 속도를 측정해보세요.

$$\frac{925\ words}{reading\ time\ (\quad)\ sec} \times 60 = (\quad)\ WPM$$

Build Your Vocabulary

cowbell
[káubèl]

n. (소를 쉽게 찾기 위해 목에 다는) 소 방울
A cowbell is a small bell that is hung around a cow's neck so that the ringing sound makes it possible to find the cow.

all the way

idiom 내내, 시종; 완전히
You use all the way to emphasize how long a distance is.

stare*
[stɛər]

v. 빤히 쳐다보다, 응시하다; n. 빤히 쳐다보기, 응시
If you stare at someone or something, you look at them for a long time.

weirdo
[wíərdou]

n. 괴짜, 별난 사람
If you describe someone as a weirdo, you disapprove of them because they behave in an unusual way which you find difficult to understand or accept.

scare**
[skɛər]

v. 겁주다, 놀라게 하다 (scared a. 무서워하는, 겁먹은)
If you are scared of someone or something, you are frightened of them.

weird*
[wiərd]

a. 기이한, 기묘한; 기괴한, 섬뜩한
If you describe something or someone as weird, you mean that they are strange.

blackboard*
[blǽkbɔ̀ːrd]

n. 칠판
A blackboard is a dark-colored board that you can write on with chalk.

discipline**
[dísəplin]

n. 규율, 훈육; 단련법, 수련법
Discipline is the practice of making people obey rules or standards of behavior, and punishing them when they do not.

recess 복습
[risés]

n. (학교의) 쉬는 시간; (의회·위원회 등의) 휴회 기간
A recess is a break between classes at a school.

cringe
[krindʒ]

v. (겁이 나서) 움츠리다, 움찔하다; 민망하다
If you cringe at something, you feel embarrassed or disgusted, and perhaps show this feeling in your expression or by making a slight movement.

charge**
[tʃaːrdʒ]

v. 급히 가다, 달려가다; (요금·값을) 청구하다; n. (상품·서비스에 대한) 요금
If you charge towars someone or something, you move quickly and aggressively toward them.

16

shrug*
[ʃrʌg]

v. (두 손바닥을 위로 하고) 어깨를 으쓱하다; n. 어깨를 으쓱하기
If you shrug, you raise your shoulders to show that you are not interested in something or that you do not know or care about something.

worth**
[wəːrθ]

a. ~해 볼 만한; (금전 등의 면에서) ~의 가치가 있는; n. 가치, 값어치
If something is worth a particular action, or if an action is worth doing, it is considered to be important enough for that action.

rumble
[rʌmbl]

n. 우르렁거리는 소리; v. 우르렁거리는 소리를 내다
A rumble is a low continuous noise.

earthquake**
[ə́ːrθkweik]

n. 지진
An earthquake is a shaking of the ground caused by movement of the earth's crust.

playground^{복습}
[pléigràund]

n. (학교의) 운동장; 놀이터
A playground is a piece of land, at school or in a public area, where children can play.

basement^{복습}
[béismənt]

n. (건물의) 지하층
The basement of a building is a floor built partly or completely below ground level.

doorway*
[dɔ́ːrwèi]

n. 출입구
A doorway is a space in a wall where a door opens and closes.

stack*
[stæk]

n. 무더기, 더미; v. (깔끔하게 정돈하여) 쌓다
A stack of things is a pile of them.

work sheet
[wə́ːrk ʃiːt]

n. (학습용) 연습 문제지
A work sheet is a specially prepared page of exercises designed to improve your knowledge or understanding of a particular subject.

blank*
[blæŋk]

a. (글자가 없는) 빈; 멍한, 무표정한; n. 빈칸, 여백
Something that is blank has nothing on it.

yard^{복습}
[jaːrd]

n. (학교의) 운동장; 마당, 뜰; 정원
A yard is a flat area of concrete or stone that is next to a building and often has a wall around it.

sack*
[sæk]

n. (종이) 봉지, 부대
A sack is a paper or plastic bag, which is used to carry things bought in a shop.

indignant*
[indígnənt]

a. 분개한, 분노한 (indignantly ad. 분개하여, 화를 내어)
If you are indignant, you are shocked and angry, because you think that something is unjust or unfair.

figure out

idiom (생각한 끝에) ~을 이해하다; (양·비용을) 계산하다
If you figure out someone or something, you come to understand them by thinking carefully.

frown^{복습}
[fraun]

v. 얼굴을 찌푸리다; n. 찡그림, 찌푸림
When someone frowns, their eyebrows become drawn together, because they are annoyed or puzzled.

Chapters 3 & 4

1. Why did Mrs. Jewls ask Bebe to come to her?
   A. Mrs. Jewls had lost Bebe's homework.
   B. Mrs. Jewls wanted to help her with her homework.
   C. Bebe had forgotten to turn in her homework.
   D. Bebe's homework had an insult against Mrs. Jewls.

2. How did Mrs. Jewls react to Bebe's explanation about her homework?
   A. Mrs. Jewls didn't believe her.
   B. Mrs. Jewls gave her an A+ and a Tootsie Roll Pop.
   C. Mrs. Jewls called her home to talk to Ray Gunn.
   D. Mrs. Jewls wanted Bebe to do her homework at school.

3. How did Bebe's mother react when Mrs. Jewls called her?
   A. Bebe's mother asked her who was Ray.
   B. Bebe's mother told her that she would stop Ray.
   C. Bebe's mother asked her to talk to Ray directly.
   D. Bebe's mother told her that Bebe was always being mean to Ray.

4. How did Mrs. Jewls react to Mac when he raised his hand?
   A. She called on him immediately.
   B. She pretended not to see him.
   C. She didn't notice his hand raised.
   D. She told him to ask questions at the end of class.

5. Which of the following was NOT one of the questions the other students asked Mac about his missing sock?
   A. They asked if he had a dog.
   B. They asked if he looked under the bed.
   C. They asked if he looked in the refrigerator.
   D. They asked if he checked the dirty clothes.

6. How did Mac say that his story related to dinosaurs?
   A. Dinosaurs loved eating watermelons.
   B. Dinosaurs never learned to grow plants.
   C. Dinosaurs didn't like vegetables or fruits.
   D. Dinosaurs must have eaten that kind of watermelon.

7. Why did Mrs. Jewls assign so much homework?
   A. She loved grading homework.
   B. She loved giving her students busy work.
   C. She wanted her students to learn at home, too.
   D. She never finished her lessons in class.

Check Your Reading Speed

1분에 몇 단어를 읽는지 리딩 속도를 측정해보세요.

$$\frac{860\ words}{reading\ time\ (\quad)\ sec} \times 60 = (\quad)\ WPM$$

Build Your Vocabulary

stay up

idiom (평상시보다 더 늦게까지) 안 자다
If you stay up, you do not go to bed.

artwork
[á:rtwə:rk]

n. (박물관의) 미술품
Artworks are paintings or sculptures which are of high quality.

sigh ^{복습}
[sai]

v. 한숨을 쉬다, 한숨짓다; n. 한숨
When you sigh, you let out a deep breath, as a way of expressing feelings such as disappointment, tiredness, or pleasure.

relief**
[rilí:f]

n. 안도, 안심; (고통·불안 등의) 경감
If you feel a sense of relief, you feel happy because something unpleasant has not happened or is no longer happening.

stern*
[stə:rn]

a. 엄중한, 근엄한; 심각한 (sternly ad. 엄격하게, 준엄하게)
Someone who is stern is very serious and strict.

hippopotamus
[hipəpátəməs]

n. [동물] 하마
A hippopotamus is a very large African animal with short legs and thick, hairless skin. Hippopotamuses live in and near rivers.

exclaim ^{복습}
[ikskléim]

v. 소리치다, 외치다
If you exclaim, you cry out suddenly in surprise, strong emotion, or pain.

instant*
[ínstənt]

a. 즉각적인; n. 순간, 아주 짧은 동안 (instantly ad. 즉각, 즉시)
You use instant to describe something that happens immediately.

sneak*
[sni:k]

v. (sneaked/snuck-sneaked/snuck) 살금살금 가다; (허락 없이) 몰래 하다
If you sneak somewhere, you go there very quietly on foot, trying to avoid being seen or heard.

trick**
[trik]

n. 속임수; (골탕을 먹이기 위한) 장난; v. 속이다, 속임수를 쓰다
A trick is an action that is intended to deceive someone.

batch
[bæʧ]

n. (일괄적으로 처리되는) 집단, 무리; (한 번에 만들어 내는 음식·기계 등의) 양
A batch of things is a group of things of the same kind, dealt with at the same time.

gripe
[graip]

v. 불평을 하다, 투덜거리다; n. 불만, 불평
If you say that someone is griping, you mean they are annoying you because they keep on complaining about something.

grump
[grʌmp]

v. 불평하다, 툴툴거리다; n. 성격이 나쁜 사람
If you grump, you complain or grumble.

20

slave[*]
[sleiv]

n. 노예; v. 고되게 일하다
You can describe someone as a slave when they are completely under the control of another person or of a powerful influence.

leak[*]
[liːk]

v. (액체·기체가) 새다; 새게 하다; n. (액체·기체가) 새는 곳
If a container leaks, there is a hole or crack in it which lets a substance such as liquid or gas escape.

nod[**]
[nad]

v. (고개를) 끄덕이다; n. (고개를) 끄덕임
If you nod, you move your head downward and upward to show that you are answering 'yes' to a question, or to show agreement, understanding, or approval.

complain[복습]
[kəmpléin]

v. 불평하다, 항의하다
If you complain about a situation, you say that you are not satisfied with it.

wreck[*]
[rek]

v. 망가뜨리다, 파괴하다; n. 난파선
To wreck something means to completely destroy or ruin it.

underwear[*]
[ʌ́ndərwɛɚr]

n. 속옷
Underwear is clothing such as vests and pants which you wear next to your skin under your other clothes.

yell[*]
[jel]

v. 고함치다, 소리 지르다; n. 고함, 외침
If you yell, you shout loudly, usually because you are excited, angry, or in pain.

darling[*]
[dáːrliŋ]

a. (대단히) 사랑하는; 굉장히 멋진; n. 사랑하는 사람을 부를 때 쓰는 표현
Some people use darling to describe someone or something that they love or like very much.

snore[*]
[snɔːr]

v. 코를 골다; n. 코 고는 소리
When someone who is asleep snores, they make a loud noise each time they breathe.

ear plug
[iər plʌ̀g]

n. 귀마개
Ear plugs are small pieces of a soft material which you put into your ears to keep out noise, water, or cold air.

shrug[복습]
[ʃrʌg]

v. (두 손바닥을 위로 하고) 어깨를 으쓱하다; n. 어깨를 으쓱하기
If you shrug, you raise your shoulders to show that you are not interested in something or that you do not know or care about something.

toothpaste
[túːθpèist]

n. 치약
Toothpaste is a thick substance which you put on your toothbrush and use to clean your teeth.

mess[복습]
[mes]

n. (지저분하고) 엉망(진창)인 상태; (많은 문제로) 엉망인 상황; v. 엉망으로 만들다
If you say that something is a mess or in a mess, you think that it is in an untidy state.

blame[**]
[bleim]

v. ~을 탓하다, ~때문으로 보다; n. 책임; 탓
If you blame a person or thing for something bad, you believe or say that they are responsible for it or that they caused it.

devil[*]
[devl]

n. 악마
A devil is an evil spirit.

1분에 몇 단어를 읽는지 리딩 속도를 측정해보세요.

$$\frac{972 \text{ words}}{\text{reading time ( ) sec}} \times 60 = (\quad) \text{ WPM}$$

Build Your Vocabulary

fraction*
[frǽkʃən]

n. 분수; 부분, 일부
A fraction is a number that can be expressed as a proportion of two whole numbers. For example, 1/2 and 1/3 are both fractions.

decimal*
[désəməl]

n. 소수; a. 십진법의
A decimal is a fraction that is written in the form of a dot followed by one or more numbers which represent tenths, hundredths, and so on: for example .5, .51, .517.

groan^{복습}
[groun]

v. (고통·짜증으로) 신음 소리를 내다; (기뻐서) 낮게 탄성을 지르다;
n. 신음, 끙 하는 소리
If you groan, you make a long, low sound because you are in pain, or because you are upset or unhappy about something.

stretch**
[streʧ]

v. (팔·다리의 근육을) 당기다; (잡아당기거나 하여 길이·폭 등을) 늘이다
When you stretch, you put your arms or legs out straight and tighten your muscles.

call on

idiom (이름을 불러서) 학생에게 시키다; (사람을) 방문하다
If a teacher calls on students in a class, he or she asks them to answer a question or give their opinion.

besides**
[bisáidz]

prep. ~외에; ad. 게다가, 뿐만 아니라
Besides means other than someone or something.

mutter^{복습}
[mʌ́tər]

v. 중얼거리다; 투덜거리다; n. 중얼거림
If you mutter, you speak very quietly so that you cannot easily be heard, often because you are complaining about something.

closet*
[klázit]

n. 벽장
A closet is a piece of furniture with doors at the front and shelves inside, which is used for storing things.

be that as it may

idiom 그것은 그렇다 치고
You say 'be that as it may' when you want to move onto another subject or go further with the discussion, without deciding whether what has just been said is right or wrong.

wax*
[wæks]

v. 왁스로 광을 내다; n. 밀랍, 왁스
If you wax a surface, you put a thin layer of wax onto it, especially in order to polish it.

impatient*
[impéiʃənt]

a. 짜증난, 안달하는; 어서 ~하고 싶어 하는 (impatiently ad. 조바심하여)
If you are impatient to do something or impatient for something to happen, you are eager to do it or for it to happen and do not want to wait.

refrigerator*
[rifrídʒərèitə:r]

n. 냉장고
A refrigerator is a large container which is kept cool inside, usually by electricity, so that the food and drink in it stays fresh.

bewilderment
[biwíldərmənt]

n. 당황, 어리둥절함
Bewilderment is the feeling of being confused.

lightning*
[láitniŋ]

n. 번개, 번갯불; a. 번개같이, 아주 빨리
Lightning is the very bright flashes of light in the sky that happen during thunderstorms.

bolt*
[boult]

n. 번개; 빗장; 볼트
A bolt of lightning is a flash of lightning that is seen as a white line in the sky.

arithmetic*
[əríθmətik]

n. 산수, 연산; 산술, 계산
Arithmetic is the part of mathematics that is concerned with the addition, subtraction, multiplication, and division of numbers.

dinosaur
[dáinəsɔ̀:r]

n. 공룡; 고루한 것
Dinosaurs were large reptiles which lived in prehistoric times.

broccoli
[brákəli]

n. 브로콜리
Broccoli is a vegetable with green stalks and green or purple tops.

explode*
[iksplóud]

v. 터지다, 폭발하다; (갑자기 강한 감정을) 터뜨리다
If an object such as a bomb explodes or if someone or something explodes it, it bursts loudly and with great force, often causing damage or injury.

watermelon
[wɔ́:tərmèlən]

n. 수박
A watermelon is a large round fruit with green skin, pink flesh, and black seeds.

seed**
[si:d]

n. 씨, 씨앗, 종자
A seed is the small, hard part of a plant from which a new plant grows.

otherwise**
[ʌ́ðərwàiz]

ad. (만약) 그렇지 않으면; 그 외에는; (~와는) 다르게, 달리
You use otherwise after stating a situation or fact, in order to say what the result or consequence would be if this situation or fact was not the case.

stomach**
[stʌ́mək]

n. 위(胃), 속, 복부, 배
Your stomach is the organ inside your body where food goes after it has been eaten and where it starts to be digested.

assign*
[əsáin]

v. (일·책임 등을) 맡기다; 선임하다, 파견하다
If you assign a piece of work to someone, you give them the work to do.

spell^{복습}
[spel]

v. 철자를 맞게 쓰다, 맞춤법에 맞게 글을 쓰다; (어떤 단어의) 철자를 말하다 (spelling n. 철자법, 맞춤법)
When you spell a word, you write or speak each letter in the word in the correct order.

Chapters 5 & 6

1. Which of the following was true about Bob, the hobo?

    A. He always took money from kids.

    B. He used to be a student at Wayside School.

    C. He wore shoes that looked too big for him.

    D. He wore a coat that was bigger than Sharie's coat.

2. Why would nobody hire Bob?

    A. He never took baths.

    B. He never wore socks.

    C. He never took money.

    D. He never wore shirts.

3. Why did Bob never wear socks?

    A. His hero, Albert Einstein, never wore socks.

    B. He kept losing them in strange places.

    C. He thought socks felt uncomfortable on his feet.

    D. He had forgotten to wear socks on the day he won a spelling bee.

4. Why did Mrs. Jewls wait before starting the weekly spelling test?

    A. She waited for everyone to sharpen their pencils.

    B. She waited for everyone to write down their names.

    C. She waited for everyone to take off their socks.

    D. She waited for everyone to say goodbye to Bob.

5. How had Paul been when he had last pulled Leslie's pigtails before he knew better?

   A. He was younger and immature.

   B. He was angry and confused.

   C. He was mean and annoying.

   D. He was cute and innocent.

6. What caused Paul to fall out the window?

   A. Leslie pushed him after he tried to pull her pigtails.

   B. He hit his head and fell after Leslie said she was trimming her hair.

   C. He wanted to see the kids playing on the playground more closely.

   D. A sudden earthquake caused him to fall out the window.

7. How did Leslie save Paul's life?

   A. She used an extension cord to pull Paul up.

   B. She used her pigtails to help pull Paul up.

   C. She used a rope to help pull Paul up.

   D. She went to go get Louis to help her pull Paul up.

$$\frac{1{,}002 \text{ words}}{\text{reading time ( ) sec}} \times 60 = (\quad) \text{ WPM}$$

Build Your Vocabulary

hobo
[hóubou]

n. 부랑자, 떠돌이
A hobo is a person who has no home, especially one who travels from place to place and gets money by begging.

side by side

idiom 나란히; 함께 (아무런 어려움 없이)
If two people or things are side by side, they are next to each other.

neat**
[ni:t]

a. 뛰어난, 훌륭한; 정돈된, 단정한, 말쑥한
If you say that something is neat, you mean that it is very good.

scraggly
[skrǽgli]

a. 듬성듬성 자란
Scraggly hair or plants are thin and untidy.

beard*
[biərd]

n. (턱)수염
A man's beard is the hair that grows on his chin and cheeks.

stain*
[stein]

n. (지우기 힘든) 얼룩; v. 얼룩지게 하다, 더럽히다
A stain is a mark on something that is difficult to remove.

patch*
[pætʃ]

n. (구멍을 때우는 데 쓰이는) 조각; (주변과는 다른 조그만) 부분; v. 덧대다, 때우다
A patch is a piece of material which you use to cover a hole in something.

spare
[spɛər]

a. (현재 쓰지 않아서) 남는; v. (시간·돈 등을) 할애하다
You use spare to describe something that is not being used by anyone, and is therefore available for someone to use.

change***
[tʃeindʒ]

n. 동전, 잔돈; 거스름돈; 변화; v. 변하다, 달라지다
Change is coins, rather than paper money.

quarter**
[kwɔ́:rtər]

n. (미국·캐나다의) 25센트짜리 동전; 4분의 1
A quarter is an American or Canadian coin that is worth 25 cents.

bound*
[baund]

a. ~행의, ~로 향하는; 꼭 ~할 것 같은; v. 껑충껑충 달리다
If a vehicle or person is bound for a particular place, they are traveling toward it.

nod^{복습}
[nad]

v. (고개를) 끄덕이다; n. (고개를) 끄덕임
If you nod, you move your head downward and upward to show that you are answering 'yes' to a question, or to show agreement, understanding, or approval.

pigtail
[pígtèil]

n. (하나 또는 두 갈래로) 땋은 머리
If someone has a pigtail or pigtails, their hair is plaited or braided into one or two lengths.

turn into

idiom (~에서) ~이 되다, ~으로 변하다
To turn or be turned into something means to become that thing.

dentist*
[déntist]

n. 치과 의사
A dentist is a person who is qualified to examine and treat people's teeth.

president***
[prézədənt]

n. 장(長), 회장; 대통령
The president of an organization is the person who has the highest position in it.

hire*
[haiər]

v. (사람을) 고용하다; 빌리다, 세내다
If you hire someone, you employ them or pay them to do a particular job for you.

scrap*
[skræp]

n. (pl.) (식사 때 먹고) 남은 음식; (종이·옷감 등의) 조각; v. 폐기하다, 버리다
Scraps are pieces of unwanted food which are thrown away or given to animals.

pot**
[pat]

n. (둥글고 속이 깊은) 냄비, 솥; 병, 항아리
A pot is a deep round container used for cooking stews, soups, and other food.

tasty
[téisti]

a. (풍미가 강하고) 맛있는
If you say that food is tasty, you mean that it has a fairly strong and pleasant flavor which makes it good to eat.

cannibal
[kǽnəbl]

n. 식인종; 육식 동물
Cannibals are people who eat the flesh of other human beings.

yuck
[jʌk]

int. 윽(역겨울 때 내는 소리)
'Yuck' is an expression of disgust.

confuse**
[kənfjúːz]

v. (사람을) 혼란시키다; (주제를) 혼란스럽게 만들다 (confused a. 혼란스러워 하는)
If you are confused, you do not know exactly what is happening or what to do.

cannonball
[kǽnənbɔ̀ːl]

n. 포탄
A cannonball is a heavy metal ball that is fired from a cannon.

scare^{복습}
[skɛər]

v. 겁주다, 놀라게 하다
If something scares you, it frightens or worries you.

refrigerator^{복습}
[rifrídʒərèitəːr]

n. 냉장고
A refrigerator is a large container which is kept cool inside, usually by electricity, so that the food and drink in it stays fresh.

cowbell^{복습}
[káubèl]

n. (소를 쉽게 찾기 위해 목에 다는) 소 방울
A cowbell is a small bell that is hung around a cow's neck so that the ringing sound makes it possible to find the cow.

announce**
[ənáuns]

v. 발표하다, 알리다; (공공장소에서) 방송으로 알리다
If you announce something, you tell people about it publicly or officially.

wave**
[weiv]

v. (손·팔을) 흔들다; (바람 등에) 흔들리다; n. 파도, 물결; (팔·손·몸을) 흔들기
If you wave, you move your hand from side to side in the air, usually in order to say hello or goodbye to someone.

Check Your Reading Speed

1분에 몇 단어를 읽는지 리딩 속도를 측정해보세요.

$$\frac{846 \text{ words}}{\text{reading time (} \quad \text{) sec}} \times 60 = (\quad) \text{ WPM}$$

Build Your Vocabulary

pigtail^{복습}
[pígtèil]

n. (하나 또는 두 갈래로) 땋은 머리
If someone has a pigtail or pigtails, their hair is plaited or braided into one or two lengths.

immature
[ìməʧúər]

a. 미숙한, 치기 어린; 다 자라지 못한
If you describe someone as immature, you are being critical of them because they do not behave in a sensible or responsible way.

know better

idiom (~할 정도로) 어리석지는 않다
If someone knows better than to do something, they are old enough or experienced enough to know it is the wrong thing to do.

recess^{복습}
[risés]

n. (학교의) 쉬는 시간; (의회·위원회 등의) 휴회 기간
A recess is a break between classes at a school.

rush**
[rʌʃ]

v. 급(속)히 움직이다; (너무 급히) 서두르다; n. 혼잡, 분주함
If you rush somewhere, you go there quickly.

lounge*
[laundʒ]

n. (호텔·클럽 등의) 휴게실; (공항 등의) 대합실; v. 느긋하게 있다
In a hotel, club, or other public place, a lounge is a room where people can sit and relax.

chuckle*
[ʧʌkl]

v. 빙그레 웃다
When you chuckle, you laugh quietly.

beg*
[beg]

v. 간청하다, 애원하다; 구걸하다
If you beg someone to do something, you ask them very anxiously or eagerly to do it.

come over

idiom (어떤 기분이) 갑자기 들다
If a feeling comes over, you suddenly start to feel that way.

disgust*
[disgʌ́st]

n. 혐오감, 역겨움, 넌더리; v. 혐오감을 유발하다, 역겹게 만들다
Disgust is a feeling of very strong dislike or disapproval.

waggle
[wǽgl]

v. (상하·좌우로) 흔들다; 흔들리다, 움직이다
If you waggle something, or if something waggles, it moves up and down or from side to side with short quick movements.

yuck^{복습}
[jʌk]

int. 윽(역겨울 때 내는 소리)
'Yuck' is an expression of disgust.

gross*
[grous]

a. 역겨운; 전체의
If you describe something as gross, you think it is very unpleasant.

march***
[ma:rʧ]

v. (단호한 태도로 급히) 걸어가다; 행진하다; n. 행군, 행진; 3월
If you say that someone marches somewhere, you mean that they walk there quickly and in a determined way, for example because they are angry.

wave^{복습}
[weiv]

v. (손·팔을) 흔들다; (바람 등에) 흔들리다; n. 파도, 물결; (팔·손·몸을) 흔들기
If you wave, you move your hand from side to side in the air, usually in order to say hello or goodbye to someone.

slap*
[slæp]

v. (손바닥으로) 철썩 때리다; 털썩 놓다; n. (손바닥으로) 철썩 때리기
If you slap someone, you hit them with the palm of your hand.

lean**
[li:n]

v. ~에 기대다; 기울다, (몸을) 숙이다; a. 군살이 없는, (탄탄하게) 호리호리한
If you lean on or against someone or something, you rest against them so that they partly support your weight.

counter^{복습}
[káuntər]

n. (식당·바 등의) 카운터, 스탠드; (은행·상점 등의) 계산대
In a place such as a shop or café a counter is a long narrow table or flat surface at which customers are served.

playground^{복습}
[pléigràund]

n. (학교의) 운동장; 놀이터
A playground is a piece of land, at school or in a public area, where children can play.

trim*
[trim]

v. 다듬다, 손질하다; n. 다듬기, 약간 자르기; a. 잘 가꾼, 깔끔한
If you trim something you cut off small amounts of it in order to make it look neater and tidier.

announce^{복습}
[ənáuns]

v. 발표하다, 알리다; (공공장소에서) 방송으로 알리다
If you announce something, you tell people about it publicly or officially.

split**
[split]

v. 찢다, 쪼개다; 분열되다; (몫 등을) 나누다; n. 분열, 불화; 분할; 몫
(split end n. 끝이 갈라진 머리카락)
If something such as wood or a piece of clothing splits or is split, a long crack or tear appears in it.

bash
[bæʃ]

v. 후려치다, 세게 치다; 맹비난하다; n. 강타
If you bash something, you hit it hard in a rough or careless way.

window frame
[wíndou frèim]

n. 창틀
A window frame is a frame around the edges of a window, which glass is fixed into.

bounce*
[bauns]

v. 튀다; 튀기다; 깡충깡충 뛰다; n. 튐, 튀어 오름
If something bounces or if something bounces it, it swings or moves up and down.

topple
[tapl]

v. 넘어지다; 넘어뜨리다; 실각시키다
If someone or something topples somewhere or if you topple them, they become unsteady or unstable and fall over.

stare^{복습}
[stɛər]

v. 빤히 쳐다보다, 응시하다; n. 빤히 쳐다보기, 응시
If you stare at someone or something, you look at them for a long time.

horror* [hɔ́ːrər]

n. 공포(감), 경악
Horror is a feeling of great shock, fear, and worry caused by something extremely unpleasant.

gasp^{복습} [gæsp]

v. 숨이 턱 막히다, 헉 하고 숨을 쉬다; n. (숨이 막히는 듯) 헉 하는 소리를 냄
When you gasp, you take a short quick breath through your mouth, especially when you are surprised, shocked, or in pain.

brick** [brik]

n. 벽돌
Bricks are rectangular blocks of baked clay used for building walls, which are usually red or brown.

desperate** [déspərət]

a. 필사적인, 극단적인; 간절히 필요로 하는 (desperately ad. 필사적으로)
If you are desperate, you are in such a bad situation that you are willing to try anything to change it.

slip^{복습} [slip]

v. 미끄러지다; 슬며시 가다; (재빨리·슬며시) 놓다; n. (작은) 실수; 미끄러짐
If something slips, it slides out of place or out of your hand.

grab^{복습} [græb]

v. (와락·단단히) 붙잡다; ~을 잡아채려고 하다; n. 와락 잡아채려고 함
If you grab something, you take it or pick it up suddenly and roughly.

clutch* [klʌtʃ]

v. 움켜잡다; n. (자동차의) 클러치판; 움켜짐
If you clutch at something or clutch something, you hold it tightly, usually because you are afraid or anxious.

extension cord [iksténʃən kɔ̀ːrd]

n. (전기 기구용) 연장 코드
An extension cord is a part which is connected to a piece of equipment in order to make it reach something further away.

wince [wins]

v. (통증·당혹감으로 얼굴 표정이) 움찔하고 놀라다
If you wince, the muscles of your face tighten suddenly because you have felt a pain or because you have just seen, heard, or remembered something unpleasant.

yelp [jelp]

v. (아파서) 꺅 하고 비명을 내지르다
If a person or dog yelps, they give a sudden short cry, often because of fear or pain.

dangle [dæŋgl]

v. (달랑) 매달리다, 달랑거리다
If something dangles from somewhere or if you dangle it somewhere, it hangs or swings loosely.

water*** [wɔ́ːtər]

v. 눈물이 나다; (화초 등에) 물을 주다; 침이 괴다; n. 물
If your eyes water, tears build up in them because they are hurting or because you are upset.

swing** [swiŋ]

v. (swung-swung) 빙 돌(리)다; (전후·좌우로) 흔들(리)다; 휙 움직이다; n. 흔들기; 휘두르기
If something swings in a particular direction or if you swing it in that direction, it moves in that direction with a smooth, curving movement.

jut [dʒʌt]

v. 돌출하다, 튀어나오다; 돌출시키다, 내밀다
If something juts out, it sticks out above or beyond a surface.

windowsill
[wíndousìl]

n. 창턱
A windowsill is a shelf along the bottom of a window, either inside or outside a building.

collapse ^{복습}
[kəlǽps]

v. (의식을 잃고) 쓰러지다; 붕괴되다, 무너지다; n. 실패, 붕괴
If you collapse, you suddenly faint or fall down because you are very ill or weak.

sore ^{복습}
[sɔːr]

a. 아픈, 따가운; n. 상처
If part of your body is sore, it causes you pain and discomfort.

Chapters 7 & 8

1. How did Myron feel about his desk?
   A. He thought that it was like a cage.
   B. He thought that it was too small.
   C. He thought that it was dirty.
   D. He thought that Oddly, the bird, could live inside it.

2. Why did Myron go to the basement?
   A. He wanted to see a dead rat.
   B. He wanted to be free.
   C. He wanted to skip a math test.
   D. He wanted to find his lost socks.

3. How did Myron find his way around the basement?
   A. He used a pipe to guide him.
   B. He used a flashlight to light the way.
   C. He used an old map of the basement.
   D. He used his ears to listen for odd sounds.

4. What did the three men in the basement offer Myron?
   A. They offered Myron a chance to go to a different school.
   B. They offered Myron another pair of shoes.
   C. They offered a choice to be free or be safe.
   D. They offered a chance for good grades for the rest of the year.

5. How did Joy feel about Todd's toy?
   A. She wanted to break it.
   B. She didn't like it but decided to steal it.
   C. She wanted Todd to let her play with it.
   D. She thought that he should have left it at home.

6. How did Mrs. Jewls feel after Todd brought his toy to her?
   A. She was so upset that she sent him home early on the kindergarten bus.
   B. She decided to keep it at her desk and give it back to him at the end of the day.
   C. She made him write a check next to his name on the board under DISCIPLINE.
   D. She let him off this time and let him erase his name from the board under DISCIPLINE.

7. What happened to the toy when Todd tried showing them the best part about it at recess?
   A. It turned into a mean looking wolf.
   B. It turned into an even cuter dog.
   C. It bit his finger and wouldn't let go.
   D. It started to walk and bark on its own.

$$\frac{\text{1,478 words}}{\text{reading time ( ) sec}} \times 60 = (\quad) \text{ WPM}$$

Build Your Vocabulary

crumble
[krʌmbl]

v. 바스러뜨리다; 바스러지다; 허물어지다, 무너지다
If something crumbles, or if you crumble it, it breaks into a lot of small pieces.

windowsill^{복습}
[wíndousìl]

n. 창턱
A windowsill is a shelf along the bottom of a window, either inside or outside a building.

crumb
[krʌm]

n. (빵·케이크의) 부스러기; 작은 것; 약간, 소량
Crumbs are tiny pieces that fall from bread, biscuits, or cake when you cut it or eat it.

out of the corner of one's eye

idiom 곁눈질로
If you see something out of the corner of your eye, you see it not very clearly because you see it from the side of your eye and are not looking straight at it.

breast**
[brest]

n. (새의) 가슴; (새·동물의) 가슴살
A bird's breast is the front part of its body.

odd**
[ad]

a. 이상한, 특이한; 홀수의 (oddly ad. 이상하게)
If you describe someone or something as odd, you think that they are strange or unusual.

dumb*
[dʌm]

a. 멍청한, 바보 같은; 벙어리의, 말을 못 하는
If you call a person dumb, you mean that they are stupid or foolish.

cage*
[keidʒ]

n. 새장, 우리; v. 우리에 가두다
A cage is a structure of wire or metal bars in which birds or animals are kept.

reluctant*
[rilʌ́ktənt]

a. 꺼리는, 마지못한, 주저하는 (reluctantly ad. 마지못해서, 꺼려하여)
If you are reluctant to do something, you are unwilling to do it and hesitate before doing it, or do it slowly and without enthusiasm.

rush^{복습}
[rʌʃ]

v. 급(속)히 움직이다, (너무 급히) 서두르다; n. 혼잡, 분주함
If you rush somewhere, you go there quickly.

staircase*
[stéərkèis]

n. (건물 내부에 난간으로 죽 이어져 있는) 계단
A staircase is a set of stairs inside a building.

declare***
[diklέər]

v. 분명히 말하다; 선언하다, 공표하다
If you declare something, you state something clearly and definitely.

34

ease**
[iːz]

v. 조심조심 움직이다; 편해지다, 편하게 해 주다; n. 쉬움, 용이함
If you ease your way somewhere or ease somewhere, you move there slowly, carefully, and gently.

basement^{복습}
[béismənt]

n. (건물의) 지하층
The basement of a building is a floor built partly or completely below ground level.

creaky
[kríːki]

a. 삐걱거리는
A creaky object makes a short, high-pitched sound when it moves.

story^{복습}
[stɔ́ːri]

① n. (건물의) 층 ② n. 이야기, 소설; 설명
A story of a building is one of its different levels, which is situated above or below other levels.

take over

idiom (~로부터) (~을) 인계받다, (기업 등을) 인수하다
If you take over something from someone, you do it instead of them.

lurk
[ləːrk]

v. (나쁜 짓을 하려고 기다리며) 숨어 있다; (불쾌한 일·위험이) 도사리다
If someone lurks somewhere, they wait there secretly so that they cannot be seen, usually because they intend to do something bad.

drip*
[drip]

n. (액체가) 뚝뚝 떨어지는 소리; (작은 액체) 방울; v. 방울방울 흐르다
A drip is the sound or action of liquid falling in drops.

echo*
[ékou]

v. (소리가) 울리다, 메아리치다; n. (소리의) 울림, 메아리
If a sound echoes, it is reflected off a surface and can be heard again after the original sound has stopped.

damp*
[dæmp]

a. 축축한, 눅눅한
Something that is damp is slightly wet.

outstretch
[àutstrétʃ]

v. 펴다, 뻗다; 확장하다 (outstretched a. 한껏 뻗은)
If a part of the body of a person or animal is outstretched, it is stretched out as far as possible.

gritty
[gríti]

a. 모래가 든, 모래 같은
Something that is gritty is covered with small pieces of stone, or has a texture like that of sand.

spiderweb
[spáidərwèb]

n. 거미줄
A spiderweb is the thin net made by a spider from a sticky substance which it produces in its body.

crawl**
[krɔːl]

v. (곤충이) 기어가다; (엎드려) 기다; n. 기어가기, 서행
When an insect crawls somewhere, it moves there quite slowly.

footstep*
[fútstèp]

n. 발소리; 발자국
A footstep is the sound or mark that is made by someone walking each time their foot touches the ground.

blind**
[blaind]

a. 앞이 안 보이는; 맹목적인; 눈이 먼, 맹인인; v. 눈이 멀게 만들다
(blindly ad. 앞이 안 보이는 채)
If you are blind with something such as tears or a bright light, you are unable to see for a short time because of the tears or light.

bend**
[bend]

v. (bent-bent) (몸이나 머리를) 굽히다, 숙이다; (무엇을) 구부리다; n. 굽이, 굽은 곳
When you bend, you move the top part of your body downward and forward.

untie
[ʌntái]

v. (매듭 등을) 풀다
If you untie something such as string or rope, you undo it so that there is no knot or so that it is no longer tying something.

sneaker
[sníːkər]

n. (pl.) 고무창 운동화
Sneakers are casual shoes with rubber soles.

slip^{복습}
[slip]

v. 미끄러지다; 슬며시 가다; (재빨리·슬며시) 놓다; n. (작은) 실수; 미끄러짐
If you slip, you accidentally slide and lose your balance.

spot**
[spat]

n. (특정한) 곳; (작은) 점; v. 발견하다, 찾다, 알아채다
You can refer to a particular place as a spot.

slime
[slaim]

n. 끈적끈적한 물질, 점액
Slime is a thick, wet substance which covers a surface or comes from the bodies of animals such as snails.

hold one's breath

idiom 숨을 죽이다
If you say that someone is holding their breath, you mean that they are waiting anxiously or excitedly for something to happen.

bald*
[bɔːld]

a. 대머리의, 머리가 벗겨진
Someone who is bald has little or no hair on the top of their head.

mustache*
[mʌ́stæʃ]

n. 콧수염
A man's mustache is the hair that grows on his upper lip.

attaché case
[ətaéʃei kèis]

n. (작은) 서류 가방
An attaché case is a flat case for holding documents.

glance*
[glæns]

v. 흘낏 보다; 대충 훑어보다; n. 흘낏 봄
If you glance at something or someone, you look at them very quickly and then look away again immediately.

make up

idiom (이야기 등을) 지어 내다; ~을 이루다
If you make up something, you invent it, often in order to trick someone.

fake*
[feik]

a. 가짜의, 거짓된; 모조의; v. 위조하다; n. 모조품
A fake fur or a fake painting, for example, is a fur or painting that has been made to look valuable or genuine, usually in order to deceive people.

thumb through

idiom (책 등을) 휙휙 넘겨 보다
If you thumb through a book or magazine, you turn the pages of it quickly and read only small parts.

chirp*
[tʃəːrp]

v. 재잘거리다; (새나 곤충이) 짹짹거리다
If someone chirps, they say something in a lively and cheerful way.

wipe*
[waip]

v. (먼지·물기 등을 없애기 위해 무엇을) 닦다; n. (행주·걸레를 써서) 닦기
If you wipe something, you rub its surface to remove dirt or liquid from it.

36

foreign**
[fɔ́:rən]

a. 외국의; 이질적인 (foreign langnage n. 외국어)
Something or someone that is foreign comes from or relates to a country that is not your own.

hop*
[hap]

v. 깡충깡충 뛰다; 급히 가다; n. 깡충 뛰기
If you hop, you move along by jumping on one foot.

all the way^{복습}

idiom 내내, 시종; 완전히
You use all the way to emphasize how long a distance is.

sore^{복습}
[sɔ:r]

a. 아픈, 따가운; n. 상처
If part of your body is sore, it causes you pain and discomfort.

discipline^{복습}
[dísəplin]

n. 규율, 훈육; 단련법, 수련법
Discipline is the practice of making people obey rules or standards of behavior, and punishing them when they do not.

arithmetic^{복습}
[əríθmətik]

n. 산수, 연산; 산술, 계산
Arithmetic is the part of mathematics that is concerned with the addition, subtraction, multiplication, and division of numbers.

definite**
[défənit]

a. 분명한, 뚜렷한; 확실한, 확고한 (definitely ad. 분명히, 틀림없이)
You use definitely to emphasize that something is the case, or to emphasize the strength of your intention or opinion.

lounge^{복습}
[laundʒ]

n. (호텔·클럽 등의) 휴게실; (공항 등의) 대합실; v. 느긋하게 있다
In a hotel, club, or other public place, a lounge is a room where people can sit and relax.

1분에 몇 단어를 읽는지 리딩 속도를 측정해보세요.

$$\frac{954 \text{ words}}{\text{reading time ( ) sec}} \times 60 = (\quad) \text{ WPM}$$

Build Your Vocabulary

adorable
[ədɔ́:rəbl]

a. 사랑스러운
If you say that someone or something is adorable, you are emphasizing that they are very attractive and you feel great affection for them.

darling^{복습}
[dá:rliŋ]

a. (대단히) 사랑하는; 굉장히 멋진; n. 사랑하는 사람을 부를 때 쓰는 표현
Some people use darling to describe someone or something that they love or like very much.

big deal
[bíg dí:l]

int. 그게 무슨 대수라고!; n. 대단한 것, 큰 일
You can say 'big deal' to someone to show that you are not impressed by something that they consider important or impressive.

hunk
[hʌŋk]

n. 큰 덩어리, 두꺼운 조각
A hunk of something is a large piece of it.

command**
[kəmǽnd]

v. 명령하다, 지시하다; (군대에서) 지휘하다; n. 명령; 지휘, 통솔
If someone in authority commands you to do something, they tell you that you must do it.

blackboard^{복습}
[blǽkbɔ̀:rd]

n. 칠판
A blackboard is a dark-colored board that you can write on with chalk.

typical**
[típikəl]

a. 늘 하는 식의; 전형적인; 보통의
If you say that something is typical of a person, situation, or thing, you are criticizing them or complaining about them and saying that they are just as bad or disappointing as you expected them to be.

kindergarten
[kíndərgà:rtn]

n. 유치원
A kindergarten is an informal kind of school for very young children, where they learn things by playing.

make it

idiom 성공하다, 해내다; 가다
If you make it, you become successful in your job.

feel around

idiom 여기저기 더듬거리다
If you feel around for someone or something, you try to find them by feel rather than sight.

precious*
[préʃəs]

a. (개인에게) 소중한; 귀중한, 값비싼
If something is precious to you, you regard it as important and do not want to lose it.

coo
[kuː]
v. 달콤하게 속삭이다; (비둘기가) 울다
When someone coos, they speak in a very soft, quiet voice which is intended to sound attractive.

lovable
[lávəbl]
a. 사랑스러운, 매력적인
If you describe someone as lovable, you mean that they have attractive qualities, and are easy to like.

let off
idiom (처벌하지 않거나 가벼운 처벌로) ~를 봐주다
If you let off someone who has committed a crime or done something wrong, you do not punish them or do not punish them severely enough.

erase[*]
[iréis]
v. (지우개 등으로) 지우다; (완전히) 없애다
If you erase something such as writing or a mark, you remove it, usually by rubbing it with a cloth.

hardly[***]
[háːrdli]
ad. 거의 ~할 수가 없다; 거의 ~아니다; 막 (~하기 시작한)
When you say you can hardly do something, you are emphasizing that it is very difficult for you to do it.

amaze[*]
[əméiz]
v. (대단히) 놀라게 하다 (amazed a. (대단히) 놀란)
If something amazes you, it surprises you very much.

crank
[kræŋk]
n. (기계의) 크랭크; 괴짜; v. 크랭크로 돌리다
A crank is a machine part with a handle that can be turned in a circular motion to move something.

floppy
[flápi]
a. 헐렁한, 축 늘어진
Something that is floppy is loose rather than stiff, and tends to hang downward.

fang
[fæŋ]
n. (뱀·개 등의) 송곳니
Fangs are the two long, sharp, upper teeth that some animals have.

stretch[복습]
[streʧ]
v. (잡아당기거나 하여 길이·폭 등을) 늘이다; (팔·다리의 근육을) 당기다
When something soft or elastic stretches or is stretched, it becomes longer or bigger as well as thinner, usually because it is pulled.

cheek[**]
[ʧiːk]
n. 볼, 뺨
Your cheeks are the sides of your face below your eyes.

bony
[bóuni]
a. 뼈가 다 드러나는, 앙상한; 뼈의, 뼈 같은
Someone who has a bony face or bony hands, for example, has a very thin face or very thin hands, with very little flesh covering their bones.

grim[*]
[grim]
a. 엄숙한, 단호한; 암울한; 음침한
If a person or their behavior is grim, they are very serious, usually because they are worried about something.

frighten[**]
[fraitn]
v. 겁먹게 만들다, 놀라게 만들다 (frightening a. 무서운)
f something is frightening, it makes you feel afraid, anxious, or nervous.

turn into[복습]
idiom (~에서) ~이 되다, ~으로 변하다
To turn or be turned into something means to become that thing.

man-eating
[mǽn-iːtiŋ]

a. 사람을 잡아먹는, 식인의
A man-eating animal is one that has killed and eaten human beings, or that people think might do so.

lap*
[læp]

n. 무릎; (경주에서 트랙의) 한 바퀴
If you have something on your lap, it is on top of your legs and near to your body.

carton*
[kaːrtn]

n. (음식이나 음료를 담는) 곽; 상자
A carton is a plastic or cardboard container in which food or drink is sold.

straw*
[strɔː]

n. 빨대; 짚, 밀짚
A straw is a thin tube of paper or plastic, which you use to suck a drink into your mouth.

suck**
[sʌk]

v. (액체·공기 등을) 빨아 먹다; (입에 넣고 계속) 빨다; (특정한 방향으로) 빨아들이다; n. 빨기, 빨아 먹기
If you suck something, you hold it in your mouth and pull at it with the muscles in your cheeks and tongue, for example in order to get liquid out of it.

splatter
[splǽtər]

v. 튀다, 튀기다; n. 튀기기; 철벅철벅 소리
If a thick wet substance splatters on something or is splattered on it, it drops or is thrown over it.

slap 복습
[slæp]

v. (손바닥으로) 철썩 때리다; 털썩 놓다; n. (손바닥으로) 철썩 때리기
If you slap someone, you hit them with the palm of your hand.

aim***
[eim]

n. 겨냥, 조준; 목적, 목표; v. (무엇을 성취하는 것을) 목표하다; 겨누다
When you take aim, you point a weapon or object at someone or something, before firing or throwing it.

fire***
[faiər]

v. 발사하다, 사격하다; 해고하다; n. 불; 발사, 총격
If someone fires a gun or a bullet, or if they fire, a bullet is sent from a gun that they are using.

rub**
[rʌb]

v. (손·손수건 등을 대고) 문지르다; (두 손 등을) 맞비비다; n. 문지르기, 비비기
If you rub a substance into a surface or rub something such as dirt from a surface, you spread it over the surface or remove it from the surface using your hand or something such as a cloth.

advantage**
[ædvǽntidʒ]

n. (누구에게) 유리한 점, 이점, 장점 (take advantage idiom ~을 이용해 먹다)
If someone takes advantage of you, they treat you unfairly for their own benefit, especially when you are trying to be kind or to help them.

wave 복습
[weiv]

v. (손·팔을) 흔들다; (바람 등에) 흔들리다; n. 파도, 물결; (팔·손·몸을) 흔들기
If you wave, you move your hand from side to side in the air, usually in order to say hello or goodbye to someone.

bite**
[bait]

v. 물다, 베어 물다; n. 물기; 한 입 (베어 문 조각)
If an animal or person bites you, they use their teeth to hurt or injure you.

pinky
[píŋki]

n. 새끼손가락
Your pinky is the smallest finger on your hand.

hop ^{복습}
[hap]

v. 깡충깡충 뛰다; 급히 가다; n. 깡충 뛰기
If you hop, you move along by jumping on one foot.

Chapters 9 & 10

1. What did the students before Ron order from Miss Mush?
   A. Mushroom Surprise
   B. Potato salad
   C. Peanut butter and jelly sandwiches
   D. Milk

2. Why had Ron not brought a lunch to school?
   A. He had forgotten it at home.
   B. He had run out of bread.
   C. He had run out of peanut butter.
   D. He had eaten it on the way to school.

3. Why was the special called Mushroom Surprise?
   A. It would be a surprise if anybody ordered it.
   B. It would be a surprise if there were mushrooms in in.
   C. It would be a surprise if you ate it and lived.
   D. It would be a surprise if Louis ate it.

4. Which of the following did NOT happen after Ron ate the Mushroom Surprise?
   A. He kissed Deedee.
   B. His whole body began to shake.
   C. His face flushed and his eyes changed color.
   D. He threw up.

5. Which of the following was NOT how Benjamin felt about Mark Miller?

   A. Mark Miller was smarter than Benjamin.

   B. Mark Miller was a better kicker than Benjamin.

   C. Mark Miller was richer than Benjamin.

   D. Mark Miller was better looking than Benjamin.

6. Why was Benjamin NOT playing the tambourine?

   A. He wanted to play the triangle.

   B. He didn't know how to play the tambourine.

   C. He wanted to tell Mrs. Jewls his real name.

   D. His tambourine was broken.

7. Why did Mrs. Jewls think that the principal had come to her class?

   A. He wanted to tell them to play louder.

   B. He wanted to tell them to play quieter.

   C. He wanted to hear the music more clearly.

   D. He wanted to help them play better.

1분에 몇 단어를 읽는지 리딩 속도를 측정해보세요.

$$\frac{893 \text{ words}}{\text{reading time ( ) sec}} \times 60 = (\quad) \text{ WPM}$$

Build Your Vocabulary

wipe^{복습}
[waip]

v. (먼지·물기 등을 없애기 위해 무엇을) 닦다; n. (행주·걸레를 써서) 닦기
If you wipe something, you rub its surface to remove dirt or liquid from it.

apron[*]
[éiprən]

n. 앞치마
An apron is a piece of clothing that you put on over the front of your normal clothes and tie round your waist, especially when you are cooking.

cafeteria^{복습}
[kæfətíəriə]

n. 카페테리아, 구내식당
A cafeteria is a restaurant where you choose your food from a counter and take it to your table after paying for it.

mushroom^{복습}
[mʌʃruːm]

n. 버섯
Mushrooms are fungi that you can eat.

carton^{복습}
[ka:rtn]

n. (음식이나 음료를 담는) 곽; 상자
A carton is a plastic or cardboard container in which food or drink is sold.

brilliant[*]
[bríljənt]

a. 훌륭한, 멋진; 아주 밝은, 선명한, 눈부신
A brilliant person, idea, or performance is extremely clever or skillful.

in a row

idiom (며칠·몇 달·몇 년 등을) 계속해서; (여러 번을) 잇달아
If something happens several days in a row, it happens on each of those days.

be left over

idiom (필요한 것을 쓰고 난 뒤) 남다
If food or money is left over, it remains when the rest has been eaten or used up.

squeak[*]
[skwiːk]

v. 끽 하는 소리를 내다; n. 끼익 하는 소리
If something or someone squeaks, they make a short, high-pitched sound.

blow one's nose

idiom 코를 풀다
When you blow your nose, you force air out of it through your nostrils in order to clear it.

dump[*]
[dʌmp]

v. (아무렇게나) 내려놓다; 버리다; n. (쓰레기) 폐기장
If you dump something somewhere, you put it or unload it there quickly and carelessly.

lump[*]
[lʌmp]

n. 덩어리, 응어리
A lump of something is a solid piece of it.

plate^{**}
[pleit]

n. 접시, 그릇; 한 접시 (분량의 음식)
A plate is a round or oval flat dish that is used to hold food.

tray[*]
[trei]

n. 쟁반
A tray is a flat piece of wood, plastic, or metal, which usually has raised edges and which is used for carrying things, especially food and drinks.

cash register
[kǽʃ rèdʒistər]

n. 금전 등록기
A cash register is a machine in a shop, pub, or restaurant that is used to add up and record how much money people pay, and in which the money is kept.

lounge^{복습}
[laundʒ]

n. (호텔·클럽 등의) 휴게실; (공항 등의) 대합실; v. 느긋하게 있다
In a hotel, club, or other public place, a lounge is a room where people can sit and relax.

burst^{**}
[bəːrst]

v. (burst-burst) 불쑥 ~하다; 터지다, 파열하다; n. (갑자기) 한바탕 ~을 함; 파열
To burst into or out of a place means to enter or leave it suddenly with a lot of energy or force.

alongside
[əlɔ́ːŋsáid]

prep. ~옆에, 나란히; ~와 함께; ~와 동시에
If one thing is alongside another thing, the first thing is next to the second.

immune
[imjúːn]

a. 면역성이 있는, ~의 영향을 받지 않는
If you are immune to a particular disease, you cannot be affected by it.

dig^{복습}
[dig]

v. (dug-dug) ~을 찌르다; (구멍 등을) 파다; n. 쿡 찌르기; 발굴
If you dig one thing into another or if one thing digs into another, the first thing is pushed hard into the second, or presses hard into it.

goop
[guːp]

n. 절꺽절꺽 들러붙는 것
Goop is a thick, slimy substance.

exclaim^{복습}
[ikskléim]

v. 소리치다, 외치다
If you exclaim, you cry out suddenly in surprise, strong emotion, or pain.

chew[*]
[ʧuː]

v. (음식을) 씹다
If you chew gum or tobacco, you keep biting it and moving it around your mouth to taste the flavor of it. You do not swallow it.

swallow^{**}
[swálou]

v. (음식 등을) 삼키다; 마른침을 삼키다; n. [동물] 제비
If you swallow something, you cause it to go from your mouth down into your stomach.

mixture[*]
[míksʧər]

n. (서로 다른 것들이 섞인) 혼합물
A mixture of things consists of several different things together.

spinach
[spínitʃ]

n. 시금치
Spinach is a vegetable with large dark green leaves that you chop up and boil in water before eating.

flush★
[flʌʃ]

v. (사람의) 얼굴이 붉어지다, 상기되다; (변기의) 물이 쏟아지다; n. 홍조
If you flush, your face goes red because you are hot or ill, or because you are feeling a strong emotion such as embarrassment or anger.

washing machine★
[wáʃiŋ məʃìːn]

n. 세탁기
A washing machine is a machine that you use to wash clothes in.

throw up

idiom 토하다
When someone throws up, they vomit.

get away

idiom (~에서) 탈출하다, 벗어나다
If you get away from someone or some place, you escape from them or that place.

smack
[smæk]

ad. 정통으로; v. 탁 소리가 나게 치다; n. 탁 하는 소리
Something that is smack in a particular place is exactly in that place.

sleeve★
[sliːv]

n. 소매
The sleeves of a coat, shirt, or other item of clothing are the parts that cover your arms.

shrug복습
[ʃrʌg]

v. (두 손바닥을 위로 하고) 어깨를 으쓱하다; n. 어깨를 으쓱하기
If you shrug, you raise your shoulders to show that you are not interested in something or that you do not know or care about something.

run away

idiom (~에서) 달아나다
If you run away, you leave quickly in order to avoid or escape someone or something.

mouthful★
[máuθfùl]

n. (음식) 한 입, 한 모금; 길고 복잡한 말
A mouthful of drink or food is the amount that you put or have in your mouth.

$$\frac{675 \text{ words}}{\text{reading time ( ) sec}} \times 60 = (\quad) \text{ WPM}$$

Build Your Vocabulary

kickball
[kíkbɔ:l]

n. 발야구
Kickball is an informal game combining elements of baseball and soccer, in which a soccer ball is thrown to a person who kicks it and proceeds to run the bases.

unfortunate[*]
[ʌnfɔ́:rtʃənət]

a. 운이 없는, 불운한, 불행한 (unfortunately ad. 불행하게도, 유감스럽게도)
You can use unfortunately to introduce or refer to a statement when you consider that it is sad or disappointing, or when you want to express regret.

sigh[복습]
[sai]

v. 한숨을 쉬다, 한숨짓다; n. 한숨
When you sigh, you let out a deep breath, as a way of expressing feelings such as disappointment, tiredness, or pleasure.

instrument[**]
[ínstrəmənt]

n. 악기; 기구, 도구
A musical instrument is an object such as a piano, guitar, or flute, which you play in order to produce music.

invent[**]
[invént]

v. 발명하다; (사실이 아닌 것을) 지어내다
If you invent something such as a machine or process, you are the first person to think of it or make it.

obvious[**]
[ábviəs]

a. 분명한, 명백한
If something is obvious, it is easy to see or understand.

snare
[snεər]

v. ~을 손에 넣다; 덫으로 잡다; n. 덫; 향현, 울림줄
If you snare something, you get or achieve it by skillful action or good luck.

bang[*]
[bæŋ]

v. 쾅 하고 치다; 쾅 하고 닫다; n. 쾅 하는 소리
If something bangs, it makes a sudden loud noise, once or several times.

eardrum
[íərdrʌm]

n. 고막
Your eardrums are the thin pieces of tightly stretched skin inside each ear, which vibrate when sound waves reach them.

rattle[*]
[rætl]

v. 달가닥거리다, 덜컹거리다; n. 덜거덕거리는 소리
When something rattles or when you rattle it, it makes short sharp knocking sounds because it is being shaken or it keeps hitting against something hard.

rock[**]
[rak]

v. (전후·좌우로 부드럽게) 흔들다; (큰 충격·공포로) 뒤흔들다; n. 암석
When something rocks or when you rock it, it moves slowly and regularly backward and forward or from side to side.

bong
[baŋ]

v. 둥 소리를 내다; n. 둥 하고 울리는 소리
If something such as a bell bongs, it makes a deep ringing noise.

gong
[gɔːŋ]

v. 징을 울리다; n. 징; 공
If something gongs, it makes a sound like that of a gong being struck.

jingle
[dʒiŋgl]

v. 짤랑짤랑 소리를 내다; n. 딸랑딸랑 울리는 소리
When something jingles or when you jingle it, it makes a gentle ringing noise, like small bells.

ting
[tiŋ]

n. 쨍그렁하는 소리; v. 쨍그렁하는 소리가 나다
A ting is a high metallic sound such as that made by a small bell.

bash^{복습}
[bæʃ]

v. 후려치다, 세게 치다; 맹비난하다; n. 강타
If you bash something, you hit it hard in a rough or careless way.

crash**
[kræʃ]

v. (굉음과 함께) 부딪치다; 충돌하다; 들이받다;
n. (자동차 충돌·항공기 추락) 사고; 요란한 소리, 굉음
If something crashes somewhere, it moves and hits something else violently, making a loud noise.

holler
[hálər]

v. 소리지르다, 고함치다
If you holler, you shout loudly.

yell^{복습}
[jel]

v. 고함치다, 소리 지르다; n. 고함, 외침
If you yell, you shout loudly, usually because you are excited, angry, or in pain.

charge^{복습}
[ʧɑːrdʒ]

v. 급히 가다, 달려가다; (요금·값을) 청구하다; n. (상품·서비스에 대한) 요금
If you charge toward someone or something, you move quickly and aggressively toward them.

principal*
[prínsəpəl]

n. 교장; 학장, 총장; a. 주요한, 주된
A principal is a teacher who is in charge of a school.

screech*
[skriːtʃ]

v. 끼익 하는 소리를 내다; n. 끼익, 귀에 거슬리는 날카로운 소리
If a vehicle screeches somewhere or if its tires screech, its tires make an unpleasant high-pitched noise on the road.

halt*
[hɔːlt]

n. 멈춤, 중단; v. 멈추다, 서다; 세우다, 중단시키다
If someone or something comes to a halt, they stop moving.

in time

idiom 제때에, 시간 맞춰, 늦지 않게
If you are in time for a particular event, you are not too late for it.

complain^{복습}
[kəmpléin]

v. 불평하다, 항의하다
If you complain about a situation, you say that you are not satisfied with it.

musician**
[mjuːzíʃən]

n. 음악가
A musician is a person who plays a musical instrument as their job or hobby.

Chapters 11 & 12

1. Why did the children across the playground quit their games?
   A. Nobody could have fun when Kathy was singing a depressing song.
   B. Nobody could have fun when Terrence was being mean.
   C. Nobody could have fun when D.J. looked so sad.
   D. It was beginning to rain.

2. Why was D.J. so sad about losing his watch?
   A. His parents would ground him.
   B. His grandfather would hate him.
   C. He would pay for it out of his allowance.
   D. He was afraid a bird might choke on it.

3. Why did Mrs. Jewls give D.J. a sheet of black construction paper?
   A. He wanted to draw a picture using a white crayon.
   B. He held it under his nose because his smile was so bright.
   C. He used it to cut out a mustache and put it under his nose.
   D. He held it above his head to fold it into a hat.

4. What was Allison's pencil like after Jason gave it back to her?

   A. It was full of teeth marks.

   B. It was missing the eraser.

   C. It was broken in half.

   D. It was too short to use to use anymore.

5. How did Jason think that Mrs. Jewls was going to help him stop chewing pencils?

   A. He thought she would give him a Tootsie Roll Pop.

   B. He thought she would give him a pen instead of a pencil.

   C. He thought that she was going to not make him do his work.

   D. He thought that she was going to give him a dirty pencil.

6. How did Mrs. Jewls help Jason stop chewing pencils?

   A. She gave him a pen.

   B. She taped his mouth shut.

   C. She gave him a Tootsie Roll Pop.

   D. She watched him closely as he worked.

1분에 몇 단어를 읽는지 리딩 속도를 측정해보세요.

$$\frac{991 \text{ words}}{\text{reading time ( ) sec}} \times 60 = (\qquad) \text{ WPM}$$

Build Your Vocabulary

playground^{복습}
[pléigràund]

n. (학교의) 운동장; 놀이터
A playground is a piece of land, at school or in a public area, where children can play.

splat
[splæt]

n. 철퍼덕 하는 소리
Splat is used to describe the sound of something wet hitting a surface with a lot of force.

jolly*
[dʒáli]

a. 행복한, 쾌활한
Someone who is jolly is happy and cheerful in their appearance or behavior.

upside down
[ʌ́psàid dáun]

ad. (아래위가) 거꾸로
If something has been moved upside down, it has been turned round so that the part that is usually lowest is above the part that is usually highest.

kickball^{복습}
[kíkbɔːl]

n. 발야구
Kickball is an informal game combining elements of baseball and soccer, in which a soccer ball is thrown to a person who kicks it and proceeds to run the bases.

gore
[gɔːr]

n. 피, 선혈
Gore is blood from a wound that has become thick.

snap out of it

idiom (침울해 하지 말고) 기운을 내다
If you say 'snap out of it' to someone, you mean they should try to stop feeling unhappy or depressed.

stare^{복습}
[stɛər]

v. 빤히 쳐다보다, 응시하다; n. 빤히 쳐다보기, 응시
If you stare at someone or something, you look at them for a long time.

mumble
[mʌ́mbl]

v. 중얼거리다, 웅얼거리다; n. 중얼거림
If you mumble, you speak very quietly and not at all clearly with the result that the words are difficult to understand.

halfway*
[hǽfwèi]

ad. (거리·시간상으로) 중간에, 가운데쯤에
Halfway means in the middle of a place or between two points, at an equal distance from each of them.

burst^{복습}
[bəːrst]

v. (burst-burst) 불쑥 ~하다; 터지다, 파열하다; n. (갑자기) 한바탕 ~을 함; 파열
If you burst out laughing, you suddenly start laughing.

stand over

idiom ~를 옆에서 지켜보다
If you stand over someone, you remain close to them and watch them.

dumb^{복습}
[dʌm]

a. 멍청한, 바보 같은; 벙어리의, 말을 못 하는
If you call a person dumb, you mean that they are stupid or foolish.

jerk*
[dʒəːrk]

n. 얼간이; 홱 움직임; v. 홱 움직이다
If you call someone a jerk, you are insulting them because you think they are stupid or you do not like them.

glee
[gliː]

n. 신이 남; (남이 잘못되는 것에 대한) 고소한 기분
Glee is a feeling of happiness and excitement, often caused by someone else's misfortune.

plop
[plap]

v. 털썩 주저앉다; 퐁당 하고 떨어지다; n. 퐁당 하는 소리
If something plops somewhere, it drops there with a soft, gentle sound.

divorce*
[divɔ́ːrs]

v. 이혼하다; n. 이혼
If a man and woman divorce, their marriage is legally ended.

hopeful**
[hóupfəl]

a. 희망에 찬; 전도 유망한; n. (전도) 유망한 사람 (hopefully ad. 희망에 차서)
If you are hopeful, you are fairly confident that something that you want to happen will happen.

delight*
[diláit]

n. 기쁨, 즐거움; v. 많은 기쁨을 주다, 아주 즐겁게 하다
Delight is a feeling of very great pleasure.

nod^{복습}
[nad]

v. (고개를) 끄덕이다; n. (고개를) 끄덕임
If you nod, you move your head downward and upward to show that you are answering 'yes' to a question, or to show agreement, understanding, or approval.

rub^{복습}
[rʌb]

v. (두 손 등을) 맞비비다; (손·손수건 등을 대고) 문지르다; n. 문지르기, 비비기
If you rub two things together or if they rub together, they move backward and forward, pressing against each other.

ground***
[graund]

v. (자녀에 대한 벌로) 외출하지 못하게 하다; n. 땅바닥, 지면; 땅, 토양
When parents ground a child, they forbid them to go out and enjoy themselves for a period of time, as a punishment.

punish***
[pʌ́niʃ]

v. 처벌하다, 벌주다; (형벌·형에) 처하다
To punish someone means to make them suffer in some way because they have done something wrong.

no matter

idiom ~일지라도 (상관없다)
If you say that you are going to do something no matter what, you are emphasizing that you are definitely going to do it, even if there are obstacles or difficulties.

worth^{복습}
[wəːrθ]

a. (금전 등의 면에서) ~의 가치가 있는; ~해 볼 만한; n. 가치, 값어치
If something is worth a particular amount of money, it can be sold for that amount or is considered to have that value.

allowance*
[əláuəns]

n. 용돈; (특정 목적을 위한) 비용; 허용량
A child's allowance is money that is given to him or her every week or every month by his or her parents.

triumphant
[traiʌ́mfənt]

a. 의기양양한; 크게 성공한, 큰 승리를 거둔 (triumphantly ad. 의기양양하여)
Someone who is triumphant has gained a victory or succeeded in something and feels very happy about it.

frown^{복습}
[fraun]

v. 얼굴을 찌푸리다; n. 찡그림, 찌푸림
When someone frowns, their eyebrows become drawn together, because they are annoyed or puzzled.

squawk
[skwɔːk]

v. (화·놀람 등으로) 꽥꽥거리다; 새가 (크게) 꽥꽥 울다
If a person squawks, they complain loudly, often in a high-pitched, harsh tone.

closet^{복습}
[klázit]

n. 벽장
A closet is a piece of furniture with doors at the front and shelves inside, which is used for storing things.

glare*
[glɛər]

v. 노려보다; 환하다, 눈부시다; n. 노려봄; 환한 빛, 눈부심
If you glare at someone, you look at them with an angry expression on your face.

choke**
[tʃouk]

v. 숨이 막히다, 질식할 지경이다; 목을 조르다; n. 숨이 막힘, 질식
When you choke or when something chokes you, you cannot breathe properly or get enough air into your lungs.

shriek*
[ʃriːk]

v. (날카롭게) 악을 쓰며 말하다; 비명을 지르다; n. 비명
If you shriek something, you shout it in a loud, high-pitched voice.

nest*
[nest]

n. (새의) 둥지
A bird's nest is the home that it makes to lay its eggs in.

grumble*
[grʌmbl]

v. 투덜거리다; 우르릉거리다; n. 불만 사항
If someone grumbles, they complain about something in a bad-tempered way.

windowsill^{복습}
[wíndousil]

n. 창턱
A windowsill is a shelf along the bottom of a window, either inside or outside a building.

gripe^{복습}
[graip]

v. 불평을 하다, 투덜거리다; n. 불만, 불평
If you say that someone is griping, you mean they are annoying you because they keep on complaining about something.

wrist*
[rist]

n. 손목
Your wrist is the part of your body between your hand and your arm which bends when you move your hand.

grouse
[graus]

v. 불평하다, 투덜대다
If you grouse, you complain.

projector
[prədʒéktər]

n. 영사기
A projector is a machine that projects films or slides onto a screen or wall.

shade**
[ʃeid]

n. (창문에 치는) 블라인드; (시원한) 그늘; 색조; v. 그늘지게 하다
A shade is a piece of stiff cloth or heavy paper that you can pull down over a window as a covering.

1분에 몇 단어를 읽는지 리딩 속도를 측정해보세요.

$$\frac{957 \text{ words}}{\text{reading time (}\quad\text{) sec}} \times 60 = (\quad\quad) \text{ WPM}$$

Build Your Vocabulary

mark***
[maːrk]
n. 자국, 흔적; 표시, 부호; 점수, 평점; v. (표·기호 등으로) 표시하다
(teeth mark n. 잇자국)
A mark is a small area of something such as dirt that has accidentally got onto a surface or piece of clothing.

point***
[pɔint]
n. (사물의 뾰족한) 끝; (말·글에서 제시하는) 의견; 요점; 점수; 점;
v. (손가락 등으로) 가리키다
The point of something such as a pin, needle, or knife is the thin, sharp end of it.

yuck복습
[jʌk]
int. 윽(역겨울 때 내는 소리)
'Yuck' is an expression of disgust.

chew복습
[ʧuː]
v. (음식을) 씹다
If you chew gum or tobacco, you keep biting it and moving it around your mouth to taste the flavor of it. You do not swallow it.

awful**
[ɔ́ːfəl]
a. 끔찍한, 지독한; (양적으로 많음을 강조하는 의미로) 엄청
If you say that someone or something is awful, you dislike that person or thing or you think that they are not very good.

embarrass**
[imbǽrəs]
v. 당황스럽게 만들다, 쑥스럽게 하다; 곤란하게 만들다
(embarrassing a. 난처한, 쑥스러운)
Something that is embarrassing makes you feel shy or ashamed.

on purpose
idiom 고의로, 일부러
If you do something on purpose, you do it intentionally.

slobber
[slábər]
v. 침을 흘리다
If a person or an animal slobbers, they let liquid fall from their mouth.

disgust복습
[disgʌ́st]
v. 혐오감을 유발하다, 역겹게 만들다; n. 혐오감, 역겨움, 넌더리
(disgusting a. 역겨운, 구역질나는)
If you say that something is disgusting, you mean that you find it completely unacceptable.

blackboard복습
[blǽkbɔ̀ːrd]
n. 칠판
A blackboard is a dark-colored board that you can write on with chalk.

discipline복습
[dísəplin]
n. 규율, 훈육; 단련법, 수련법
Discipline is the practice of making people obey rules or standards of behavior, and punishing them when they do not.

spell^{복습}
[spel]

v. 철자를 맞게 쓰다, 맞춤법에 맞게 글을 쓰다; (어떤 단어의) 철자를 말하다
(spelling n. 철자법, 맞춤법)
When you spell a word, you write or speak each letter in the word in the correct order.

slap^{복습}
[slæp]

v. (손바닥으로) 철썩 때리다; 털썩 놓다; n. (손바닥으로) 철썩 때리기
If you slap someone, you hit them with the palm of your hand.

forehead*
[fɔ́:rhèd]

n. 이마
Your forehead is the area at the front of your head between your eyebrows and your hair.

make a face

idiom 얼굴을 찌푸리다, 침울한 표정을 짓다
If you make a face, you twist your face to indicate a certain mental or emotional state.

sharpen*
[ʃɑ́:rpən]

v. 날카롭게 하다, (날카롭게) 깎다; 날카로워지다, 선명해지다
If you sharpen an object, you make its edge very thin or you make its end pointed.

erase^{복습}
[iréis]

v. (지우개 등으로) 지우다; (완전히) 없애다 (eraser n. 고무 지우개)
An eraser is an object, usually a piece of rubber or plastic, which is used for removing something that has been written using a pencil or a pen.

horror^{복습}
[hɔ́:rər]

n. 공포(감), 경악
Horror is a feeling of great shock, fear, and worry caused by something extremely unpleasant.

chalk**
[tʃɔ:k]

n. 분필
A chalk is a small piece of soft white rock, used for writing or drawing with.

stack^{복습}
[stæk]

n. 무더기, 더미; v. (깔끔하게 정돈하여) 쌓다
A stack of things is a pile of them.

work sheet^{복습}
[wɔ́:rk ʃì:t]

n. (학습용) 연습 문제지
A work sheet is a specially prepared page of exercises designed to improve your knowledge or understanding of a particular subject.

contain**
[kəntéin]

v. (무엇의 안에 또는 그 일부로) ~이 들어 있다; (감정을) 억누르다
If writing, speech, or film contains particular information, ideas, or images, it includes them.

arithmetic^{복습}
[əríθmətik]

n. 산수, 연산; 산술, 계산
Arithmetic is the part of mathematics that is concerned with the addition, subtraction, multiplication, and division of numbers.

stuff*
[stʌf]

v. (재빨리·되는대로) 쑤셔 넣다; (빽빽히) 채워 넣다; n. 일, 것; 물건
If you stuff something somewhere, you push it there quickly and roughly.

suck^{복습}
[sʌk]

v. (입에 넣고 계속) 빨다; (액체·공기 등을) 빨아 먹다; (특정한 방향으로) 빨아들이다;
n. 빨기, 빨아 먹기
If you suck something, you hold it in your mouth and pull at it with the muscles in your cheeks and tongue, for example in order to get liquid out of it.

56

heavy-duty
[hèvi-djúːti]

a. 튼튼한; 아주 진지한
A heavy-duty piece of equipment is very strong and can be used a lot.

masking tape
[mǽskiŋ tèip]

n. 보호 테이프
Masking tape is plastic or paper tape which is sticky on one side and is used, for example, to protect part of a surface that you are painting.

tease*
[tiːz]

v. 놀리다, 장난하다; n. 남을 놀리기 좋아하는 사람; 장난, 놀림
To tease someone means to laugh at them or make jokes about them in order to embarrass, annoy, or upset them.

mummy*
[mʌ́mi]

n. 미라
A mummy is a dead body which was preserved long ago by being rubbed with special oils and wrapped in cloth.

sneeze*
[sniːz]

v. 재채기하다; n. 재채기
When you sneeze, you suddenly take in your breath and then blow it down your nose noisily without being able to stop yourself, for example because you have a cold.

rip*
[rip]

v. (갑자기·거칠게) 찢다; 떼어 내다; n. (옷감·종이 등에 길게) 찢어진 곳
When something rips or when you rip it, you tear it forcefully with your hands or with a tool such as a knife.

crash^{복습}
[kræʃ]

v. (굉음과 함께) 부딪치다; 충돌하다, 들이받다;
n. (자동차 충돌·항공기 추락) 사고; 요란한 소리, 굉음
If something crashes somewhere, it moves and hits something else violently, making a loud noise.

protect**
[prətékt]

v. 보호하다, 지키다
To protect someone or something means to prevent them from being harmed or damaged.

Chapters 13 & 14

1. What kind of story did Dana hope that Mrs. Jewls would read?
   A. Dana hoped that Mrs. Jewls would read a funny story.
   B. Dana hoped that Mrs. Jewls would read a sad story.
   C. Dana hoped that Mrs. Jewls would read a scary story.
   D. Dana hoped that Mrs. Jewls would read a boring story.

2. Why did John call Dana a foghorn?
   A. Dana always cried.
   B. Dana laughed loudly.
   C. Dana shouted loudly.
   D. Dana blew her nose loudly.

3. How did Mrs. Jewls feel about Dana and stories?
   A. Mrs. Jewls wished that Dana would become a writer.
   B. Mrs. Jewls wished that everybody laughed and cried as much as her.
   C. Mrs. Jewls wished that Dana would leave the room when she read stories.
   D. Mrs. Jewls wished that Dana would help her read stories to the class.

4. What was the most fun part of Calvin's birthday party?
   A. Eating the cupcakes
   B. Singing 'Happy Birthday'
   C. Trading jelly beans
   D. Opening presents

5. Why did Calvin think it was easy for others to give suggestions about his tattoo?
   A. Calvin thought it was easy, because they wouldn't have to live with it.
   B. Calvin thought it was easy, because the other children already had tattoos.
   C. Calvin thought it was easy, because they could draw better than him.
   D. Calvin thought it was easy, because they had seen more tattoo examples.

6. How did Calvin's dad feel about him getting a tattoo?
   A. He said it was like getting married.
   B. He said it was like getting a second nose.
   C. He said it was like being a piece of art.
   D. He said it was like making a new friend.

Check Your Reading Speed

1분에 몇 단어를 읽는지 리딩 속도를 측정해보세요.

$$\frac{943 \text{ words}}{\text{reading time ( ) sec}} \times 60 = (\qquad) \text{ WPM}$$

Build Your Vocabulary

wise***
[waiz]

a. 지혜로운, 현명한, 슬기로운
A wise person is able to use their experience and knowledge in order to make sensible decisions and judgments.

horrible**
[hɔ́ːrəbl]

a. 지긋지긋한, 끔찍한; 소름끼치는, 무시무시한
If you describe something or someone as horrible, you do not like them at all.

embarrass^{복습}
[imbǽrəs]

v. 당황스럽게 만들다, 쑥스럽게 하다; 곤란하게 만들다
(embarrassing a. 난처한, 쑥스러운)
Something that is embarrassing makes you feel shy or ashamed.

break out

idiom 갑자기 ~하기 시작하다; 발발하다
If you break out something, you begin it, or you begin using or doing it.

giggle*
[gigl]

v. 피식 웃다, 킥킥거리다; n. 피식 웃음, 킥킥거림
If someone giggles, they laugh in a childlike way, because they are amused, nervous, or embarrassed.

arithmetic^{복습}
[əríθmətik]

n. 산수, 연산; 산술, 계산
Arithmetic is the part of mathematics that is concerned with the addition, subtraction, multiplication, and division of numbers.

silly**
[síli]

a. 어리석은, 바보 같은; n. 바보
If you say that someone or something is silly, you mean that they are foolish, childish, or ridiculous.

squash^{복습}
[skwaʃ]

v. 짓누르다, 으깨다, 찌부러뜨리다; n. 스쿼시; 호박
If someone or something is squashed, they are pressed or crushed with such force that they become injured or lose their shape.

leak^{복습}
[liːk]

v. (액체·기체가) 새다; 새게 하다; n. (액체·기체가) 새는 곳
(leaky a. 물·가스가) 새는, 구멍이 난)
Something that is leaky has holes, cracks, or other faults which allow liquids and gases to pass through.

faucet*
[fɔ́ːsit]

n. (수도)꼭지
A faucet is a device that controls the flow of a liquid or gas from a pipe or container.

plumber
[plʌ́mər]

n. 배관공
A plumber is a person whose job is to connect and repair things such as water and drainage pipes, baths, and toilets.

60

cave*
[keiv]

n. 동굴
A cave is a large hole in the side of a cliff or hill, or one that is under the ground.

recess^{복습}
[risés]

n. (학교의) 쉬는 시간; (의회·위원회 등의) 휴회 기간
A recess is a break between classes at a school.

chase**
[ʧeis]

v. 뒤쫓다, 추적하다; (돈·성공 등을) 좇다; n. 추적, 추격
If you chase someone, or chase after them, you run after them or follow them quickly in order to catch or reach them.

stream**
[stri:m]

v. (액체·기체가) 줄줄 흐르다; 줄을 지어 이어지다; n. 개울; (액체·기체의) 줄기
If a liquid streams somewhere, it flows or comes out in large amounts.

bore*
[bɔ:r]

v. 지루하게 하다 (boring a. 재미없는, 지루한)
Someone or something boring is so dull and uninteresting that they make people tired and impatient.

wrap**
[ræp]

v. (포장지 등으로) 싸다, 포장하다; 두르다; n. 포장지 (wrapping paper n. 포장지)
When you wrap something, you fold paper or cloth tightly round it to cover it completely, for example in order to protect it or so that you can give it to someone as a present.

bow*
[bou]

① n. (매듭·리본의) 나비 모양; 활
② v. (허리를 굽혀) 절하다; (고개를) 숙이다; n. 절, (고개 숙여 하는) 인사
A bow is a knot with two loops and two loose ends that is used in tying shoelaces and ribbons.

tease^{복습}
[ti:z]

v. 놀리다, 장난하다; n. 남을 놀리기 좋아하는 사람; 장난, 놀림
To tease someone means to laugh at them or make jokes about them in order to embarrass, annoy, or upset them.

snicker
[sníkər]

v. 낄낄 웃다, 숨죽여 웃다; n. 낄낄 웃음, 숨죽여 웃는 웃음
If you snicker, you laugh quietly in a disrespectful way, for example at something rude or embarrassing.

tear^{복습}
[tɛər]

① v. (tore-torn) 찢다, 뜯다; 구멍을 뚫다; n. 찢어진 곳, 구멍 ② n. 눈물
If you tear paper, cloth, or another material, or if it tears, you pull it into two pieces or you pull it so that a hole appears in it.

hysterical
[histérikəl]

a. 히스테리 상태의, (히스테리) 발작적인 (hysterically ad. 히스테리적인)
Hysterical laughter is loud and uncontrolled.

fist*
[fist]

n. 주먹
Your hand is referred to as your fist when you have bent your fingers in toward the palm in order to hit someone.

cowbell^{복습}
[káubèl]

n. (소를 쉽게 찾기 위해 목에 다는) 소 방울
A cowbell is a small bell that is hung around a cow's neck so that the ringing sound makes it possible to find the cow.

stinky
[stíŋki]

a. 악취가 나는; 지독한, 역겨운
If something is stinky, it smells extremely unpleasant.

playful**
[pleifl]

a. 장난기 많은; 놀기 좋아하는
A playful animal is lively and cheerful.

skunk
[skʌŋk]

n. [동물] 스컹크
A skunk is a small black and white animal which releases an unpleasant smelling liquid if it is frightened or attacked.

gasp^{복습}
[gæsp]

v. 숨이 턱 막히다, 헉 하고 숨을 쉬다; n. (숨이 막히는 듯) 헉 하는 소리를 냄
When you gasp, you take a short quick breath through your mouth, especially when you are surprised, shocked, or in pain.

hunter*
[hʌ́ntər]

n. 사냥꾼
A hunter is a person who hunts wild animals for food or as a sport.

chipmunk
[ʧípmʌŋk]

n. [동물] 얼룩 다람쥐
A chipmunk is a small animal with a large furry tail and a striped back.

come along

idiom (명령형으로 쓰여) 서둘러; 함께 가다
If you say 'come along' to someone, you encourage them or tell them to hurry up.

thunder*
[θʌ́ndər]

n. 천둥, 우레; v. 천둥이 치다
Thunder is the loud noise that you hear from the sky after a flash of lightning, especially during a storm.

speed*
[spiːd]

v. 빨리 가다; 더 빠르게 하다, 가속화하다; n. (물체의 이동) 속도
If you speed somewhere, you move or travel there quickly, usually in a vehicle.

look out

idiom 조심해!
If you say or shout 'look out!' to someone, you are warning them that they are in danger.

onrushing
[ɔ́nrʌ̀ʃiŋ]

a. 돌진하는; 앞뒤를 헤아리지 않고 내닫는
Onrushing describes something such as a vehicle that is moving forward so quickly or forcefully that it would be very difficult to stop.

in time^{복습}

idiom 제때에, 시간 맞춰, 늦지 않게
If you are in time for a particular event, you are not too late for it.

unfortunate^{복습}
[ʌ̀nfɔ́ːrʧənət]

a. 운이 없는, 불운한, 불행한 (unfortunately ad. 불행하게도, 유감스럽게도)
You can use unfortunately to introduce or refer to a statement when you consider that it is sad or disappointing, or when you want to express regret.

run over

idiom (차량이나 운전자가) ~을 치다
If someone runs over, they hit and drive over someone or something with a vehicle.

sob*
[sab]

v. (흑흑) 흐느끼다, 흐느껴 울다; n. 흐느껴 울기, 흐느낌
When someone sobs, they cry in a noisy way, breathing in short breaths.

sniffle
[snifl]

v. (계속) 훌쩍거리다; n. 훌쩍거림; 훌쩍거리는 소리
If you sniffle, you keep sniffing, usually because you are crying or have a cold.

62

wipe ^{복습}
[waip]

v. (먼지·물기 등을 없애기 위해 무엇을) 닦다; n. (행주·걸레를 써서) 닦기
If you wipe something, you rub its surface to remove dirt or liquid from it.

blow one's nose ^{복습}

idiom 코를 풀다
When you blow your nose, you force air out of it through your nostrils in order to clear it.

foggy
[fɔ́:gi]

a. 안개가 낀
When it is foggy, there are tiny drops of water in the air which form a thick cloud and make it difficult to see things.

flight of stairs

idiom 한 줄로 이어진 계단
A flight of stairs is a set of steps or stairs that lead from one level to another without changing direction.

make a face ^{복습}

idiom 얼굴을 찌푸리다, 침울한 표정을 짓다
If you make a face, you twist your face to indicate a certain mental or emotional state.

Check Your Reading Speed

1분에 몇 단어를 읽는지 리딩 속도를 측정해보세요.

$$\frac{993 \text{ words}}{\text{reading time ( ) sec}} \times 60 = (\quad) \text{ WPM}$$

Build Your Vocabulary

trade***
[treid]

v. 주고받다, 교환하다, 맞바꾸다; 거래하다; n. 거래, 교역, 무역
If someone trades one thing for another or if two people trade things, they agree to exchange one thing for the other thing.

mumble^{복습}
[mʌmbl]

v. 중얼거리다, 웅얼거리다; n. 중얼거림
If you mumble, you speak very quietly and not at all clearly with the result that the words are difficult to understand.

tattoo
[tætúː]

n. 문신; v. 문신을 새기다
A tattoo is a design that is drawn on someone's skin using needles to make little holes and filling them with colored dye.

neat^{복습}
[niːt]

a. 뛰어난, 훌륭한; 정돈된, 단정한, 말쑥한
If you say that something is neat, you mean that it is very good.

exclaim^{복습}
[ikskléim]

v. 소리치다, 외치다
If you exclaim, you cry out suddenly in surprise, strong emotion, or pain.

complain^{복습}
[kəmpléin]

v. 불평하다, 항의하다
If you complain about a situation, you say that you are not satisfied with it.

parlor*
[páːrlər]

n. (특정한 상품·서비스를 제공하는) 상점; 응접실, 거실
Parlor is used in the names of some types of shops which provide a service, rather than selling things.

big deal^{복습}
[big díːl]

int. 그게 무슨 대수라고!; n. 대단한 것, 큰 일
You can say 'big deal' to someone to show that you are not impressed by something that they consider important or impressive.

spit*
[spit]

v. (입에 든 음식 등을) 뱉다; 침을 뱉다; n. 침; (침 등을) 뱉기
If you spit liquid or food somewhere, you force a small amount of it out of your mouth.

naked*
[néikid]

a. 벌거벗은, 아무것도 걸치지 않은
Someone who is naked is not wearing any clothes.

chest**
[ʧest]

n. 가슴, 흉부; (나무로 만든) 상자
Your chest is the top part of the front of your body where your ribs, lungs, and heart are.

giggle^{복습}
[gigl]

v. 피식 웃다, 킥킥거리다; n. 피식 웃음, 킥킥거림
If someone giggles, they laugh in a childlike way, because they are amused, nervous, or embarrassed.

64

maniac
[méiniæk]

n. 미치광이; ~에 광적으로 열중하는 사람; a. 광적인, 광란의
A maniac is a mad person who is violent and dangerous.

forehead^{복습}
[fɔ́:rhèd]

n. 이마
Your forehead is the area at the front of your head between your eyebrows and your hair.

cheek^{복습}
[ʧi:k]

n. 볼, 뺨
Your cheeks are the sides of your face below your eyes.

anchor*
[ǽŋkər]

n. 닻; v. 닻을 내리다, 정박하다
An anchor is a heavy hooked object that is dropped from a boat into the water at the end of a chain in order to make the boat stay in one place.

buffalo*
[bʌ́fəlòu]

n. [동물] 버팔로, 물소
A buffalo is a wild animal like a large cow with horns that curve upward.

trace*
[treis]

v. (지도·그림 등을 투명한 종이 밑에 받쳐 놓고) 베끼다; 추적하다; n. 자취, 흔적
If you trace a picture, you copy it by covering it with a piece of transparent paper and drawing over the lines underneath.

mutter^{복습}
[mʌ́tər]

v. 중얼거리다; 투덜거리다; n. 중얼거림
If you mutter, you speak very quietly so that you cannot easily be heard, often because you are complaining about something.

pick up

idiom ~를 (차에) 태우러 가다
If you pick someone up, you go to their home or a place you have arranged and take them somewhere in your car.

leopard
[lépərd]

n. [동물] 표범
A leopard is a type of large, wild cat, which has yellow fur and black spots, and live in Africa and Asia.

stuff^{복습}
[stʌf]

v. (빽빽이) 채워 넣다; (재빨리·되는대로) 쑤셔 넣다; n. 일, 것; 물건
If you stuff a container or space with something, you fill it with something or with a quantity of things until it is full.

wise^{복습}
[waiz]

a. 지혜로운, 현명한, 슬기로운
A wise person is able to use their experience and knowledge in order to make sensible decisions and judgments.

exact***
[igzǽkt]

a. 정확한, 정밀한; 꼼꼼한, 빈틈없는 (exactly ad. 정확히, 꼭, 틀림없이)
Exact means correct in every detail.

ankle*
[ǽŋkl]

n. 발목
Your ankle is the joint where your foot joins your leg.

dumb^{복습}
[dʌm]

a. 멍청한, 바보 같은; 벙어리의, 말을 못 하는
If you call a person dumb, you mean that they are stupid or foolish.

soar*
[sɔ:r]

v. (하늘 높이) 날아오르다; (가치·물가 등이) 급증하다
If something such as a bird soars into the air, it goes quickly up into the air.

lightning ^{복습}
[láitniŋ]

n. 번개, 번갯불; a. 번개같이, 아주 빨리
Lightning is the very bright flashes of light in the sky that happen during thunderstorms.

bolt ^{복습}
[boult]

n. 번개; 빗장; 볼트
A bolt of lightning is a flash of lightning that is seen as a white line in the sky.

creature**
[kríːʧər]

n. 생명이 있는 존재, 생물; (~한) 사람
You can refer to any living thing that is not a plant as a creature, especially when it is of an unknown or unfamiliar kind.

outer space
[áutər speis]

n. (대기권 외) 우주 공간
Outer space is the area outside the earth's atmosphere where the other planets and stars are situated.

know better ^{복습}

idiom (~할 정도로) 어리석지는 않다
If someone knows better than to do something, they are old enough or experienced enough to know it is the wrong thing to do.

Chapters 15 & 16

1. Why was Deedee running across the playground screaming?
    A. She was playing a game with her friends.
    B. She was being bullied by another student.
    C. She had seen Mrs. Gorf on the monkey bars.
    D. She had fallen off the monkey bars and hurt herself.

2. Why did Louis think Deedee was talking about a hippopotamus?
    A. The hippopotamus was Deedee's favorite animal.
    B. The hippopotamus wiggles its ears when its mad.
    C. Deedee had just seen a hippopotamus at the zoo.
    D. Mrs. Jewls class had watched a video about a hippopotamus.

3. How did Louis's mother know when he got in trouble when he was younger?
    A. He would come home from school late.
    B. His teacher would call her during dinner.
    C. He would have dirty fingernails when he came home.
    D. He had bits of trash stuck in his hair when he came home.

4. Why was Dameon always doing nice things for Mrs. Jewls?

   A. He was in love with Mrs. Jewls.

   B. He wanted to get good grades.

   C. He wanted to impress his friends.

   D. He wanted to get a Tootsie Roll Pop.

5. How did Joy want Dameon to prove that he was not in love with Mrs. Jewls?

   A. Joy wanted Dameon to not come to class.

   B. Joy wanted Dameon to steal Mrs. Jewls's lunch.

   C. Joy wanted Dameon to put a dead rat in Mrs. Jewls's desk.

   D. Joy wanted Dameon to tell Mrs. Jewls's that he hated her.

6. How did the dead rat react to Dameon and Mrs. Jewls?

   A. It tried to scare them both.

   B. It died again.

   C. It didn't react, because it was already dead.

   D. It said it was disgusting and walked out of the room.

1분에 몇 단어를 읽는지 리딩 속도를 측정해보세요.

$$\frac{911 \text{ words}}{\text{reading time ( ) sec}} \times 60 = (\quad) \text{ WPM}$$

Build Your Vocabulary

playground ^{복습}
[pléigràund]

n. (학교의) 운동장; 놀이터
A playground is a piece of land, at school or in a public area, where children can play.

grab ^{복습}
[græb]

v. (와락·단단히) 붙잡다; ~을 잡아채려고 하다; n. 와락 잡아채려고 함
If you grab something, you take it or pick it up suddenly and roughly.

stare ^{복습}
[stɛər]

v. 빤히 쳐다보다, 응시하다; n. 빤히 쳐다보기, 응시
If you stare at someone or something, you look at them for a long time.

wide-eyed
[wáid-aid]

a. 눈을 크게 뜬, 깜짝 놀란
If you describe someone as wide-eyed, you mean that they are having their eyes wide open as a result of surprise or fear.

gather ^{복습}
[gǽðər]

v. (사람들이) 모이다; 모으다, 챙기다
If people gather somewhere or if someone gathers people somewhere, they come together in a group.

hiccup
[híkʌp]

v. 딸꾹질을 하다, 딸꾹 하는 소리를 내다; n. 딸꾹 하는 소리; 딸꾹질
When you hiccup, you make repeated sharp sounds in your throat.

tremble*
[trembl]

v. (몸을) 떨다, 떨리다; (가볍게) 흔들리다; n. 떨림, 전율
If you tremble, you shake slightly because you are frightened or cold.

upside down ^{복습}
[ápsàid dáun]

ad. (아래위가) 거꾸로
If something has been moved upside down, it has been turned round so that the part that is usually lowest is above the part that is usually highest.

wiggle
[wigl]

v. (좌우·상하로 짧게) 씰룩씰룩 움직이다
If you wiggle something or if it wiggles, it moves up and down or from side to side in small quick movements.

run away ^{복습}

idiom (~에서) 달아나다
If you run away, you leave quickly in order to avoid or escape someone or something.

hippopotamus ^{복습}
[hìpəpátəməs]

n. [동물] 하마
A hippopotamus is a very large African animal with short legs and thick, hairless skin. Hippopotamuses live in and near rivers.

70

fountain*
[fáuntən]

n. 분수
A fountain is an ornamental feature in a pool or lake which consists of a long narrow stream of water that is forced up into the air by a pump.

bend^{복습}
[bend]

v. (bent-bent) (몸이나 머리를) 굽히다, 숙이다; (무엇을) 구부리다; n. 굽이, 굽은 곳
When you bend, you move the top part of your body downward and forward.

faucet^{복습}
[fɔ́:sit]

n. (수도)꼭지
A faucet is a device that controls the flow of a liquid or gas from a pipe or container.

banister
[bǽnəstər]

n. 난간
A banister is a rail supported by posts and fixed along the side of a staircase.

shiver*
[ʃívər]

n. 전율; 몸서리, 오싹(한 느낌); v. (추위·두려움·흥분 등으로) 몸을 떨다
A shiver is a feeling of being frightened of someone or something.

shrug^{복습}
[ʃrʌg]

n. (두 손바닥을 위로 하고) 어깨를 으쓱하기; v. 어깨를 으쓱하다
A shrug is an act of raising your shoulders and then dropping them to show that you do not know or care about something.

take over^{복습}

idiom (~로부터) (~을) 인계받다, (기업 등을) 인수하다
If you take over something from someone, you do it instead of them.

get rid of

idiom ~을 처리하다, 없애다
When you get rid of someone or something that is annoying you or that you do not want, you make yourself free of them or throw something away.

insist**
[insíst]

v. 고집하다, 주장하다, 우기다
If you insist that something is the case, you say so very firmly and refuse to say otherwise, even though other people do not believe you.

nightmare*
[náitmeər]

n. 악몽
A nightmare is a very frightening dream.

horrible^{복습}
[hɔ́:rəbl]

a. 지긋지긋한, 끔찍한; 소름끼치는, 무시무시한
If you describe something or someone as horrible, you do not like them at all.

fingernail*
[fíŋgərnèil]

n. 손톱
Your fingernails are the thin hard areas at the end of each of your fingers.

nasty*
[nǽsti]

a. 끔찍한, 형편없는; 못된, 고약한
Something that is nasty is very unpleasant to see, experience, or feel.

wastepaper
[wéistpeipər]

n. 휴지 (wastepaper basket n. 휴지통)
Wastepaper is paper discarded after use.

mustache^{복습}
[mʌ́stæʃ]

n. 콧수염
A man's mustache is the hair that grows on his upper lip.

slap[복습]
[slæp]

v. (손바닥으로) 철썩 때리다; 털썩 놓다; n. (손바닥으로) 철썩 때리기
If you slap someone, you hit them with the palm of your hand.

declare[복습]
[diklέər]

v. 분명히 말하다; 선언하다, 공표하다
If you declare that something is true, you say that it is true in a firm, deliberate way.

dare*
[dɛər]

v. ~할 용기가 있다, 감히 ~하다, ~할 엄두를 내다
If you dare to do something, you do something which requires a lot of courage.

somewhat*
[sʌ́mhwʌt]

ad. 어느 정도, 약간, 다소
You use somewhat to indicate that something is the case to a limited extent or degree.

hook**
[huk]

v. ~에 걸다; 갈고리로 잠그다; n. (갈)고리, 걸이
If you hook one thing to another, you attach it there using a hook.

hop[복습]
[hap]

v. 깡충깡충 뛰다; 급히 가다; n. 깡충 뛰기
If you hop, you move along by jumping on one foot.

hand in hand

idiom (두 사람이) 서로 손을 잡고
If two people are hand in hand, they are holding each other's nearest hand, usually while they are walking.

scare[복습]
[skɛər]

v. 겁주다, 놀라게 하다 (scared a. 무서워하는, 겁먹은)
If you are scared of someone or something, you are frightened of them.

chew[복습]
[tʃuː]

v. (음식을) 씹다
If you chew gum or tobacco, you keep biting it and moving it around your mouth to taste the flavour of it. You do not swallow it.

footprint
[fútprint]

n. (사람·동물의) 발자국
A footprint is a mark in the shape of a foot that a person or animal makes in or on a surface.

1분에 몇 단어를 읽는지 리딩 속도를 측정해보세요.

$$\frac{1,002 \text{ words}}{\text{reading time ( ) sec}} \times 60 = (\quad) \text{ WPM}$$

Build Your Vocabulary

bounce^{복습}
[bauns]

v. 튀다; 튀기다; 깡충깡충 뛰다; n. 튐, 튀어 오름
When an object such as a ball bounces or when you bounce it, it moves upward from a surface or away from it immediately after hitting it.

blush*
[blʌʃ]

v. 얼굴을 붉히다, 얼굴이 빨개지다; n. (당황하거나 수치스러워) 얼굴이 붉어짐
When you blush, your face becomes redder than usual because you are ashamed or embarrassed.

stack^{복습}
[stæk]

n. 무더기, 더미; v. (깔끔하게 정돈하여) 쌓다
A stack of things is a pile of them.

workbook
[wə́ːrkbùk]

n. 연습 문제집
A workbook is a book to help you learn a particular subject which has questions in it with spaces for the answers.

assure*
[əʃúər]

v. 장담하다, 확언하다; 확인하다
If you assure someone that something is true or will happen, you tell them that it is definitely true or will definitely happen, often in order to make them less worried.

accuse*
[əkjúːz]

v. 비난하다, 혐의를 제기하다
If you accuse someone of doing something wrong or dishonest, you say or tell them that you believe that they did it.

watch out

idiom (위험하니까) 조심해라
You say 'watch out,' when you warn someone about something dangerous.

prove**
[pruːv]

v. 입증하다, 증명하다; (~임이) 드러나다
If you prove that something is true, you show by means of argument or evidence that it is definitely true.

sack^{복습}
[sæk]

n. (종이) 봉지, 부대
A sack is a paper or plastic bag, which is used to carry things bought in a shop.

mutter^{복습}
[mʌ́tər]

v. 중얼거리다; 투덜거리다; n. 중얼거림
If you mutter, you speak very quietly so that you cannot easily be heard, often because you are complaining about something.

closet^{복습}
[klázit]

n. 벽장
A closet is a piece of furniture with doors at the front and shelves inside, which is used for storing things.

drawer**
[drɔːr]

n. 서랍
A drawer is part of a desk, chest, or other piece of furniture that is shaped like a box and is designed for putting things in.

dump^{복습}
[dʌmp]

v. (아무렇게나) 내려놓다; 버리다; n. (쓰레기) 폐기장
If you dump something somewhere, you put it or unload it there quickly and carelessly.

awful^{복습}
[ɔ́ːfəl]

a. 끔찍한, 지독한; (양적으로 많음을 강조하는 의미로) 엄청
If you say that someone or something is awful, you dislike that person or thing or you think that they are not very good.

pay attention

idiom 관심을 갖다
If you pay attention to someone, you watch them, listen to them, or take notice of them.

snowflake
[snóuflèik]

n. 눈송이
A snowflake is one of the soft, white bits of frozen water that fall as snow.

discipline^{복습}
[dísəplin]

n. 규율, 훈육; 단련법, 수련법
Discipline is the practice of making people obey rules or standards of behavior, and punishing them when they do not.

necessary***
[nésəsèri]

a. 필요한; 필연적인, 불가피한
Something that is necessary is needed in order for something else to happen.

rotten*
[ratn]

a. 형편없는, 끔찍한; 썩은, 부패한
If you feel rotten, you feel bad, either because you are ill or because you are sorry about something.

grade**
[greid]

v. 성적을 매기다; (등급을) 나누다; n. (상품의) 품질; 성적, 학점; 학년
If something is graded, its quality is judged, and it is often given a number or a name that indicates how good or bad it is.

erase^{복습}
[iréis]

v. (지우개 등으로) 지우다; (완전히) 없애다
If you erase something such as writing or a mark, you remove it, usually by rubbing it with a cloth.

all the way^{복습}

idiom 내내, 시종; 완전히
You use all the way to emphasize how long a distance is.

chalk^{복습}
[tʃɔːk]

n. 분필
A chalk is a small piece of soft white rock, used for writing or drawing with.

end up

idiom 결국 (어떤 처지에) 처하게 되다
If you end up doing something or end up in a particular state, you reach or come to a particular place or situation that you did not expect or intend to be in.

give away

idiom ~을 선물로 주다, 기부하다; (비밀을) 누설하다
If you give away something, you give it to someone as a gift.

74

disgust ^{복습}
[disgΛst]

v. 혐오감을 유발하다, 역겹게 만들다; n. 혐오감, 역겨움, 넌더리
(disgusting a. 역겨운, 구역질나는)
If you say that something is disgusting, you mean that you find it completely unacceptable.

1. How did Mrs. Jewls suggest that Jenny read the story?

    A. She told her to read the story backward.

    B. She told her to read the story upside down.

    C. She told her to read the story out loud.

    D. She told her to listen to the story read to her.

2. Why did Jenny miss the bus to school?

    A. She woke up after it left.

    B. She was finishing her prune juice.

    C. She was looking for her homework.

    D. She was packing her lunch.

3. How did Jenny get to school?

    A. She walked.

    B. She rode her bicycle.

    C. Her father gave her a ride on his motorcycle.

    D. Her mother gave her a ride in her car.

4. Why did Mrs. Jewls's class love having a substitute teacher?

    A. They loved being nice to them.

    B. They loved playing mean tricks on them.

    C. They felt that they learned much more.

    D. They loved taking a break from their usual routine.

5. Why was Benjamin upset about having a substitute teacher?

   A. He didn't know any tricks to play.

   B. He wanted to ask Mrs. Jewls a very important question.

   C. He finally had the courage to tell Mrs. Jewls his real name.

   D. He was afraid that the substitute teacher would know his real name.

6. What did the students all want to do when called upon by Mrs. Franklin, the substitute teacher?

   A. They all wanted to drop their books on the floor.

   B. They all wanted to leave the classroom.

   C. They all wanted to tell her a funny joke.

   D. They all wanted to tell her their names were Benjamin.

7. Why did the students work hard and listen closely to Mrs. Franklin?

   A. They all wanted her to call on them.

   B. They all wanted to know her real name.

   C. They all wanted to call her Benjamin.

   D. They all wanted to learn their lesson and not have homework.

$$\frac{502 \text{ words}}{\text{reading time ( ) sec}} \times 60 = (\quad) \text{ WPM}$$

Build Your Vocabulary

throw up 복습

idiom 토하다
When someone throws up, they vomit.

hysterical 복습
[histérikəl]

a. 히스테리 상태의, (히스테리) 발작적인 (hysterically ad. 히스테리적인)
Hysterical laughter is loud and uncontrolled.

interrupt 복습
[intərʌ́pt]

v. (말·행동을) 방해하다, 중단시키다 (interruption n. (말을) 가로막음)
If you interrupt someone who is speaking, you say or do something that causes them to stop.

make a face 복습

idiom 얼굴을 찌푸리다, 침울한 표정을 짓다
If you make a face, you twist your face to indicate a certain mental or emotional state.

awful 복습
[ɔ́:fəl]

a. 끔찍한, 지독한; (양적으로 많음을 강조하는 의미로) 엄청
If you say that someone or something is awful, you dislike that person or thing or you think that they are not very good.

prune
[pru:n]

n. 말린 자두; v. (가지를) 잘라 내다
A prune is a dried plum.

blackboard 복습
[blǽkbɔ̀:rd]

n. 칠판
A blackboard is a dark-colored board that you can write on with chalk.

gripe 복습
[graip]

v. 불평을 하다, 투덜거리다; n. 불만, 불평
If you say that someone is griping, you mean they are annoying you because they keep on complaining about something.

catch one's breath

idiom 숨을 고르다, 숨을 돌리다
When you catch your breath while you are doing something energetic, you stop for a short time so that you can start breathing normally again.

motocycle
[móutərsàikl]

n. 오토바이
A motorcycle is a vehicle with two wheels and an engine.

charge 복습
[ʧa:rdʒ]

v. 급히 가다, 달려가다; (요금·값을) 청구하다; n. (상품·서비스에 대한) 요금
If you charge toward someone or something, you move quickly and aggressively toward them.

stomach 복습
[stʌ́mək]

n. 위(胃), 속; 복부, 배
Your stomach is the organ inside your body where food goes after it has been eaten and where it starts to be digested.

bumpy
[bʌ́mpi]

a. (바닥이) 울퉁불퉁한, 평탄하지 않은
A bumpy road or path has a lot of bumps on it.

grumble 복습
[grʌmbl]

v. 투덜거리다; 우르릉거리다; n. 불만 사항
If someone grumbles, they complain about something in a bad-tempered way.

pull away

idiom 움직이기 시작하다, 떠나다; ~에서 떼어놓다
When a vehicle or driver pulls away, the vehicle starts moving forward.

sigh 복습
[sai]

v. 한숨을 쉬다, 한숨짓다; n. 한숨
When you sigh, you let out a deep breath, as a way of expressing feelings such as disappointment, tiredness, or pleasure.

$$\frac{911 \text{ words}}{\text{reading time ( ) sec}} \times 60 = (\quad) \text{ WPM}$$

Build Your Vocabulary

take it

idiom (비난·고통 등을) 견디다, 참다; 믿다, 생각하다
If you say that you can take it, you mean that you are able to bear or tolerate something difficult or unpleasant such as stress, criticism or pain.

mark^{복습}
[ma:rk]

n. 점수, 평점; 자국, 흔적; 표시, 부호; v. (표·기호 등으로) 표시하다
(get high marks idiom 높은 점수를 얻다)
If someone gets high marks for doing something, they have done it well.

glum
[glʌm]

a. 침울한 (glumly ad. 무뚝뚝하게, 침울하게)
Someone who is glum is sad and quiet because they are disappointed or unhappy about something.

substitute*
[sʌ́bstətjùːt]

n. (= substitute teacher) 대리 교사; 대신하는 사람; v. 대신하다
A substitute is a teacher whose job is to take the place of other teachers at different schools when they are unable to be there.

trick^{복습}
[trik]

n. 속임수; (골탕을 먹이기 위한) 장난; v. 속이다, 속임수를 쓰다
A trick is an action that is intended to deceive someone.

frown^{복습}
[fraun]

v. 얼굴을 찌푸리다; n. 찡그림, 찌푸림
When someone frowns, their eyebrows become drawn together, because they are annoyed or puzzled.

lock**
[lak]

v. (자물쇠로) 잠그다; n. 자물쇠 (unlock v. (열쇠로) 열다)
When you lock something such as a door, drawer, or case, you fasten it, usually with a key, so that other people cannot open it.

bonkers
[báŋkərz]

a. 완전히 제정신이 아닌
If you say that someone is bonkers, you mean that they are silly or act in a crazy way.

spectacle*
[spéktəkl]

n. (pl.) 안경; (굉장한) 구경거리
Glasses are sometimes referred to as spectacles.

ponytail
[póunitèil]

n. 뒤에서 묶어 늘어뜨린 머리
A ponytail is a hairstyle in which someone's hair is tied up at the back of the head and hangs down like a tail.

bold*
[bould]

a. 용감한, 대담한; 선명한, 굵은 (boldly ad. 대담하게)
Someone who is bold is not afraid to do things which involve risk or danger.

snicker ^{복습}
[sníkər]

v. 낄낄 웃다, 숨죽여 웃다; n. 낄낄 웃음, 숨죽여 웃는 웃음
If you snicker, you laugh quietly in a disrespectful way, for example at something rude or embarrassing.

assert *
[əsə́:rt]

v. (사실임을 강하게) 주장하다; 확고히 하다
If someone asserts a fact or belief, they state it firmly.

giggle ^{복습}
[gigl]

v. 피식 웃다, 킥킥거리다; n. 피식 웃음, 킥킥거림
If someone giggles, they laugh in a childlike way, because they are amused, nervous, or embarrassed.

blurt
[blə:rt]

v. 불쑥 내뱉다
If someone blurts something, they say it suddenly, after trying hard to keep quiet or to keep it secret.

hysterical ^{복습}
[histérikəl]

a. 히스테리 상태의, (히스테리) 발작적인
Someone who is hysterical is in a state of uncontrolled excitement, anger, or panic.

recess ^{복습}
[risés]

n. (학교의) 쉬는 시간; (의회·위원회 등의) 휴회 기간
A recess is a break between classes at a school.

congratulate **
[kəngrǽʧuleit]

v. 축하하다; 기뻐하다
If you congratulate someone, you say something to show you are pleased that something nice has happened to them.

genius *
[ʤí:njəs]

n. 천재; 천재성; 특별한 재능
A genius is a highly talented, creative, or intelligent person.

social studies
[sóuʃəl stʌdiz]

n. (학교 교과로서의) 사회
In the United States, social studies is a subject that is taught in schools, and that includes history, geography, sociology, and politics.

volunteer *
[vàləntíər]

v. (어떤 일을 하겠다고) 자원하다; 자원 봉사로 하다; n. 자원 봉사자
A volunteer is someone who offers to do a particular task or job without being forced to do it.

pay attention ^{복습}

idiom 관심을 갖다
If you pay attention to someone, you watch them, listen to them, or take notice of them.

call on ^{복습}

idiom (이름을 불러서) 학생에게 시키다; (사람을) 방문하다
If a teacher calls on students in a class, he or she asks them to answer a question or give their opinion.

plead *
[pli:d]

v. 애원하다
If you plead with someone to do something, you ask them in an intense, emotional way to do it.

gather ^{복습}
[gǽðər]

v. 모으다, 챙기다; (사람들이) 모이다
If you gather things, you collect them together so that you can use them.

straw ^{복습}
[strɔ:]

n. 짚, 밀짚; 빨대
Straw consists of the dried, yellowish stalks from crops such as wheat or barley.

Chapter 19 (1) & (2)

1. How did Allison feel about the students in her class?
   A. She thought they were all mean.
   B. She thought they were all silly.
   C. She thought that they all loved her.
   D. She thought they were all show-offs.

2. Why did Jason call his goldfish Shark?
   A. He wanted it to be scary.
   B. It had bit him once.
   C. It made him feel important.
   D. It was gray like a shark.

3. Why did Allison run down the stairs screaming?
   A. Jason had swallowed his goldfish.
   B. Deedee and Ron had pushed her.
   C. Mrs. Jewls had sent her to the principal's office.
   D. Nobody in the class could see or hear her.

4. Which of the following was NOT true about Miss Zarves's class?
   A. It was on the nineteenth floor.
   B. The desks were arranged in clusters of four.
   C. She always gave her class good grades.
   D. Anyone could leave whenever they wanted.

5. Why did Allison want to remember where she came from?
   A. She thought that she might not get back if she forgot where she came from.
   B. She wanted to remember how nice Miss Zarves was compared to Mrs. Jewls.
   C. She wanted to remember all the happy times with her old friends.
   D. She thought that what she learned from Mrs. Jewls could help her.

6. What did Miss Zarves assign her class to do?
   A. Add zero and a million
   B. Spell 'zero' and 'a million'
   C. Count from zero to a million out loud
   D. Write the numbers from zero to a million in alphabetical order

7. Why was Allison glad to talk to Ben?
   A. She knew him from her old class.
   B. He was a new kid who looked to be her age.
   C. He said that he remembered where he came from.
   D. She knew that his real name was Mark Miller.

1분에 몇 단어를 읽는지 리딩 속도를 측정해보세요.

$$\frac{1{,}041 \text{ words}}{\text{reading time ( ) sec}} \times 60 = (\quad) \text{ WPM}$$

Build Your Vocabulary

cram
[kræm]

v. (좁은 공간 속으로 억지로) 밀어 넣다
If people cram into a place or vehicle or cram a place or vehicle, so many of them enter it at one time that it is completely full.

scurry
[skə́:ri]

v. 종종걸음을 치다, 허둥지둥 가다
When people or small animals scurry somewhere, they move there quickly and hurriedly, especially because they are frightened.

peaceful**
[píːsfəl]

a. 평화로운; 평화적인, 비폭력적인
Someone who feels or looks peaceful feels or looks calm and free from worry.

story^{복습}
[stɔ́ːri]

① n. (건물의) 층 ② n. 이야기, 소설; 설명
A story of a building is one of its different levels, which is situated above or below other levels.

footstep^{복습}
[fútstèp]

n. 발소리; 발자국
A footstep is the sound or mark that is made by someone walking each time their foot touches the ground.

charge^{복습}
[tʃaːrdʒ]

v. 급히 가다, 달려가다; (요금·값을) 청구하다; n. (상품·서비스에 대한) 요금
If you charge toward someone or something, you move quickly and aggressively toward them.

race
[reis]

v. 쏜살같이 가다; 경주하다; n. 경주, 달리기 (시합); 인종, 종족
If you race somewhere, you go there as quickly as possible.

lean^{복습}
[liːn]

v. ~에 기대다; 기울다, (몸을) 숙이다; a. 군살이 없는, (탄탄하게) 호리호리한
If you lean on or against someone or something, you rest against them so that they partly support your weight.

stamp**
[stæmp]

v. (발을) 구르다; 쾅쾅거리며 걷다; n. 우표; 도장, 스탬프
If you stamp on something, you put your foot down on it very hard.

elbow**
[élbou]

n. 팔꿈치; v. (팔꿈치로) 밀치다
Your elbow is the part of your arm where the upper and lower halves of the arm are joined.

jam**
[dʒæm]

v. (세게) 밀다; 움직이지 못하게 되다; n. 잼; 혼잡, 교통 체증
If you jam something somewhere, you push or put it there roughly.

grunt^{복습}
[grʌnt]

v. 끙 앓는 소리를 내다; (돼지가) 꿀꿀거리다; n. 꿀꿀거리는 소리; 끙 하는 소리
If you grunt, you make a low sound, especially because you are annoyed or not interested in something.

fortunate ^{복습}
[fɔ́ːrʧənət]

a. 운 좋은, 다행한 (fortunately ad. 다행스럽게도, 운이 좋게도)
If you say that someone is fortunate, you mean that they are lucky.

windbreaker
[wíndbrèikər]

n. 방한용 재킷
A windbreaker is a warm casual jacket.

tear ^{복습}
[tɛər]

① v. (tore-torn) 찢다, 뜯다; 구멍을 뚫다; n. 찢어진 곳, 구멍 ② n. 눈물
If you tear paper, cloth, or another material, or if it tears, you pull it into two pieces or you pull it so that a hole appears in it.

silly ^{복습}
[síli]

a. 어리석은, 바보 같은; n. 바보
If you say that someone or something is silly, you mean that they are foolish, childish, or ridiculous.

pooped
[puːpt]

a. 녹초가 된, 기진맥진한
If you are pooped, you are very tired.

pester
[péstər]

v. 성가시게 하다, 괴롭히다, 조르다
If you say that someone is pestering you, you mean that they keep asking you to do something, or keep talking to you, and you find this annoying.

wander*
[wándər]

v. (이리저리 천천히) 돌아다니다; (있어야 할 곳에서) 다른 데로 가다; n. (이리저리) 거닐기
If you wander in a place, you walk around there in a casual way, often without intending to go in any particular direction.

goldfish
[góuldfìʃ]

n. [동물] 금붕어
A small orange or red fish. Goldfish are kept as pets in bowls or ponds.

roll one's eyes

idiom 눈을 굴리다
If you roll your eyes or if your eyes roll, they move round and upward. People sometimes roll their eyes when they are frightened, bored, or annoyed.

tiptoe
[típtòu]

n. 발끝; v. 발끝으로 살금살금 걷다
If you do something on tiptoe or on tiptoes, you do it standing or walking on the front part of your foot, without putting your heels on the ground.

nudge
[nʌdʒ]

v. (~을 특정 방향으로) 조금씩 밀다; (팔꿈치로 살짝) 쿡 찌르다; n. 쿡 찌르기
If you nudge someone or something into a place or position, you gently push them there.

topple ^{복습}
[tapl]

v. 넘어지다; 넘어뜨리다; 실각시키다
If someone or something topples somewhere or if you topple them, they become unsteady or unstable and fall over.

gulp
[gʌlp]

v. 꿀꺽꿀꺽 삼키다; (공포·놀라움에 질려) 침을 꿀떡 삼키다; n. 꿀꺽 한 입
If you gulp something, you eat or drink it very quickly by swallowing large quantities of it at once.

yell ^{복습}
[jel]

v. 고함치다, 소리 지르다; n. 고함, 외침
If you yell, you shout loudly, usually because you are excited, angry, or in pain.

upside down^{복습}
[ápsàid dáun]

ad. (아래위가) 거꾸로
If something has been moved upside down, it has been turned round so that the part that is usually lowest is above the part that is usually highest.

make a face^{복습}

idiom 얼굴을 찌푸리다, 침울한 표정을 짓다
If you make a face, you twist your face to indicate a certain mental or emotional state.

swallow^{복습}
[swálou]

v. (음식 등을) 삼키다; 마른침을 삼키다; n. 제비
If you swallow something, you cause it to go from your mouth down into your stomach.

show-off
[ʃóu-ɔ̀ːf]

n. 과시적인 사람
If you say that someone is a show-off, you are criticizing them for trying to impress people by showing in a very obvious way what they can do or what they own.

cowbell^{복습}
[káubèl]

n. (소를 쉽게 찾기 위해 목에 다는) 소 방울
A cowbell is a small bell that is hung around a cow's neck so that the ringing sound makes it possible to find the cow.

roll**
[roul]

n. 명부, 명단; 통, 두루마리; v. 구르다, 굴러가다
(take roll idiom 출석을 부르다)
A roll is an official list of people's names.

absent**
[ǽbsənt]

a. 결석한, 결근한; 멍한; v. 결석하다, 불참하다
If someone or something is absent from a place or situation where they should be or where they usually are, they are not there.

besides^{복습}
[bisáidz]

prep. ~외에; ad. 게다가, 뿐만 아니라
Besides means other than someone or something.

mark^{복습}
[maːrk]

v. (표·기호 등으로) 표시하다; n. 자국, 흔적; 표시, 부호; 점수, 평점
If you mark something with a particular word or symbol, you write that word or symbol on it.

march^{복습}
[maːrʧ]

v. (단호한 태도로 급히) 걸어가다; 행진하다; n. 행군, 행진; 3월
If you say that someone marches somewhere, you mean that they walk there quickly and in a determined way, for example because they are angry.

mumble^{복습}
[mʌmbl]

v. 중얼거리다, 웅얼거리다; n. 중얼거림
If you mumble, you speak very quietly and not at all clearly with the result that the words are difficult to understand.

get off one's case

idiom 잔소리 좀 그만해라
You can say 'get off my case' to tell someone to stop criticizing you.

exclaim^{복습}
[ikskléim]

v. 소리치다, 외치다
If you exclaim, you cry out suddenly in surprise, strong emotion, or pain.

protest**
[próutest]

v. 항의하다, 이의를 제기하다; n. 항의
If you protest against something or about something, you say or show publicly that you object to it.

ignore**
[ignɔ́ːr]

v. (사람을) 못 본 척하다; 무시하다
If you ignore someone or something, you pay no attention to them.

stare^{복습}
[stɛər]

v. 빤히 쳐다보다, 응시하다; n. 빤히 쳐다보기, 응시
If you stare at someone or something, you look at them for a long time.

lick*
[lik]

v. 핥다; 핥아먹다; n. 한 번 핥기, 핥아먹기
When people or animals lick something, they move their tongue across its surface.

yuck^{복습}
[jʌk]

int. 윽(역겨울 때 내는 소리)
'Yuck' is an expression of disgust.

wipe^{복습}
[waip]

v. (먼지·물기 등을 없애기 위해 무엇을) 닦다; n. (행주·걸레를 써서) 닦기
If you wipe something, you rub its surface to remove dirt or liquid from it.

sleeve^{복습}
[sliːv]

n. 소매
The sleeves of a coat, shirt, or other item of clothing are the parts that cover your arms.

slam*
[slæm]

v. 쾅 닫다; 세게 놓다; n. 탕 하고 닫기; 탕 하는 소리
If you slam a door or window or if it slams, it shuts noisily and with great force.

stream^{복습}
[striːm]

v. (액체·기체가) 줄줄 흐르다; 줄을 지어 이어지다; n. 개울; (액체·기체의) 줄기
If a liquid streams somewhere, it flows or comes out in large amounts.

cheek^{복습}
[ʧiːk]

n. 볼, 뺨
Your cheeks are the sides of your face below your eyes.

stern^{복습}
[stəːrn]

a. 엄중한, 근엄한; 심각한 (sternly ad. 엄격하게, 준엄하게)
Someone who is stern is very serious and strict.

announce^{복습}
[ənáuns]

v. 발표하다, 알리다; (공공장소에서) 방송으로 알리다
If you announce something, you tell people about it publicly or officially.

Check Your Reading Speed

1분에 몇 단어를 읽는지 리딩 속도를 측정해보세요.

$$\frac{846 \text{ words}}{\text{reading time ( ) sec}} \times 60 = (\quad) \text{ WPM}$$

Build Your Vocabulary

arrange**
[əréindʒ]

v. 정리하다, 배열하다; 마련하다, (일을) 처리하다
If you arrange things somewhere, you place them in a particular position, usually in order to make them look attractive or tidy.

cluster*
[klʌ́stər]

n. 무리; v. 무리를 이루다, (소규모로) 모이다
A cluster of people or things is a small group of them close together.

singsong
[síŋsɔ̀ːŋ]

a. 단조로운, 억양이 없는; n. 단조로운 가락의 시
Something that is singsong is having a regular or monotonous rising and falling rhythm.

on purpose^{복습}

idiom 고의로, 일부러
If you do something on purpose, you do it intentionally.

include**
[inklúːd]

v. 포함하다; ~을 (~에) 포함시키다
If one thing includes another thing, it has the other thing as one of its parts.

related*
[riléitid]

a. 친척의; (~에) 관련된
People who are related belong to the same family.

alphabetical*
[ælfəbétikəl]

a. 알파벳순의
Alphabetical means arranged according to the normal order of the letters in the alphabet.

order***
[ɔ́ːrdər]

n. 순서, ~순(順); 질서; 명령, 지시; 주문; v. 명령하다; (상품을) 주문하다
If a set of things are arranged or done in a particular order, they are arranged or done so one thing follows another, often according to a particular factor such as importance.

run out of

idiom ~을 다 써버리다, ~이 없어지다
If you are running out of something, you do not have much of it left.

closet^{복습}
[klázit]

n. 벽장
A closet is a piece of furniture with doors at the front and shelves inside, which is used for storing things.

horror^{복습}
[hɔ́ːrər]

n. 공포(감), 경악
Horror is a feeling of great shock, fear, and worry caused by something extremely unpleasant.

cheerful***
[tʃíərfəl]

a. 발랄한, 쾌활한; 생기를 주는, 쾌적한 (cheerfully ad. 쾌활하게, 명랑하게)
Someone who is cheerful is happy and shows this in their behavior.

88

break***
[breik]

n. (학교의) 쉬는 시간; (작업 중의) 휴식; v. 깨어지다, 부서지다; 깨다, 부수다
Break is the regular time in the middle of the morning or afternoon, for school students to talk or play, and sometimes have food or drink.

big deal^{복습}
[bíg díːl]

int. 그게 무슨 대수라고!; n. 대단한 것, 큰 일
You can say 'big deal' to someone to show that you are not impressed by something that they consider important or impressive.

figure out^{복습}

idiom (생각한 끝에) ~을 이해하다; (양·비용을) 계산하다
If you figure out someone or something, you come to understand them by thinking carefully.

turn into^{복습}

idiom (~에서) ~이 되다, ~으로 변하다
To turn or be turned into something means to become that thing.

Chapters 19 (3), 20, 21, & 22

1. How did Allison feel about Mrs. Jewls's class after she remembered them again?

   A. She missed everyone except for Jason.

   B. She thought that Miss Zarves was a much better teacher.

   C. She missed everyone and thought they were all wonderful.

   D. She thought that they would all like to meet Miss Zarves.

2. What did Allison realize about Miss Zarves and her plan?

   A. She assigned busy work so that they wouldn't have time to think.

   B. She gave them good grades so that they could go to a better school.

   C. She assigned busy work so that they could learn important things.

   D. She gave them good grades so that their parents would be happy.

3. How did Allison try to get back to Mrs. Jewls's class?

   A. She tried to phone Mrs. Jewls's class.

   B. She tried to act like she was in Mrs. Jewls's class.

   C. She tried to ask Miss Zarves if she could go back.

   D. She tried to walk out the door and up the stairs to Mrs. Jewls's class.

4. How did Mrs. Jewls choose to send Eric Fry to the principal first?
   A. She chose the closest Eric.
   B. She chose the biggest Eric.
   C. She chose the shortest Eric.
   D. She chose the Eric with the worst grades.

5. What did Eric Ovens ask Mr. Kidswatter?
   A. He asked why he was there.
   B. He asked if he could leave.
   C. He asked what happened to Eric Fry.
   D. He asked what a Mugworm Griblick was.

6. How did Eric Bacon react to being called to Mr. Kidswatter's office?
   A. He trembled as he slowly stood up.
   B. He shivered and his eyes filled with tears.
   C. He turned pale and begged not to go.
   D. He hopped out of his chair and bounced down the stairs.

7. Why did Mr. Kidswatter call the Erics to his office?
   A. He wanted to know who had insulted him.
   B. He wanted to know where they had their haircuts.
   C. He wanted to know who had lost a pencil.
   D. He wanted to know who had nice handwriting.

$$\frac{1{,}061 \text{ words}}{\text{reading time ( ) sec}} \times 60 = (\quad) \text{ WPM}$$

Build Your Vocabulary

dictionary**
[díkʃənèri]

n. 사전
A dictionary is a book in which the words and phrases of a language are listed alphabetically, together with their meanings or their translations in another language.

memorize*
[méməràiz]

v. 암기하다
If you memorize something, you learn it so that you can remember it exactly.

assure^{복습}
[əʃúər]

v. 장담하다, 확언하다; 확인하다
If you assure someone that something is true or will happen, you tell them that it is definitely true or will definitely happen, often in order to make them less worried.

sigh^{복습}
[sai]

v. 한숨을 쉬다, 한숨짓다; n. 한숨
When you sigh, you let out a deep breath, as a way of expressing feelings such as disappointment, tiredness, or pleasure.

relief^{복습}
[rilíːf]

n. 안도, 안심; (고통·불안 등의) 경감
If you feel a sense of relief, you feel happy because something unpleasant has not happened or is no longer happening.

break^{복습}
[breik]

n. (학교의) 쉬는 시간; (작업 중의) 휴식; v. 깨어지다, 부서지다; 깨다, 부수다
Break is the regular time in the middle of the morning or afternoon, for school students to talk or play, and sometimes have food or drink.

chill*
[ʧil]

n. 오싹한 느낌; 냉기, 한기; v. 아주 춥게 만들다
If something sends a chill through you, it gives you a sudden feeling of fear or anxiety.

spine
[spain]

n. 척추, 등뼈
Your spine is the row of bones down your back.

devil^{복습}
[devl]

n. 악마
A devil is an evil spirit.

punish^{복습}
[pániʃ]

v. 처벌하다, 벌주다; (형벌·형에) 처하다
To punish someone means to make them suffer in some way because they have done something wrong.

expert*
[ékspəːrt]

n. 전문가; a. 전문가의, 전문적인; 숙련된
An expert is a person who is very skilled at doing something or who knows a lot about a particular subject.

shiver ^{복습}
[ʃívər]

v. (추위·두려움·흥분 등으로) 몸을 떨다; n. 전율; 몸서리, 오싹(한 느낌)
When you shiver, your body shakes slightly because you are cold or frightened.

assign ^{복습}
[əsáin]

v. (일·책임 등을) 맡기다; 선임하다, 파견하다
If you assign a piece of work to someone, you give them the work to do.

sleeve ^{복습}
[sliːv]

n. 소매 (up one's sleeve idiom 몰래 준비해 둔)
If you have something up your sleeve, you have an idea or plan which you have not told anyone about.

take a chance

idiom 모험을 하다, (~을) 운에 맡기다
When you take a chance, you try to do something although there is a large risk of danger or failure.

suck ^{복습}
[sʌk]

v. (입에 넣고 계속) 빨다; (액체·공기 등을) 빨아 먹다; (특정한 방향으로) 빨아들이다; n. 빨기, 빨아 먹기
If you suck something, you hold it in your mouth and pull at it with the muscles in your cheeks and tongue, for example in order to get liquid out of it.

get off one's case ^{복습}

idiom 잔소리 좀 그만해라
You can say 'get off my case' to tell someone to stop criticizing you.

furious *
[fjúəriəs]

a. 몹시 화가 난; 맹렬한
Someone who is furious is extremely angry.

clap *
[klæp]

v. 박수를 치다, 손뼉을 치다; n. 박수 (소리)
When you clap, you hit your hands together to show appreciation or attract attention.

slam ^{복습}
[slæm]

v. 세게 놓다; 쾅 닫다; n. 탕 하고 닫기; 탕 하는 소리
If you slam something down, you put it there quickly and with great force.

jam ^{복습}
[dʒæm]

v. (세게) 밀다; 움직이지 못하게 되다; n. 잼; 혼잡, 교통 체증
If you jam something somewhere, you push or put it there roughly.

stomach ^{복습}
[stʌ́mək]

n. 복부, 배; 위(胃), 속
You can refer to the front part of your body below your waist as your stomach.

grunt ^{복습}
[grʌnt]

v. 끙 앓는 소리를 내다; (돼지가) 꿀꿀거리다; n. 꿀꿀거리는 소리; 끙 하는 소리
If you grunt, you make a low sound, especially because you are annoyed or not interested in something.

race ^{복습}
[reis]

v. 쏜살같이 가다; 경주하다; n. 경주, 달리기 (시합); 인종, 종족
If you race somewhere, you go there as quickly as possible.

knock ^{복습}
[nak]

v. (때리거나 타격을 가해) ~한 상태가 되게 만들다; (문 등을) 두드리다; 치다, 부딪치다; n. 문 두드리는 소리
To knock someone into a particular position or condition means to hit them very hard so that they fall over or become unconscious.

rip ^{복습}
[rip]

v. (갑자기·거칠게) 찢다; 떼어 내다; n. (옷감·종이 등에 길게) 찢어진 곳
When something rips or when you rip it, you tear it forcefully with your hands or with a tool such as a knife.

windbreaker ^{복습}
[wíndbrèikər]

n. 방한용 재킷
A windbreaker is a warm casual jacket.

pooped ^{복습}
[puːpt]

a. 녹초가 된, 기진맥진한
If you are pooped, you are very tired.

absent ^{복습}
[ǽbsənt]

a. 결석한, 결근한; 멍한; v. 결석하다, 불참하다
If someone or something is absent from a place or situation where they should be or where they usually are, they are not there.

giggle ^{복습}
[gigl]

v. 피식 웃다, 킥킥거리다; n. 피식 웃음, 킥킥거림
If someone giggles, they laugh in a childlike way, because they are amused, nervous, or embarrassed.

goldfish ^{복습}
[góuldfiʃ]

n. [동물] 금붕어
A small orange or red fish. Goldfish are kept as pets in bowls or ponds.

closet ^{복습}
[klázit]

n. 벽장
A closet is a piece of furniture with doors at the front and shelves inside, which is used for storing things.

tiptoe ^{복습}
[típtòu]

n. 발끝; v. 발끝으로 살금살금 걷다
If you do something on tiptoe or on tiptoes, you do it standing or walking on the front part of your foot, without putting your heels on the ground.

nudge ^{복습}
[nʌdʒ]

v. (~을 특정 방향으로) 조금씩 밀다; (팔꿈치로 살짝) 쿡 찌르다; n. 쿡 찌르기
If you nudge someone or something into a place or position, you gently push them there.

94

1분에 몇 단어를 읽는지 리딩 속도를 측정해보세요.

$$\frac{1{,}278 \text{ words}}{\text{reading time (} \quad \text{) sec}} \times 60 = (\quad) \text{ WPM}$$

Build Your Vocabulary

crackle
[krǽkl]

v. 치직 소리를 내다; n. 치직하는 소리
If something crackles, it makes a rapid series of short, harsh noises.

loudspeaker
[láudspìːkər]

n. 확성기, 스피커
A loudspeaker is a piece of equipment that converts electric signals to audible sound.

at once

idiom 즉시, 당장; 동시에, 한꺼번에
If you do something at once, you do it immediately.

confuse^{복습}
[kənfjúːz]

v. (사람을) 혼란시키다; (주제를) 혼란스럽게 만들다
(confused a. 혼란스러워 하는)
If you are confused, you do not know exactly what is happening or what to do.

tremble^{복습}
[trémbl]

v. (몸을) 떨다, 떨리다; (가볍게) 흔들리다; n. 떨림, 전율
If you tremble, you shake slightly because you are frightened or cold.

principal^{복습}
[prínsəpəl]

n. 교장; 학장, 총장; a. 주요한, 주된
A principal is a teacher who is in charge of a school.

knock^{복습}
[nak]

v. (문 등을) 두드리다; 치다, 부딪치다; (때리거나 타격을 가해) ~한 상태가 되게 만들다;
n. 문 두드리는 소리
If you knock on something such as a door or window, you hit it, usually several times, to attract someone's attention.

boom[*]
[buːm]

v. 굵은 목소리로 말하다; 쾅 하는 소리를 내다; n. 쾅, 탕 하는 소리
When something such as someone's voice, a cannon, or a big drum booms, it makes a loud, deep sound that lasts for several seconds.

doorknob
[dɔ́ːrnàb]

n. (문의) 손잡이
A doorknob is a round handle on a door.

enormous[*]
[inɔ́ːrməs]

a. 거대한, 막대한
Something that is enormous is extremely large in size or amount.

bare[*]
[bɛər]

a. 아무것도 안 덮인; 벌거벗은
A bare surface is not covered or decorated with anything.

light bulb
[láit bʌ̀lb]

n. 백열 전구
A light bulb or bulb is the round glass part of an electric light or lamp which light shines from.

crack**
[kræk]

v. 날카로운 소리를 내다; 갈라지다, 금이 가다;
n. (무엇이 갈라져 생긴) 금; 찢어지는 듯한 소리
If something cracks, or if you crack it, it makes a sharp sound like
the sound of a piece of wood breaking.

knuckle
[nʌkl]

n. 손가락 관절
Your knuckles are the rounded pieces of bone that form lumps on
your hands where your fingers join your hands, and where your
fingers bend.

**one way or
another**

idiom 어떻게 해서든
You can use one way or another when you want to say that
something definitely happens, but without giving any details about
how it happens.

pound*
[paund]

v. 치다, 두드리다; n. (화폐 단위·무게 단위) 파운드
If you pound something or pound on it, you hit it with great force,
usually loudly and repeatedly.

fist^{복습}
[fist]

n. 주먹
Your hand is referred to as your fist when you have bent your
fingers in toward the palm in order to hit someone.

sharpen^{복습}
[ʃáːrpən]

v. 날카롭게 하다, (날카롭게) 깎다; 날카로워지다, 선명해지다
If you sharpen an object, you make its edge very thin or you make
its end pointed.

stammer*
[stǽmər]

v. 말을 더듬다, 더듬으며 말하다; n. 말 더듬기
If you stammer, you speak with difficulty, hesitating and repeating
words or sounds.

spell^{복습}
[spel]

v. 철자를 맞게 쓰다, 맞춤법에 맞게 글을 쓰다; (어떤 단어의) 철자를 말하다
(spelling n. 철자법, 맞춤법)
When you spell a word, you write or speak each letter in the word in
the correct order.

kickball^{복습}
[kíkbɔːl]

n. 발야구
Kickball is an informal game combining elements of baseball and
soccer, in which a soccer ball is thrown to a person who kicks it and
proceeds to run the bases.

grumble^{복습}
[grʌmbl]

v. 투덜거리다; 우르릉거리다; n. 불만 사항
If someone grumbles, they complain about something in a bad-
tempered way.

barber*
[báːrbər]

n. 이발사
A barber is a man whose job is cutting men's hair.

pale**
[peil]

a. 창백한, 핼쑥한; (색깔이) 옅은; v. 창백해지다
If someone looks pale, their face looks a lighter color than usual,
usually because they are ill, frightened, or shocked.

beg^{복습}
[beg]

v. 간청하다, 애원하다; 구걸하다
If you beg someone to do something, you ask them very anxiously
or eagerly to do it.

innocent[*]
[ínəsənt]

a. 아무 잘못이 없는, 무죄인, 결백한; 순결한, 순진한
If someone is innocent, they did not commit a crime which they have been accused of.

scowl
[skaul]

v. 노려보다, 쏘아보다; n. 노려봄, 쏘아봄
When someone scowls, an angry or hostile expression appears on their face.

flick
[flik]

v. (버튼·스위치를) 탁 누르다; (손가락 등으로) 튀기다; n. 휙 움직임
If you flick a switch, or flick an electrical appliance on or off, you press the switch sharply so that it moves into a different position and works the equipment.

shiver^{복습}
[ʃívər]

v. (추위·두려움·흥분 등으로) (몸을) 떨다; n. 전율; 몸서리, 오싹(한 느낌)
When you shiver, your body shakes slightly because you are cold or frightened.

tap[*]
[tæp]

v. (가볍게) 톡톡 두드리다; 박자를 맞추다; n. 수도꼭지; (가볍게) 두드리기
If you tap something, you hit it with a quick light blow or a series of quick light blows.

bellow
[bélou]

v. (우렁찬 소리로) 고함치다
If someone bellows, they shout angrily in a loud, deep voice.

gulp^{복습}
[gʌlp]

v. (공포·놀라움에 질려) 침을 꿀떡 삼키다; 꿀꺽꿀꺽 삼키다; n. 꿀꺽 한 입
If you gulp, you swallow air, often making a noise in your throat as you do so, because you are nervous or excited.

so long as

idiom ~하는 동안은, ~하는 한은
If you say that something is the case so long as something else is the case, you mean that it is only the case if the second thing is the case.

scare^{복습}
[skɛər]

v. 겁주다, 놀라게 하다 (scared a. 무서워하는, 겁먹은)
If you are scared of someone or something, you are frightened of them.

sly[*]
[slai]

a. 교활한, 음흉한; (남들은 모르는 비밀을 자기는) 다 알고 있다는 듯한
(slyly ad. 음흉하게)
A sly look, expression, or remark shows that you know something that other people do not know or that was meant to be a secret.

accidental[*]
[æksədéntl]

a. 우연한, 돌발적인 (accidentally ad. 우연히, 뜻하지 않게)
An accidental event happens by chance or as the result of an accident, and is not deliberately intended.

toss[*]
[tɔːs]

v. (가볍게·아무렇게나) 던지다; n. (무엇을 결정하기 위한) 동전 던지기
If you toss something somewhere, you throw it there lightly, often in a rather careless way.

stapler
[stéiplər]

n. 스테이플러, 서류 철하는 기구
A stapler is a device used for putting staples into sheets of paper.

resound
[rizáund]

v. (소리·목소리 등이) 울려 퍼지다
When a noise resounds, it is heard very loudly and clearly.

hop^{복습}
[hap]

v. 깡충깡충 뛰다; 급히 가다; n. 깡충 뛰기
If you hop, you move along by jumping on one foot.

bounce^{복습}
[bauns]

v. 깡충깡충 뛰다; 튀다; 튀기다; n. 튐, 튀어 오름
If someone bounces somewhere, they move there in an energetic way, because they are feeling happy.

bother*
[báðər]

v. 신경 쓰다, 애를 쓰다; 귀찮게 하다, 귀찮게 말을 걸다; n. 성가심
If you do not bother to do something or if you do not bother with it, you do not do it, consider it, or use it because you think it is unnecessary or because you are too lazy.

lean^{복습}
[li:n]

v. ~에 기대다; 기울다, (몸을) 숙이다; a. 군살이 없는, (탄탄하게) 호리호리한
If you lean on or against someone or something, you rest against them so that they partly support your weight.

comb*
[koum]

n. 빗; 빗질; v. 빗다, 빗질하다
A comb is a flat piece of plastic or metal with narrow pointed teeth along one side, which you use to tidy your hair.

neat^{복습}
[ni:t]

a. 정돈된, 단정한, 말쑥한; 뛰어난, 훌륭한
A neat place, thing, or person is tidy and smart, and has everything in the correct place.

trim^{복습}
[trim]

a. 잘 가꾼, 깔끔한; v. 다듬다, 손질하다; n. 다듬기, 약간 자르기
Something that is trim is neat, tidy, and attractive.

right away^{복습}

idiom 즉시, 곧바로
If you do something right away, you do it immediately.

bald^{복습}
[bɔ:ld]

a. 대머리의, 머리가 벗겨진
Someone who is bald has little or no hair on the top of their head.

wig
[wig]

n. 가발
A wig is a covering of false hair which you wear on your head.

glare^{복습}
[glɛər]

v. 노려보다; 환하다, 눈부시다; n. 노려봄; 환한 빛, 눈부심
If you glare at someone, you look at them with an angry expression on your face.

dictionary^{복습}
[díkʃənèri]

n. 사전
A dictionary is a book in which the words and phrases of a language are listed alphabetically, together with their meanings or their translations in another language.

rub^{복습}
[rʌb]

v. (손·손수건 등을 대고) 문지르다; (두 손 등을) 맞비비다; n. 문지르기, 비비기
If you rub a part of your body, you move your hand or fingers backward and forward over it while pressing firmly.

chin**
[ʧin]

n. 턱
Your chin is the part of your face that is below your mouth and above your neck.

crawl^{복습}
[krɔ:l]

v. (엎드려) 기다; (곤충이) 기어가다; n. 기어가기, 서행
When you crawl, you move forward on your hands and knees.

come clean

idiom (비밀로 하던 것을) 자백하고 나서다
If you come clean about something that you have been keeping secret, you admit it or tell people about it.

98

stand***
[stænd]

n. 가판대, 좌판; 태도, 의견; v. 서다, 서 있다; 일어서다
A stand is a small shop or stall, outdoors or in a large public building.

Chapters 23 & 24

1. Why was Rondi afraid after she grew two new front teeth?
   A. She was afraid that food would taste different.
   B. She was afraid that she wouldn't be able to whistle anymore.
   C. She was afraid that she might accidentally bite her tongue.
   D. She was afraid that nobody would think she was cute anymore.

2. Why did Louis say that he could not kick Rondi in the teeth?
   A. If he kicked her in the teeth, she might cry.
   B. If he kicked her in the teeth, she might get hurt.
   C. If he kicked her in the teeth, he might get fired.
   D. If he kicked her in the teeth, then the other kids would want it too.

3. Why did Louis want Rondi to get the ball back from Terrence?
   A. He was too busy to take care of it.
   B. Terrence would punch her teeth out.
   C. Terrence would listen to Rondi.
   D. Rondi was the one who wanted to play with the ball.

4. How did the class react to Rondi's new teeth?

    A. They all thought that she looked cuter before.

    B. They all thought that she looked cuter now.

    C. Twelve kids thought that she should keep just one tooth.

    D. Some thought she looked cuter before and some thought she
       looked cuter now.

5. What did John add to his potato salad?

    A. Mushroom Surprise

    B. Salt and pepper

    C. Ketchup and mustard

    D. Nothing

6. Who did the potato salad resemble?

    A. Joe

    B. Mrs. Gorf

    C. Mrs. Jewls

    D. Miss Mush

7. Why did John and Joe eat the potato salad as fast as they
   could?

    A. They wanted to stop Mrs. Gorf.

    B. They didn't want it to get cold.

    C. They wanted to go to recess quickly.

    D. They were very hungry.

$$\frac{775 \text{ words}}{\text{reading time (} \quad \text{) sec}} \times 60 = (\quad) \text{ WPM}$$

Build Your Vocabulary

terrible*
[térəbl]

a. 끔찍한, 소름끼치는; 심한, 지독한
A terrible experience or situation is very serious or very unpleasant.

scrub*
[skrʌb]

v. (비눗물과 솔로) 문질러 씻다; n. 문질러 씻기, 청소하기
If you scrub something, you rub it hard in order to clean it, using a stiff brush and water.

toothpaste^{복습}
[túːθpèist]

n. 치약
Toothpaste is a thick substance which you put on your toothbrush and use to clean your teeth.

exclaim^{복습}
[ikskléim]

v. 소리치다, 외치다
If you exclaim, you cry out suddenly in surprise, strong emotion, or pain.

discipline^{복습}
[dísəplin]

n. 규율, 훈육; 단련법, 수련법
Discipline is the practice of making people obey rules or standards of behavior, and punishing them when they do not.

recess^{복습}
[risés]

n. (학교의) 쉬는 시간; (의회·위원회 등의) 휴회 기간
A recess is a break between classes at a school.

storm**
[stɔːrm]

v. 쿵쾅대며 가다, 뛰쳐나가다; 기습하다; n. 폭풍, 폭풍우
If you storm into or out of a place, you enter or leave it quickly and noisily, because you are angry.

seashell
[síːʃèl]

n. 조개껍데기, 조가비
Seashells are the empty shells of small sea creatures.

seashore**
[síːʃɔːr]

n. 해안
The seashore is the part of a coast where the land slopes down into the sea.

complain^{복습}
[kəmpléin]

v. 불평하다, 항의하다
If you complain about a situation, you say that you are not satisfied with it.

count***
[kaunt]

v. (정식으로) 인정되다; 수를 세다, 계산하다; 중요하다; n. 셈, 계산
If something counts or is counted as a particular thing, it is regarded as being that thing, especially in particular circumstances or under particular rules.

scowl^{복습}
[skaul]

v. 노려보다, 쏘아보다; n. 노려봄, 쏘아봄
When someone scowls, an angry or hostile expression appears on their face.

102

bush**
[buʃ]

n. 관목, 덤불
A bush is a large plant which is smaller than a tree and has a lot of branches.

twirl*
[twəːrl]

v. (손가락으로) 배배 꼬다; 빙글빙글 돌다; n. 빙그르르 돌기
If you twirl something such as your hair, you twist it around your finger.

multicolored
[mÀltiká lərd]

a. 색깔이 다채로운, 화려한
A multicolored object has many different colors.

mustache^{복습}
[mÁstæʃ]

n. 콧수염
A man's mustache is the hair that grows on his upper lip.

wink*
[wiŋk]

v. 윙크하다; (빛이) 깜박거리다; n. 윙크
When you wink at someone, you look toward them and close one eye very briefly, usually as a signal that something is a joke or a secret.

light up

idiom (얼굴이) 환해지다; 빛나게 만들다
If someone's eyes or face light up, or something lights them up, they become bright with excitement or happiness.

playground^{복습}
[pléigràund]

n. (학교의) 운동장; 놀이터
A playground is a piece of land, at school or in a public area, where children can play.

drop dead

idiom (명령문으로 써서) 꺼져 버려
If you tell someone to drop dead, you are saying that you are very angry with them and ask them to go away.

stare^{복습}
[stɛər]

v. 빤히 쳐다보다, 응시하다; n. 빤히 쳐다보기, 응시
If you stare at someone or something, you look at them for a long time.

collect oneself

idiom 마음을 가라앉히다
If you collect yourself, you make an effort to calm yourself or prepare yourself mentally.

mole*
[moul]

n. [동물] 두더지; (피부 위에 작게 돋은 진갈색) 점; (조직 내부에 있는) 스파이
A mole is a small animal with black fur that lives underground.

dig^{복습}
[dig]

v. (구멍 등을) 파다; ~을 찌르다; n. 쿡 찌르기; 발굴
If people or animals dig, they make a hole in the ground or in a pile of earth, stones, or rubbish.

goose*
[guːs]

n. [동물] 거위
A goose is a large bird that has a long neck and webbed feet.

jail*
[dʒeil]

n. 교도소, 감옥
A jail is a place where criminals are kept in order to punish them, or where people waiting to be tried are kept.

garbage^{복습}
[gáːrbidʒ]

n. 쓰레기(통)
Garbage is rubbish, especially waste from a kitchen.

pail*
[peil]

n. 들통, 버킷 (garbage pail n. 쓰레기통)
A pail is a bucket, usually made of metal or wood.

hold one's ground

idiom 한 걸음도 물러서지 않다; 자신의 입장을 고수하다
If you hold your ground, you do not run away from a situation, but face it bravely.

retort*
[ritɔ́:t]

v. 말대꾸하다, 맞받아 응수하다; 반박하다, 항변하다; n. 말대꾸
To retort means to reply angrily to someone.

impress*
[imprés]

v. 깊은 인상을 주다, 감명을 주다; 강하게 남다
(impressed a. 감명을 받은, 인상 깊게 생각하는)
If something impresses you, you feel great admiration for it.

gleam*
[gli:m]

v. 어슴푸레 빛나다; (눈빛이 어떤 감정을 보이며) 반짝거리다; n. 어슴푸레한 빛
If an object or a surface gleams, it reflects light because it is shiny and clean.

vote**
[vout]

n. 투표, 표결; (선거 등에서의) 표; v. 의사 표시를 하다, 표를 던지다, 투표하다
A vote is an occasion when a group of people make a decision by each person indicating his or her choice.

bite^{복습}
[bait]

v. 물다, 베어 물다; n. 물기; 한 입 (베어 문 조각)
If you bite something, you use your teeth to cut into it, for example in order to eat it or break it.

carrot*
[kǽrət]

n. 당근; 보상, 미끼
Carrots are long, thin, orange-colored vegetables.

duck
[dʌk]

v. (머리나 몸을) 휙 수그리다; (머리나 몸을 움직여) 피하다; n. 오리
If you duck, you move your head or the top half of your body quickly downward to avoid something that might hit you, or to avoid being seen.

in time^{복습}

idiom 제때에, 시간 맞춰, 늦지 않게
If you are in time for a particular event, you are not too late for it.

$$\frac{686 \text{ words}}{\text{reading time ( ) sec}} \times 60 = (\quad) \text{ WPM}$$

Build Your Vocabulary

mushroom 복습
[mʌʃruːm]

n. 버섯
Mushrooms are fungi that you can eat.

scoop
[skuːp]

v. (큰 숟갈 같은 것으로) 뜨다; 재빨리 들어올리다; n. 숟갈; 한 숟갈(의 양)
If you scoop something from a container, you remove it with something such as a spoon.

glop
[glap]

n. (기분 나쁘게) 질척거리는 것
Glop is a sticky, thick substance, such as food, that appears unpleasant.

vat
[væt]

n. (액체를 담는 데 쓰는 대형) 통
A vat is a large barrel or tank in which liquids can be stored.

plop 복습
[plap]

v. 풍당 하고 떨어지다; 털썩 주저앉다; n. 풍당 하는 소리
If something plops somewhere, it drops there with a soft, gentle sound.

plate 복습
[pleit]

n. 접시, 그릇; 한 접시 (분량의 음식)
A plate is a round or oval flat dish that is used to hold food.

cash register 복습
[kæʃ rèdʒistər]

n. 금전 등록기
A cash register is a machine in a shop, pub, or restaurant that is used to add up and record how much money people pay, and in which the money is kept.

grayish
[gréiiʃ]

a. 회색을 띤
Grayish means slightly gray in color.

mound*
[maund]

n. 더미, 무더기; 흙더미; 언덕
A mound of something is a large rounded pile of it.

squirt
[skwəːrt]

v. (액체·가스 등을 가늘게) 찍 짜다; 찍 나오다
If you squirt a liquid somewhere or if it squirts somewhere, the liquid comes out of a narrow opening in a thin fast stream.

squiggle
[skwigl]

n. 구불구불한 선 (squiggly ad. 구불구불한)
Squiggly lines are lines that bend and curl in an irregular way.

dollop
[dáləp]

n. (숟가락으로 덜어낸) 덩이; 소량, 약간
A dollop of soft or sticky food is a large spoonful of it.

pal*
[pæl]

n. 친구
Your pals are your friends.

buddy*
[bʌ́di]

n. 친구
A buddy is a close friend, usually a male friend of a man.

polka dot
[póulkə dàt]

n. 물방울무늬
Polka dot is a pattern consisting of an array of filled circles.

second***
[sékənd]

n. (pl.) (방금 먹은 음식으로) 한 그릇 더; 초; a. (순서상으로) 두 번째의
If you have seconds, you have a second helping of food.

run out of^{복습}

idiom ~을 다 써버리다, ~이 없어지다
If you are running out of something, you do not have much of it left.

lump^{복습}
[lʌmp]

n. 덩어리, 응어리 (lumpy a. 덩어리가 많은)
Something that is lumpy contains lumps or is covered with lumps.

gooey
[gúːi]

a. 부드럽고 끈적거리는
If you describe a food or other substance as gooey, you mean that it is very soft and sticky.

drag*
[dræg]

v. 질질 끌다; (힘들여) 끌다; (원치 않는 곳에) 가게 하다; n. ~에 대한 장애물
If you drag something, you pull it along the ground, often with difficulty.

swirl
[swəːrl]

v. 빙빙 돌게 하다; 빙빙 돌다, 소용돌이치다; n. 소용돌이
If you swirl something liquid or flowing, or if it swirls, it moves round and round quickly.

spongy
[spʌ́ndʒi]

a. 부드럽고 흡수성이 좋은
Something that is spongy is soft and can be pressed in, like a sponge.

pale^{복습}
[peil]

a. (색깔이) 옅은; 창백한, 핼쑥한; v. 창백해지다
If something is pale, it is very light in color or almost white.

pile**
[pail]

v. 쌓다, 포개다; n. 포개 놓은 것, 더미
If you pile things somewhere, you put them there so that they form a pile.

dig^{복습}
[dig]

v. (dug-dug) (구멍 등을) 파다; ~을 찌르다; n. 쿡 찌르기; 발굴
If people or animals dig, they make a hole in the ground or in a pile of earth, stones, or rubbish.

eyebrow*
[áibràu]

n. 눈썹
Your eyebrows are the lines of hair which grow above your eyes.

pointy
[pɔ́inti]

a. 끝이 뾰족한; 가시가 돋은
Something that is pointy has a point at one end.

creation*
[kriéiʃən]

n. 창작품; 창조, 창작, 창출
You can refer to something that someone has made as a creation, especially if it shows skill, imagination, or artistic ability.

abrupt*
[əbrʌ́pt]

a. 돌연한, 갑작스런; 퉁명스러운 (abruptly ad. 갑자기, 불쑥)
An abrupt change or action is very sudden, often in a way which is unpleasant.

turn into^{복습}

idiom (~에서) ~이 되다, ~으로 변하다
To turn or be turned into something means to become that thing.

frown ^{복습}
[fraun]

n. 찡그림, 찌푸림; v. 얼굴을 찌푸리다
A frown is a facial expression that usually shows dislike or displeasure.

terror[*]
[térər]

n. (극심한) 두려움, 공포(심); 테러 (행위·협박)
Terror is very great fear.

figure out ^{복습}

idiom (생각한 끝에) ~을 이해하다; (양·비용을) 계산하다
If you figure out someone or something, you come to understand them by thinking carefully.

get away ^{복습}

idiom (~에서) 탈출하다, 벗어나다
If you get away from someone or some place, you escape from them or that place.

wiggle ^{복습}
[wigl]

v. (좌우·상하로 짧게) 씰룩씰룩 움직이다
If you wiggle something or if it wiggles, it moves up and down or from side to side in small quick movements.

utensil[*]
[juːténsəl]

n. 기구, 도구
Utensils are tools or objects that you use in order to help you to cook or to do other tasks in your home.

shovel[*]
[ʃʌ́vəl]

v. 삽질하다, 삽으로 파다; n. 삽, 부삽
If you shovel something somewhere, you push a lot of it quickly into that place.

swallow ^{복습}
[swálou]

v. (음식 등을) 삼키다; 마른침을 삼키다; n. 제비
If you swallow something, you cause it to go from your mouth down into your stomach.

mouthful ^{복습}
[máuθfùl]

n. (음식) 한 입, 한 모금; 길고 복잡한 말
A mouthful of drink or food is the amount that you put or have in your mouth.

rub ^{복습}
[rʌb]

v. (손·손수건 등을 대고) 문지르다; (두 손 등을) 맞비비다; n. 문지르기, 비비기
If you rub a part of your body, you move your hand or fingers backward and forward over it while pressing firmly.

belly[*]
[béli]

n. 배
The belly of a person or animal is their stomach or abdomen.

sigh ^{복습}
[sai]

v. 한숨을 쉬다, 한숨짓다; n. 한숨
When you sigh, you let out a deep breath, as a way of expressing feelings such as disappointment, tiredness, or pleasure.

Chapters 25 & 26

1. How did Stephen dress for class picture day?
   A. He wore a three-piece suit.
   B. He wore a school uniform.
   C. He wore white shorts and a Hawaiian shirt.
   D. He wore a toga made out of a bed sheet.

2. How did Stephen feel about his tie?
   A. He thought that it kept his neck warm.
   B. He thought that it kept his shirt on.
   C. He thought that it made him look better.
   D. He thought that it made him look older.

3. Why did the students tell Stephen to pull his tie tighter?
   A. They wanted to see him laugh.
   B. They wanted him to look even better.
   C. They wanted him to rip his tie in half.
   D. They wanted to see his face turn blue.

4. What did Mrs. Jewls say made someone important?
   A. She said that it was what's underneath that counted.
   B. She said that it was how you felt that counted.
   C. She said it was how other people thought you looked that counted.
   D. She said it was how hard you studied in school that counted.

5. How did Mrs. Jewls feel about busy work?

   A. She liked to give busy work only as homework.

   B. She thought that it was the best way for children to learn.

   C. She thought that it was the easiest way to teach.

   D. She didn't like giving busy work and wanted to teach new things instead.

6. Which of the following was NOT one of the things Mrs. Jewls tried to teach her class?

   A. The capital of England

   B. Seven plus four

   C. How to spell England

   D. How to make pickles

7. How did Paul save Leslie?

   A. He pushed the vat of brine away from Leslie.

   B. He pulled her pigtails away from Mrs. Jewls.

   C. He answered the third question correctly for Leslie.

   D. He jumped in front of Leslie and got drenched in pickle juice.

$$\frac{667 \text{ words}}{\text{reading time ( ) sec}} \times 60 = (\qquad) \text{ WPM}$$

Build Your Vocabulary

dress up

idiom 옷을 갖춰 입다; 변장을 하다
If you dress up, you put on clothes that are more formal than the clothes you usually wear.

suit**
[su:t]

n. 정장; (특정한 활동 때 입는) 옷; v. (~에게) 괜찮다; 어울리다
A man's suit consists of a jacket, trousers, and sometimes a waistcoat, all made from the same fabric.

trouser
[tráuzər]

n. (pl.) 바지
Trousers are a piece of clothing that you wear over your body from the waist downward, and that cover each leg separately.

vest
[vest]

n. 조끼; (셔츠 같은 옷 안에 입는) 속옷
A vest is a sleeveless piece of clothing with buttons which people usually wear over a shirt.

stripe*
[straip]

n. 줄무늬 (striped a. 줄무늬가 있는)
Something that is striped has stripes on it.

silly**ᵇᵇ
[síli]

a. 어리석은, 바보 같은; n. 바보
If you say that someone or something is silly, you mean that they are foolish, childish, or ridiculous.

costume*
[kástju:m]

n. 의상, 복장
A costume is a set of clothes worn in order to look like someone or something else, especially for a party or as part of an entertainment.

polka dotᵇᵇ
[póulkə dàt]

n. 물방울무늬
Polka dot is a pattern consisting of an array of filled circles.

floppyᵇᵇ
[flápi]

a. 헐렁한, 축 늘어진
Something that is floppy is loose rather than stiff, and tends to hang downward.

stand around

idiom 우두커니 서 있다
If you stand around, you stand in a place doing nothing, either waiting for someone or with no particular purpose.

wrinkle*
[riŋkl]

v. 주름이 생기다; (얼굴에) 주름을 잡다, 찡그리다; n. 주름
If cloth wrinkles, or if someone or something wrinkles it, it gets folds or lines in it.

knock^{복습}
[nak]

v. (문 등을) 두드리다; 치다, 부딪치다; (때리거나 타격을 가해) ~한 상태가 되게 만들다;
n. 문 두드리는 소리
If you knock something, you touch or hit it roughly, especially so that it falls or moves.

fist^{복습}
[fist]

n. 주먹
Your hand is referred to as your fist when you have bent your fingers in toward the palm in order to hit someone.

sparkle*
[spaːrkl]

v. 반짝이다; n. 반짝거림, 광채 (sparkling a. 반짝거리는)
If something sparkles, it is clear and bright and shines with a lot of very small points of light.

goddess*
[gádis]

n. 여신
In many religions, a goddess is a female spirit or being that is believed to have power over a particular part of the world or nature.

bet*
[bet]

v. 틀림없다, 분명하다; 돈을 걸다; n. 내기; 내기 돈; 짐작, 추측
You use expression 'I bet' to indicate that you are sure something is true.

kickball^{복습}
[kíkbɔːl]

n. 발야구
Kickball is an informal game combining elements of baseball and soccer, in which a soccer ball is thrown to a person who kicks it and proceeds to run the bases.

choke^{복습}
[tʃouk]

v. 목을 조르다; 숨이 막히다, 질식할 지경이다; n. 숨이 막힘, 질식
To choke someone means to squeeze their neck.

tighten*
[taitn]

v. 조여지다; 조이다; 팽팽해지다; 팽팽하게 하다
If you tighten a rope or chain, or if it tightens, it is stretched or pulled hard until it is straight.

gasp^{복습}
[gæsp]

v. 숨이 턱 막히다, 헉 하고 숨을 쉬다; n. (숨이 막히는 듯) 헉 하는 소리를 냄
When you gasp, you take a short quick breath through your mouth, especially when you are surprised, shocked, or in pain.

bed sheet
[béd ʃiːt]

n. 시트, (침대에) 까는 천
A bed sheet is a large rectangular piece of cotton or other cloth that you sleep on or cover yourself with in a bed.

yell^{복습}
[jel]

v. 고함치다, 소리 지르다; n. 고함, 외침
If you yell, you shout loudly, usually because you are excited, angry, or in pain.

bulge
[bʌldʒ]

v. 툭 튀어 나오다; (~으로) 가득 차다; n. 툭 튀어 나온 것
If someone's eyes or veins are bulging, they seem to stick out a lot, often because the person is making a strong physical effort or is experiencing a strong emotion.

rip^{복습}
[rip]

v. (갑자기·거칠게) 찢다; 떼어 내다; n. (옷감·종이 등에 길게) 찢어진 곳
When something rips or when you rip it, you tear it forcefully with your hands or with a tool such as a knife.

groan^{복습}
[groun]

v. (고통·짜증으로) 신음 소리를 내다; (기뻐서) 낮게 탄성을 지르다;
n. 신음, 끙 하는 소리
If you groan, you make a long, low sound because you are in pain, or because you are upset or unhappy about something.

count^{복습}
[kaunt]

v. 중요하다; 수를 세다, 계산하다; (정식으로) 인정되다; n. 셈, 계산

If something or someone counts for something or counts, they are important or valuable.

underpant
[ʌ́ndərpænts]

n. (남성용·여성용) 팬티

Underpants are a piece of underwear which have two holes to put your legs through and elastic around the top to hold them up round your waist or hips.

flowered
[fláuərd]

a. 꽃무늬의

Flowered paper or cloth has a pattern of flowers on it.

$$\frac{1,289 \text{ words}}{\text{reading time ( ) sec}} \times 60 = (\quad) \text{ WPM}$$

Build Your Vocabulary

rotten^{복습}
[ratn]

a. 형편없는, 끔찍한; 썩은, 부패한
If you describe someone as rotten, you are insulting them or criticizing them because you think that they are very unpleasant or unkind.

burst^{복습}
[bəːrst]

v. 불쑥 ~하다; 터지다, 파열하다; n. (갑자기) 한바탕 ~을 함; 파열
To burst into or out of a place means to enter or leave it suddenly with a lot of energy or force.

bulletin board*
[búlitən bɔːrd]

n. 게시판
A bulletin board is a board which is usually attached to a wall in order to display notices giving information about something.

handwriting*
[hǽndràitiŋ]

n. 손으로 쓰기, 필적
Your handwriting is your style of writing with a pen or pencil.

ignore^{복습}
[ignɔ́ːr]

v. (사람을) 못 본 척하다; 무시하다
If you ignore someone or something, you pay no attention to them.

eventually**
[ivéntʃuəli]

ad. 결국, 마침내
Eventually means at the end of a situation or process or as the final result of it.

punish^{복습}
[pʌ́niʃ]

v. 처벌하다, 벌주다; (형벌·형에) 처하다
To punish someone means to make them suffer in some way because they have done something wrong.

yardstick
[jáːrdstik]

n. 야드 자; 기준, 척도
A yardstick is a long, flat tool that is one yard long and is used to measure things.

scurry^{복습}
[skə́ːri]

v. 종종걸음을 치다, 허둥지둥 가다
When people or small animals scurry somewhere, they move there quickly and hurriedly, especially because they are frightened.

announce^{복습}
[ənáuns]

v. 발표하다, 알리다; (공공장소에서) 방송으로 알리다
If you announce something, you tell people about it publicly or officially.

capital**
[kǽpətl]

n. 수도; 자본금, 자금; 대문자; a. 대문자의
The capital of a country is the city or town where its government or parliament meets.

pay attention ^{복습}

idiom 관심을 갖다
If you pay attention to someone, you watch them, listen to them, or take notice of them.

equal*
[íːkwəl]

v. (수·양·가치 등이) 같다, ~이다; a. (수·양·가치 등이) 동일한
If something equals a particular number or amount, it is the same as that amount or the equivalent of that amount.

cucumber
[kjúːkʌmbər]

n. 오이
A cucumber is a long thin vegetable with a hard green skin and wet transparent flesh. It is eaten raw in salads.

brine
[brain]

n. (식품 저장용) 소금물
Brine is salty water, especially salty water that is used for preserving food.

vat ^{복습}
[væt]

n. (액체를 담는 데 쓰는 대형) 통
A vat is a large barrel or tank in which liquids can be stored.

demonstrate*
[démənstrèit]

v. (무엇의 작동 과정이나 사용법을) 보여주다; 입증하다
(demonstration n. 시범)
A demonstration of something is a talk by someone who shows you how to do it or how it works.

shrug ^{복습}
[ʃrʌg]

v. (두 손바닥을 위로 하고) 어깨를 으쓱하다; n. 어깨를 으쓱하기
If you shrug, you raise your shoulders to show that you are not interested in something or that you do not know or care about something.

declare ^{복습}
[diklέər]

v. 분명히 말하다; 선언하다, 공표하다
If you declare that something is true, you say that it is true in a firm, deliberate way.

frown ^{복습}
[fraun]

v. 얼굴을 찌푸리다; n. 찡그림, 찌푸림
When someone frowns, their eyebrows become drawn together, because they are annoyed or puzzled.

unfortunate ^{복습}
[ʌnfɔ́ːrtʃənət]

a. 운이 없는, 불운한, 불행한 (unfortunately ad. 불행하게도, 유감스럽게도)
You can use unfortunately to introduce or refer to a statement when you consider that it is sad or disappointing, or when you want to express regret.

that does it

idiom 더 이상은 못 참아
You say 'that does it' to indicate that you will not tolerate a particular thing any longer.

blackboard ^{복습}
[blǽkbɔ̀ːrd]

n. 칠판
A blackboard is a dark-colored board that you can write on with chalk.

discipline ^{복습}
[dísəplin]

n. 규율, 훈육; 단련법, 수련법
Discipline is the practice of making people obey rules or standards of behavior, and punishing them when they do not.

come over ^{복습}

idiom (어떤 기분이) 갑자기 들다
If a feeling comes over, you suddenly start to feel that way.

snap*
[snæp]

v. 딱딱거리다, 톡 쏘다; 딱 하고 움직이다; n. 찰칵 하는 소리; a. 성급한; 불시의
If someone snaps at you, they speak to you in a sharp, unfriendly way.

make a face복습

idiom 얼굴을 찌푸리다, 침울한 표정을 짓다
If you make a face, you twist your face to indicate a certain mental or emotional state.

dare복습
[dɛər]

v. ~할 용기가 있다, 감히 ~하다, ~할 엄두를 내다
You say 'how dare you' when you are very shocked and angry about something that someone has done.

talk back

idiom 말대답하다
If you talk back to someone, you reply rudely to someone in authority.

nod복습
[nad]

v. (고개를) 끄덕이다; n. (고개를) 끄덕임
If you nod, you move your head downward and upward to show that you are answering 'yes' to a question, or to show agreement, understanding, or approval.

meek*
[miːk]

a. 온순한, 온화한 (meekly ad. 온순하게)
If you describe a person as meek, you think that they are gentle and quiet, and likely to do what other people say.

slam복습
[slæm]

v. 세게 놓다; 쾅 닫다; n. 탕 하고 닫기; 탕 하는 소리
If you slam something down, you put it there quickly and with great force.

bang복습
[bæŋ]

v. 쾅 하고 치다; 쾅 하고 닫다; n. 쾅 하는 소리
If you bang on something or if you bang it, you hit it hard, making a loud noise.

goodness*
[gúdnis]

int. (놀람을 나타내어) 와, 어머나!; n. 선량함
People sometimes say 'goodness' or 'oh my goodness' to express surprise.

mock*
[mak]

v. 놀리다, 조롱하다; a. 거짓된, 가짜의 (mocking a. 비웃는)
A mocking expression or mocking behavior indicates that you think someone or something is stupid or inferior.

pour**
[pɔːr]

v. 붓다, 따르다; 마구 쏟아지다
If you pour a liquid or other substance, you make it flow steadily out of a container by holding the container at an angle.

shrivel
[ʃrívəl]

v. 쪼글쪼글해지다; 쪼글쪼글하게 만들다
When something shrivels or when something shrivels it, it becomes dryer and smaller, often with lines in its surface, as a result of losing the water it contains.

wart
[wɔːrt]

n. (피부에 생기는) 사마귀
A wart is a small lump which grows on your skin.

aisle*
[ail]

n. 통로
An aisle is a long narrow gap that people can walk along between rows of seats in a public building.

glare 복습
[glɛər]

v. 노려보다; 환하다, 눈부시다; n. 노려봄; 환한 빛, 눈부심
If you glare at someone, you look at them with an angry expression on your face.

pigtail 복습
[pígtèil]

n. (하나 또는 두 갈래로) 땋은 머리
If someone has a pigtail or pigtails, their hair is plaited or braided into one or two lengths.

tremble 복습
[trembl]

v. (몸을) 떨다, 떨리다; (가볍게) 흔들리다; n. 떨림, 전율
If you tremble, you shake slightly because you are frightened or cold.

wiggle 복습
[wigl]

v. (좌우·상하로 짧게) 씰룩씰룩 움직이다
If you wiggle something or if it wiggles, it moves up and down or from side to side in small quick movements.

dump 복습
[dʌmp]

v. (아무렇게나) 내려놓다; 버리다; n. (쓰레기) 폐기장
If you dump something somewhere, you put it or unload it there quickly and carelessly.

gulp 복습
[gʌlp]

v. (공포·놀라움에 질려) 침을 꿀떡 삼키다; 꿀꺽꿀꺽 삼키다; n. 꿀꺽 한 입
If you gulp, you swallow air, often making a noise in your throat as you do so, because you are nervous or excited.

take a wild guess

idiom 어림짐작하다
If you take a wild guess, you give an answer which is very unlikely to be accurate.

tip*
[tip]

v. 따르다; 기울어지다, 젖혀지다; n. (뾰족한) 끝
If you tip something somewhere, you pour it there.

favor*
[féivər]

n. 호의, 친절; 지지, 인정; v. 선호하다 (return the favor idiom 은혜를 갚다)
If you do someone a favor, you do something for them even though you do not have to.

drench
[drenʧ]

v. 흠뻑 적시다
To drench something or someone means to make them completely wet.

freeze
[fri:z]

v. (froze-frozen) (두려움 등으로 몸이) 얼어붙다; 얼리다; 얼다;
n. (임금·가격 등의) 동결
If someone who is moving freezes, they suddenly stop and become completely still and quiet.

terror 복습
[térər]

n. (극심한) 두려움, 공포(심); 테러 (행위·협박)
Terror is very great fear.

blink*
[bliŋk]

v. 눈을 깜박이다; (불빛이) 깜박거리다; n. 눈을 깜박거림
When you blink or when you blink your eyes, you shut your eyes and very quickly open them again.

drip 복습
[drip]

v. 방울방울 흐르다; n. (액체가) 뚝뚝 떨어지는 소리; (작은 액체) 방울
When liquid drips somewhere, or you drip it somewhere, it falls in individual small drops.

cure
[kjuər]

v. 낫게 하다; 치유하다; n. 치유하는 약, 치유법
If doctors or medical treatments cure a person, they make the person well again after an illness or injury.

kindergarten [복습]
[kíndərgàːrtn]

n. 유치원
A kindergarten is an informal kind of school for very young children, where they learn things by playing.

Chapters 27 & 28

1. Why did Maruecia crawl in the bushes?

   A. She was looking for her lost lunch.

   B. She was looking for her lost ball.

   C. She was playing hide-and-seek.

   D. She was looking for her lost chocolate milk.

2. Why did Maurecia bring the paper bag of money to Louis?

   A. She thought that Louis could use the money.

   B. She thought that Louis would know what to do.

   C. She owed Louis money for lunch.

   D. She wanted Louis to return it to the bank robbers.

3. How did Mr. Finch make his money?

   A. He worked at an ice cream parlor.

   B. He taught at Wayside School.

   C. He robbed banks.

   D. He made pencils.

4. What was Mr. Finch going to do with his money?

   A. He was going to give half of it to Maurecia.

   B. He was going to donate it to Wayside School.

   C. He was going to open his own ice cream parlor.

   D. He was going to start his own pencil company.

5. Why did Eric Bacon say that he did not need dance lessons?
   A. He said that he already knew how to dance.
   B. He said that he had broken his leg and couldn't dance.
   C. He said that he was already taking lessons after school.
   D. He said that he was transferring to another school.

6. What kind of dancing did Mrs. Waloosh teach the class?
   A. Waltz
   B. Tango
   C. Salsa
   D. Breakdancing

7. Which of the following was NOT true about Mrs. Jewls's class after Mrs. Waloosh's dance lesson?
   A. They spoke like Mrs. Waloosh.
   B. They came out bruised and bleeding.
   C. They couldn't wait until next Wednesday.
   D. Myron was glad he had missed it.

Check Your Reading Speed

1분에 몇 단어를 읽는지 리딩 속도를 측정해보세요.

$$\frac{1{,}096 \text{ words}}{\text{reading time (\quad) sec}} \times 60 = (\quad) \text{ WPM}$$

Build Your Vocabulary

no way

idiom 절대로 아니다; (강한 거절의 의미로) 절대로 안 돼, 싫어
If you say there's no way that something will happen, you are emphasizing that you think it will definitely not happen.

carton복습
[ka:rtn]

n. (음식이나 음료를 담는) 곽; 상자
A carton is a plastic or cardboard container in which food or drink is sold.

swallow복습
[swálou]

v. (음식 등을) 삼키다; 마른침을 삼키다; n. 제비
If you swallow something, you cause it to go from your mouth down into your stomach.

crawl복습
[krɔ:l]

v. (엎드려) 기다; (곤충이) 기어가다; n. 기어가기, 서행
When you crawl, you move forward on your hands and knees.

dirt**
[də:rt]

n. 흙; 먼지, 때
You can refer to the earth on the ground as dirt, especially when it is dusty.

bush복습
[buʃ]

n. 관목, 덤불
A bush is a large plant which is smaller than a tree and has a lot of branches.

exclaim복습
[ikskléim]

v. 소리치다, 외치다
If you exclaim, you cry out suddenly in surprise, strong emotion, or pain.

cough**
[kɔ:f]

v. 기침하다; (기침을 하여 무엇을) 토하다; n. 기침
When you cough, you force air out of your throat with a sudden, harsh noise.

sack복습
[sæk]

n. (종이) 봉지, 부대
A sack is a paper or plastic bag, which is used to carry things bought in a shop.

pop*
[pap]

v. (놀라거나 흥분하여) 눈이 휘둥그레지다; 펑 하는 소리가 나다;
n. 펑 하고 터지는 소리
If your eyes pop, you look very surprised or excited when you see something.

stuff복습
[stʌf]

v. (빽빽히) 채워 넣다; (재빨리·되는대로) 쑤셔 넣다; n. 일, 것; 물건
If you stuff a container or space with something, you fill it with something or with a quantity of things until it is full.

120

bill**
[bil]

n. 지폐; 고지서, 청구서; (식당의) 계산서
A bill is a piece of paper money.

count^{복습}
[kaunt]

v. 수를 세다, 계산하다; 중요하다; (정식으로) 인정되다; n. 셈, 계산
When you count, you say all the numbers one after another up to a particular number.

split^{복습}
[split]

v. (몫 등을) 나누다; 분열되다; 찢다, 쪼개다; n. 분열, 불화; 분할; 몫
If two or more people split something, they share it between them.

fancy**
[fǽnsi]

a. 값비싼, 고급의; v. 원하다, ~하고 싶다; n. 공상, 상상
If you describe something as fancy, you mean that it is very expensive or of very high quality.

rob**
[rab]

v. 털다, 도둑질하다
If someone is robbed, they have money or property stolen from them.

jail^{복습}
[dʒeil]

n. 교도소, 감옥
A jail is a place where criminals are kept in order to punish them, or where people waiting to be tried are kept.

robber*
[rábər]

n. (협박·폭력을 이용하는) 강도
A robber is someone who steals money or property from a bank, a shop, or a vehicle, often by using force or threats.

murder**
[mə́:rdər]

v. 살해하다, 살인하다; (경기에서 상대를) 묵사발이 되게 하다; n. 살인(죄), 살해
To murder someone means to commit the crime of killing them deliberately.

protect^{복습}
[prətékt]

v. 보호하다, 지키다
To protect someone or something means to prevent them from being harmed or damaged.

pole**
[poul]

n. 막대기, 기둥, 장대
A pole is a long thin piece of wood or metal, used especially for supporting things.

untie^{복습}
[ʌntái]

v. (매듭 등을) 풀다
If you untie something such as string or rope, you undo it so that there is no knot or so that it is no longer tying something.

blink^{복습}
[bliŋk]

v. 눈을 깜박이다; (불빛이) 깜박거리다; n. 눈을 깜박거림
When you blink or when you blink your eyes, you shut your eyes and very quickly open them again.

get lost

idiom 꺼져; (거절을 나타내어) 턱도 없어
If you say 'get lost' to someone, it is an impolite way of telling them to go away, or of refusing something.

run away^{복습}

idiom (~에서) 달아나다
If you run away, you leave quickly in order to avoid or escape someone or something.

lost and found
[lɔ́:st ən faund]

n. 분실물 보관소
Lost and found is the place where lost property is kept.

claim***
[kleim]

v. 요구하다; (~이 사실이라고) 주장하다; n. 주장
If you claim something, you try to get it because you think you have a right to it.

court**
[kɔːrt]

n. (테니스 등을 하는) 코트; 법정, 법원
A court is an area in which you play a game such as tennis, basketball, badminton, or squash.

sweet potato
[swíːt pətéitou]

n. 고구마
Sweet potatoes are vegetables that look like large ordinary potatoes but taste sweet. They have pinkish-brown skins and yellow flesh.

beard^{복습}
[biərd]

n. (턱)수염
A man's beard is the hair that grows on his chin and cheeks.

nod^{복습}
[nad]

v. (고개를) 끄덕이다; n. (고개를) 끄덕임
If you nod, you move your head downward and upward to show that you are answering 'yes' to a question, or to show agreement, understanding, or approval.

saving*
[séiviŋ]

n. (pl.) 저축한 돈, 저금, 예금; 절약
Your savings are the money that you have saved, especially in a bank or a building society.

parlor^{복습}
[páːrlər]

n. (특정한 상품·서비스를 제공하는) 상점; 응접실, 거실
Parlor is used in the names of some types of shops which provide a service, rather than selling things.

blubber
[blʌ́bər]

v. 흐느껴 울다
If someone blubbers, they cry noisily and in an unattractive way.

contain^{복습}
[kəntéin]

v. (무엇의 안에 또는 그 일부로) ~이 들어 있다; (감정을) 억누르다
If something such as a box, bag, room, or place contains things, those things are inside it.

reward**
[riwɔ́ːrd]

n. 보상; 현상금, 보상금, 사례금; v. 보상하다, 사례하다
A reward is something that you are given, for example because you have behaved well, worked hard, or provided a service to the community.

involve**
[inválv]

v. (상황·사건·활동이 사람을) 관련시키다; (중요 요소로·필연적으로) 포함하다
(involved a. 관여하는, 관련된)
If you are involved in a situation or activity, you are taking part in it or have a strong connection with it.

1분에 몇 단어를 읽는지 리딩 속도를 측정해보세요.

$$\frac{1{,}023 \text{ words}}{\text{reading time ( ) sec}} \times 60 = (\quad) \text{ WPM}$$

Build Your Vocabulary

gross^{복습}
[grous]

a. 역겨운; 전체의
If you describe something as gross, you think it is very unpleasant.

yuck^{복습}
[jʌk]

int. 윽(역겨울 때 내는 소리)
'Yuck' is an expression of disgust.

obvious^{복습}
[ábviəs]

a. 분명한, 명백한 (obviously ad. 분명히, 명백히)
You use obviously to indicate that something is easily noticed, seen, or recognized.

no way^{복습}

idiom (강한 거절의 의미로) 절대로 안 돼, 싫어; 절대로 아니다
You can say no way as an emphatic way of saying no.

at once^{복습}

idiom 동시에, 한꺼번에; 즉시, 당장
If a number of different things happen at once, they all happen at the same time.

cootie
[kú:ti]

n. 이
Cooties are small insects that live on the bodies of people or animals and bite them in order to feed off their blood.

wart^{복습}
[wɔ:rt]

n. (피부에 생기는) 사마귀
A wart is a small lump which grows on your skin.

horrible^{복습}
[hɔ́:rəbl]

a. 지긋지긋한, 끔찍한; 소름끼치는, 무시무시한
Horrible is used to emphasize how bad something is.

disease^{★★}
[dizí:z]

n. 질병, 병, 질환
A disease is an illness which affects people, animals, or plants, for example one which is caused by bacteria or infection.

sarcastic[★]
[sa:rkǽstik]

a. 빈정대는, 비꼬는 (sarcastically ad. 비꼬는 투로, 풍자적으로)
Someone who is sarcastic says or does the opposite of what they really mean in order to mock or insult someone.

grace[★]
[greis]

n. 우아함; 품위; (pl.) 예의
If someone moves with grace, they move in a smooth, controlled, and attractive way.

classical^{★★}
[klǽsikəl]

a. 고전적인; 클래식 음악의
You use classical to describe something that is traditional in form, style, or content.

ballroom
[bɔ́:lrù:m]

n. 무도회장
A ballroom is a very large room that is used for dancing.

groan ^{복습}
[groun]

v. (고통·짜증으로) 신음 소리를 내다; (기뻐서) 낮게 탄성을 지르다;
n. 신음, 끙 하는 소리
If you groan, you make a long, low sound because you are in pain, or because you are upset or unhappy about something.

president ^{복습}
[prézədənt]

n. 대통령; 장(長), 회장
The president of a country that has no king or queen is the person who is the head of state of that country.

bet ^{복습}
[bet]

v. 틀림없다, 분명하다; 돈을 걸다; n. 내기; 내기 돈; 짐작, 추측
You use expression 'I bet' to indicate that you are sure something is true.

blackmail
[blǽkmèil]

v. 협박하다, 돈을 뜯어내다; n. 갈취, 협박
If one person blackmails another person, they use action of threatening to reveal a secret about them.

lampshade
[lǽmpʃèid]

n. (램프·전등의) 갓
A lampshade is a covering that is fitted round or over an electric light bulb in order to protect it or decorate it, or to make the light less harsh.

make sense

idiom 타당하다, 말이 되다; 의미가 통하다, 이해가 되다
If something makes sense, you can understand it.

sparkle ^{복습}
[spa:rkl]

v. 반짝이다; n. 반짝거림, 광채 (sparkling a. 반짝거리는)
If something sparkles, it is clear and bright and shines with a lot of very small points of light.

recess ^{복습}
[risés]

n. (학교의) 쉬는 시간; (의회·위원회 등의) 휴회 기간
A recess is a break between classes at a school.

squeak ^{복습}
[skwi:k]

v. 끽 하는 소리를 내다; n. 끼익 하는 소리
If something or someone squeaks, they make a short, high-pitched sound.

bellow ^{복습}
[bélou]

v. (우렁찬 소리로) 고함치다
If someone bellows, they shout angrily in a loud, deep voice.

waist **
[weist]

n. 허리
Your waist is the middle part of your body where it narrows slightly above your hips.

grab ^{복습}
[græb]

v. (와락·단단히) 붙잡다; ~을 잡아채려고 하다; n. 와락 잡아채려고 함
If you grab something, you take it or pick it up suddenly and roughly.

drag ^{복습}
[dræg]

v. (원치 않는 곳에) 가게 하다; 질질 끌다; (힘들여) 끌다; n. ~에 대한 장애물
If someone drags you somewhere, they pull you there, or force you to go there by physically threatening you.

stomp
[stamp]

v. 발을 구르며 춤추다; 쿵쿵거리며 걷다
If you stomp somewhere, you walk there with very heavy steps, often because you are angry.

in time ^{복습}

idiom 제때에, 시간 맞춰, 늦지 않게
If you play, dance, or sing in time to the music, you do it at the right speed.

clap ^{복습}
[klæp]

v. 박수를 치다, 손뼉을 치다; n. 박수 (소리)
When you clap, you hit your hands together to show appreciation or attract attention.

somersault
[sʌ́məːrsɔ̀ːlt]

n. 공중제비, 재주넘기; v. 공중제비를 하다
If someone or something does a somersault, they turn over completely in the air.

midair
[midéər]

n. 공중, 상공
If something happens in midair, it happens in the air, rather than on the ground.

stamp ^{복습}
[stæmp]

v. (발을) 구르다; 쾅쾅거리며 걷다; n. 우표; 도장, 스탬프
If you stamp or stamp your foot, you lift your foot and put it down very hard on the ground, for example because you are angry or because your feet are cold.

trip^{***}
[trip]

v. (발을 걸어) ~를 넘어뜨리다; 발을 헛디디다; n. 여행; 발을 헛디딤
If you trip someone who is walking or running, you put your foot or something else in front of them, so that they knock their own foot against it and fall or nearly fall.

toss ^{복습}
[tɔːs]

v. (가볍게·아무렇게나) 던지다; n. (무엇을 결정하기 위한) 동전 던지기
If you toss something somewhere, you throw it there lightly, often in a rather careless way.

crash ^{복습}
[kræʃ]

v. (굉음과 함께) 부딪치다; 충돌하다, 들이받다;
n. (자동차 충돌·항공기 추락) 사고; 요란한 소리, 굉음
If something crashes somewhere, it moves and hits something else violently, making a loud noise.

murder ^{복습}
[mə́ːrdər]

v. (경기에서 상대를) 묵사발이 되게 하다; 살해하다, 살인하다; n. 살인(죄), 살해
To murder an opponent in a game or sport means to conclusively defeat them.

stagger ^{복습}
[stǽgər]

v. 비틀거리다, 휘청거리며 가다; 큰 충격을 주다, 깜짝 놀라게 하다
If you stagger, you walk very unsteadily, for example because you are ill or drunk.

cut up

idiom 심한 부상을 입히다; ~을 난도질하다, 잡아 찢다
If you cut someone up, you injure them by cutting them with a knife or a piece of glass.

bruise[*]
[bruːz]

v. 멍이 생기다, 타박상을 입(히)다; n. 멍, 타박상
If you bruise a part of your body, a bruise appears on it, for example because something hits you.

bleed[*]
[bliːd]

v. 피를 흘리다, 출혈하다
When you bleed, you lose blood from your body as a result of injury or illness.

Chapters 29 & 30

1. Why was Benjamin determined to tell Mrs. Jewls his real name before the end of the week?

   A. Mrs. Jewls would be meeting all of their parents.

   B. Mrs. Jewls would be handing out report cards.

   C. Mrs. Jewls would be giving back school pictures.

   D. Mrs. Jewls would be assigning them new seats.

2. What did everyone in Mrs. Jewls's class agree was crazy?

   A. Reading a story backward

   B. Bringing a hobo to show-and-tell

   C. The bathrooms being on the first floor

   D. Letting people call someone the wrong name

3. Which of the following did NOT happen after Benjamin told the class his real name?

   A. Mrs. Jewls gave him his lunch that had been sitting on her desk.

   B. Allison ran into Mark Miller on the stairs.

   C. Allison had understood everything for a second.

   D. Miss Zarves gave Mark Miller his lunch that had been sitting on her desk.

4. Why was it hard for the students to find their desks when they came to class on the windy morning?

    A. The wind had blown off the name cards on their desks.

    B. The children had a hard time seeing after the wind blew leaves in their faces.

    C. All the desks were crammed together on one side of the room.

    D. The children had a hard time walking in the door because of the wind.

5. Why was Mrs. Jewls constantly ringing her cowbell during the fire drill?

    A. She rang it, because the children might not be able to see through the smoke in a real fire.

    B. She rang it, because the children would be calmer with the sound of the cowbell.

    C. She rang it, because the first alarm didn't sound.

    D. She rang it, because she had lost her cow and wanted it to come home.

6. Why were the children and teachers on the ground shouting?

    A. They wanted Mrs. Jewls and her class to come down the stairs.

    B. They wanted Mrs. Jewls and her class to wait for a helicopter.

    C. They wanted Mrs. Jewls to stop ringing her bell.

    D. They wanted Mrs. Jewls and her class to go back inside their classroom.

7. Why was Wayside School closed?

    A. It had completely fallen down.

    B. It was was turned into a farm.

    C. It was destroyed by an earthquake.

    D. It was filled with cows.

$$\frac{888 \text{ words}}{\text{reading time ( ) sec}} \times 60 = (\quad) \text{ WPM}$$

Build Your Vocabulary

mammal[*]
[mǽməl]

n. 포유동물
Mammals are animals such as humans, dogs, lions, and whales. In general, female mammals give birth to babies rather than laying eggs, and feed their young with milk.

bald[복습]
[bɔːld]

a. 대머리의, 머리가 벗겨진
Someone who is bald has little or no hair on the top of their head.

stare[복습]
[stɛər]

v. 빤히 쳐다보다, 응시하다; n. 빤히 쳐다보기, 응시
If you stare at someone or something, you look at them for a long time.

determined[*]
[ditə́ːrmind]

a. 단단히 결심한; 단호한, 완강한
If you are determined to do something, you have made a firm decision to do it and will not let anything stop you.

barber[복습]
[báːrbər]

n. 이발사
A barber is a man whose job is cutting men's hair.

ambulance[**]
[ǽmbjuləns]

n. 구급차
An ambulance is a vehicle for taking people to and from hospital.

sew[*]
[sou]

v. 바느질하다, 깁다
When you sew something such as clothes, you make them or repair them by joining pieces of cloth together by passing thread through them with a needle.

operate[**]
[ápərèit]

v. 수술하다; 작동되다; 조작하다 (operating room n. 수술실)
When surgeons operate on a patient in a hospital, they cut open a patient's body in order to remove, replace, or repair a diseased or damaged part.

refrigerator[복습]
[rifrídʒərèitəːr]

n. 냉장고
A refrigerator is a large container which is kept cool inside, usually by electricity, so that the food and drink in it stays fresh.

grumble[복습]
[grʌmbl]

v. 투덜거리다; 우르릉거리다; n. 불만 사항
If someone grumbles, they complain about something in a bad-tempered way.

pigtail[복습]
[pígtèil]

n. (하나 또는 두 갈래로) 땋은 머리
If someone has a pigtail or pigtails, their hair is plaited or braided into one or two lengths.

classmate[*]
[klǽsmeit]

n. 급우, 반 친구
Your classmates are students who are in the same class as you at school or college.

weird^{복습}
[wiərd]

a. 기이한, 기묘한; 기괴한, 섬뜩한
If you describe something or someone as weird, you mean that they are strange.

hobo^{복습}
[hóubou]

n. 부랑자, 떠돌이
A hobo is a person who has no home, especially one who travels from place to place and gets money by begging.

weirdo^{복습}
[wíərdou]

n. 괴짜, 별난 사람
If you describe someone as a weirdo, you disapprove of them because they behave in an unusual way which you find difficult to understand or accept.

choke^{복습}
[tʃouk]

v. 목을 조르다; 숨이 막히다, 질식할 지경이다; n. 숨이 막힘, 질식
To choke someone means to squeeze their neck.

bunch[*]
[bʌntʃ]

n. (한 무리의) 사람들; 다발, 송이, 묶음
A bunch of people is a group of people who share one or more characteristics or who are doing something together.

sack^{복습}
[sæk]

n. (종이) 봉지, 부대
A sack is a paper or plastic bag, which is used to carry things bought in a shop.

story^{복습}
[stɔ́:ri]

① n. (건물의) 층 ② n. 이야기, 소설; 설명
A story of a building is one of its different levels, which is situated above or below other levels.

light up^{복습}

idiom (얼굴이) 환해지다; 빛나게 만들다
If someone's eyes or face light up, or something lights them up, they become bright with excitement or happiness.

get it^{복습}

idiom 알다, 이해하다
You can say get it when you understand something or get the right answer.

confuse^{복습}
[kənfjú:z]

v. (사람을) 혼란시키다; (주제를) 혼란스럽게 만들다 (confused a. 혼란스러워 하는)
If you are confused, you do not know exactly what is happening or what to do.

never mind

idiom (중요하지 않으니까) 신경쓰지 마; 걱정하지 마
You use never mind to tell someone that they need not do something or worry about something, because it is not important or because you will do it yourself.

mumble^{복습}
[mʌmbl]

v. 중얼거리다, 웅얼거리다; n. 중얼거림
If you mumble, you speak very quietly and not at all clearly with the result that the words are difficult to understand.

1분에 몇 단어를 읽는지 리딩 속도를 측정해보세요.

$$\frac{1{,}015 \text{ words}}{\text{reading time ( ) sec}} \times 60 = (\quad) \text{ WPM}$$

Build Your Vocabulary

whoosh
[hwuːʃ]

v. 휙 하고 지나가다; n. 쉭 하는 소리
If something whooshes somewhere, it moves there quickly or suddenly.

playground^{복습}
[pléigràund]

n. (학교의) 운동장; 놀이터
A playground is a piece of land, at school or in a public area, where children can play.

dirt^{복습}
[dəːrt]

n. 흙; 먼지, 때
You can refer to the earth on the ground as dirt, especially when it is dusty.

hardly^{복습}
[háːrdli]

ad. 거의 ~할 수가 없다; 거의 ~아니다; 막 (~하기 시작한)
When you say you can hardly do something, you are emphasizing that it is very difficult for you to do it.

make it^{복습}

idiom 가다; 성공하다, 해내다
If you make it to somewhere, you succeed in reaching there.

gust
[gʌst]

n. 세찬 바람, 돌풍; v. (갑자기) 몰아치다
A gust is a short, strong, sudden rush of wind.

teeter
[tíːtər]

v. (넘어질 듯이) 불안정하게 움직이다
If someone or something teeters, they shake in an unsteady way, and seem to be about to lose their balance and fall over.

totter
[tátəːr]

v. 무너질 것 같다, 휘청거리다; 비틀거리다
If something such as a market or government is tottering, it is weak and likely to collapse or fail completely.

sway[*]
[swei]

v. (전후·좌우로 천천히) 흔들리다; (마음을) 흔들다; n. 흔들림, 진동
When people or things sway, they lean or swing slowly from one side to the other.

back and forth
[bæk ən fɔ́ːrθ]

ad. 앞뒤로; 좌우로; 여기저기에, 왔다갔다
If someone moves back and forth, they repeatedly move in one direction and then in the opposite direction.

hooray
[huréi]

int. 만세
People sometimes shout 'Hooray!' when they are very happy and excited about something.

yell^{복습}
[jel]

v. 고함치다, 소리 지르다; n. 고함, 외침
If you yell, you shout loudly, usually because you are excited, angry, or in pain.

story^{복습}
[stɔ́:ri]

① n. (건물의) 층 ② n. 이야기, 소설; 설명
A story of a building is one of its different levels, which is situated above or below other levels.

cowbell^{복습}
[káubèl]

n. (소를 쉽게 찾기 위해 목에 다는) 소 방울
A cowbell is a small bell that is hung around a cow's neck so that the ringing sound makes it possible to find the cow.

cram^{복습}
[kræm]

v. (좁은 공간 속으로 억지로) 밀어 넣다
If you cram things into a container or place, you put them into it, although there is hardly enough room for them.

plant***
[plænt]

v. (특정 장소에 단단히) 놓다; n. 식물, 초목; 공장
If you plant something somewhere, you put it there firmly.

drill*
[dril]

n. (비상시를 대비한) 훈련; 드릴, 송곳; 반복 연습
A drill is a routine exercise or activity, in which people practise what they should do in dangerous situations.

monitor^{복습}
[mánətər]

n. 감시 요원; 화면, 모니터; v. 추적 관찰하다
You can refer to a person who checks that something is done correctly, or that it is fair, as a monitor.

fireman
[fáiərmən]

n. (pl. firemen) 소방관
A fireman is a person, usually a man, whose job is to put out fires.

bleep
[bli:p]

n. (전자 장치에서 나는) 삐 소리; v. 삐 소리를 내다
A bleep is a short, high-pitched sound, usually one of a series, that is made by an electrical device.

constant*
[kánstənt]

a. 끊임없는; 거듭되는; 변함없는 (constantly ad. 끊임없이; 거듭)
You use constant to describe something that happens all the time or is always there.

all the way^{복습}

idiom 내내, 시종; 완전히
You use all the way to emphasize how long a distance is.

ladder*
[lǽdər]

n. 사다리
A ladder is a piece of equipment used for climbing up something or down from something.

trapdoor
[trǽpdɔ:r]

n. (바닥·천장에 나 있는) 작은 문
A trapdoor is a small horizontal door in a floor, a ceiling, or on a stage.

roof**
[ru:f]

n. 지붕
The roof of a building is the covering on top of it that protects the people and things inside from the weather.

rescue*
[réskju:]

v. 구하다, 구출하다; n. 구출, 구조, 구제
If you rescue someone, you get them out of a dangerous or unpleasant situation.

statue*
[stǽʧu:]

n. 조각상
A statue is a large sculpture of a person or an animal, made of stone or metal.

liberty**
[líbərti]

n. (지배·권위 등으로부터의) 자유
Liberty is the freedom to live your life in the way that you want, without interference from other people or the authorities.

funnel*
[fʌnl]

n. 깔때기
A funnel is an object with a wide, circular top and a narrow short tube at the bottom.

distance**
[dístəns]

n. (특정한 거리를 사이에 둔) 먼 곳; (공간상·시간상으로 떨어진) 거리
If you can see something in the distance, you can see it, far away from you.

suck^{복습}
[sʌk]

v. (특정한 방향으로) 빨아들이다; (액체·공기 등을) 빨아 먹다; (입에 넣고 계속) 빨다;
n. 빨기, 빨아 먹기
If something sucks a liquid, gas, or object in a particular direction, it draws it there with a powerful force.

flash**
[flæʃ]

n. 섬광, 번쩍임; v. (잠깐) 비치다; 비추다
A flash is a sudden burst of light or of something shiny or bright.

lightning^{복습}
[láitniŋ]

n. 번개, 번갯불; a. 번개같이, 아주 빨리
Lightning is the very bright flashes of light in the sky that happen during thunderstorms.

crack^{복습}
[kræk]

n. 찢어지는 듯한 소리; (무엇이 갈라져 생긴) 금;
v. 갈라지다, 금이 가다; 날카로운 소리를 내다
A crack is a sharp sound, like the sound of a piece of wood breaking.

thunder^{복습}
[θʌ́ndə:r]

n. 천둥, 우레; v. 천둥이 치다
Thunder is the loud noise that you hear from the sky after a flash of lightning, especially during a storm.

violent**
[váiələnt]

a. 격렬한, 맹렬한; 폭력적인, 난폭한 (violently ad. 격렬하게, 맹렬히)
If you describe something as violent, you mean that it is said, done, or felt very strongly.

earthquake^{복습}
[ə́:rθkweik]

n. 지진
An earthquake is a shaking of the ground caused by movement of the earth's crust.

rumble^{복습}
[rʌmbl]

v. 우르릉거리는 소리를 내다; n. 우르렁거리는 소리
If something rumbles, it makes a low, continuous noise.

rattle^{복습}
[rætl]

v. 달가닥거리다, 덜컹거리다; n. 덜거덕거리는 소리
When something rattles or when you rattle it, it makes short sharp knocking sounds because it is being shaken or it keeps hitting against something hard.

shrug^{복습}
[ʃrʌg]

v. (두 손바닥을 위로 하고) 어깨를 으쓱하다; n. 어깨를 으쓱하기
If you shrug, you raise your shoulders to show that you are not interested in something or that you do not know or care about something.

clap^{복습}
[klæp]

v. 박수를 치다, 손뼉을 치다; n. 박수 (소리)
When you clap, you hit your hands together to show appreciation or attract attention.

exclaim^{복습}
[ikskléim]

v. 소리치다, 외치다
If you exclaim, you cry out suddenly in surprise, strong emotion, or pain.

countryside*
[kántrisàid]

n. 시골 지역, 전원 지대
The countryside is land which is away from towns and cities.

heed
[hi:d]

v. (남의 충고·경고에) 주의를 기울이다
If you heed someone's advice or warning, you pay attention to it and do what they suggest.

no way^{복습}

idiom 절대로 아니다; (강한 거절의 의미로) 절대로 안 돼, 싫어
If you say there's no way that something will happen, you are emphasizing that you think it will definitely not happen.

get rid of^{복습}

idiom ~을 처리하다, 없애다
When you get rid of someone or something that is annoying you or that you do not want, you make yourself free of them or throw something away.

starve*
[sta:rv]

v. 굶기다; 굶주리다
To starve someone means not to give them any food.

bale
[beil]

n. 더미, 뭉치
A bale is a large quantity of something such as hay, cloth, or paper, tied together tightly.

hay*
[hei]

n. 건초
Hay is grass which has been cut and dried so that it can be used to feed animals.

calf*
[kæf]

n. (pl. calves) 송아지; 종아리
A calf is a young cow.

temporary**
[témpərèri]

a. 일시적인, 임시의 (temporarily ad. 일시적으로, 임시로)
Something that is temporary lasts for only a limited time.

plead^{복습}
[pli:d]

v. 애원하다
If you plead with someone to do something, you ask them in an intense, emotional way to do it.

yard^{복습}
[ja:rd]

n. (학교의) 운동장; 마당, 뜰; 정원
A yard is a flat area of concrete or stone that is next to a building and often has a wall around it.

moo
[mu:]

v. (소가) 음매 하고 울다
When cattle, especially cows, moo, they make the long low sound that cattle typically make.

수고하셨습니다!

드디어 끝까지 다 읽으셨군요! 축하드립니다! 여러분은 이 책을 통해 총 28,627개의 단어를 읽으셨고, 800개 이상의 어휘와 표현들을 익히셨습니다. 이 책에 나온 어휘는 다른 원서를 읽을 때에도 빈번히 만날 수 있는 필수 어휘들입니다. 이 책을 읽었던 경험은 비슷한 수준의 다른 원서들을 읽을 때 큰 도움이 될 것입니다.

이제 자신의 상황에 맞게 원서를 반복해서 읽거나, 오디오북을 들어 볼 수 있습니다. 혹은 비슷한 수준의 다른 원서를 찾아 읽는 것도 좋습니다. 일단 원서를 완독한 뒤에 어떻게 계속 영어 공부를 이어갈 수 있을지, 도움말을 꼼꼼히 살펴보고 각자 상황에 맞게 적용해 보세요!

리딩(Reading)을 확실하게 다지고 싶다면? 반복해서 읽어 보세요!

리딩 실력을 탄탄하게 다지고 싶다면, 같은 원서를 2~3번 반복해서 읽을 것을 권합니다. 같은 책을 여러 번 읽으면 지루할 것 같지만, 꼭 그렇지도 않습니다. 반복해서 읽을 때 처음과 주안점을 다르게 두면, 전혀 다른 느낌으로 재미있게 읽을 수 있습니다.

처음 원서를 읽을 때는 생소한 단어들과 스토리로 인해 읽으면서 곧바로 이해하기가 매우 힘들 수 있습니다. 전체 맥락을 잡고 읽어도 약간 버거운 느낌이지요. 하지만 반복해서 읽기 시작하면 달라집니다. 일단 내용을 파악한 상황이기 때문에 문장 구조나 어휘의 활용에 더 집중하게 되고, 조금 더 깊이 있게 읽을 수 있습니다. 좋은 표현과 문장을 수집하고 메모할 만한 여유도 생기게 되지요. 어휘도 많이 익숙해졌기 때문에 리딩 속도에도 탄력이 붙습니다. 처음 읽을 때는 '내용'에서 재미를 느꼈다면, 반복해서 읽을 때에는 '영어'에서 재미를 느끼게 되는 것입니다. 따라서 리딩 실력을 더욱 확고하게 다지고자 한다면, 같은 책을 2~3회 정도 반복해서 읽을 것을 권해 드립니다.

리스닝(Listening) 실력을 늘리고 싶다면?
귀를 통해서 읽어 보세요!

많은 영어 학습자들이 '리스닝이 안 돼서 문제'라고 한탄합니다. 그리고 리스닝 실력을 늘리는 방법으로 무슨 뜻인지 몰라도 반복해서 듣는 '무작정 듣기'를 선택합니다. 하지만 뜻도 모르면서 무작정 듣는 일에는 엄청난 인내력이 필요합니다. 그래서 대부분 며칠 시도하다가 포기해 버리고 말지요.

따라서 모르는 내용을 무작정 듣는 것보다는 어느 정도 알고 있는 내용을 반복해서 듣는 것이 더 효과적인 듣기 방법입니다. 그리고 이런 방식의 듣기에 활용할 수 있는 가장 좋은 교재가 오디오북입니다.

리스닝 실력을 향상하고 싶다면, 이 책에서 제공하는 오디오북을 이용해서 듣는 연습을 해 보세요. 활용법은 간단합니다. 일단 책을 한 번 완독했다면, 오디오북을 통해 다시 들어 보는 것입니다. 휴대 기기에 넣어 시간이 날 때 틈틈이 듣는 것도 좋고, 책상에 앉아 눈으로는 텍스트를 보며 귀로 읽는 것도 좋습니다. 이미 읽었던 내용이라 이해하기가 훨씬 수월하고, 애매했던 발음들도 자연스럽게 교정할 수 있습니다. 또 성우의 목소리 연기를 듣다 보면 내용이 더욱 생동감 있게 다가와 이해도가 높아지는 효과도 거둘 수 있습니다.

반대로 듣기에 자신 있는 사람이라면, 책을 읽기 전에 처음부터 오디오북을 먼저 듣는 것도 좋은 방법입니다. 귀를 통해 책을 쭉 읽어 보고, 이후에 다시 눈으로 책을 읽으면서 잘 들리지 않았던 부분을 보충하는 것이지요.

중요한 것은 내용을 따라가면서, 내용에 푹 빠져서 반복해 들어야 한다는 것입니다. 이렇게 연습을 반복해서 눈으로 읽지 않은 책이라도 '귀를 통해' 읽을 수 있을 정도가 되면, 리스닝으로 고생하는 일은 거의 없을 것입니다.

이 책은 저자 루이스 새커가 직접 읽은 오디오북을 기본으로 제공하고 있습니다. 오디오북은 MP3 파일로 제공되므로 컴퓨터 또는 휴대 기기에 옮겨서 사용하시면 됩니다. 혹시 오디오북에 이상이 있을 경우 help@ltinc.net으로 메일을 주시면 안내를 받으실 수 있습니다.

스피킹(Speaking)이 고민이라면? 소리 내어 읽어 보세요!

스피킹 역시 많은 학습자들이 고민하는 부분입니다. 스피킹이 고민이라면, 원서를 큰 소리로 읽는 낭독 훈련(Voice Reading)을 해 보세요!

'소리 내어 읽는 것이 말하기에 정말로 도움이 될까?'라고 의아한 생각이 들 수도 있습니다. 하지만 인간의 두뇌 입장에서 봤을 때, 성대 구조를 활용해서 '발화'한다는 점에서는 소리 내어 읽기와 말하기에 큰 차이가 없다고 합니다. 소리 내어 읽는 것은 '타인의 생각'을 전달하고, 직접 말하는 것은 '자신의 생각'을 전달한다는 차이가 있을 뿐, 머릿속에서 문장을 처리하고 조음기관(혀와 성대 등)을 움직여 의미를 만든다는 점에서 같은 과정인 것이지요. 따라서 소리 내어 읽는 연습을 꾸준히 하는 것은 스피킹 연습에 큰 도움이 됩니다.

소리 내어 읽기를 하는 방법은 간단합니다. 일단 오디오북을 들으면서 성우의 목소리를 최대한 따라 하며 같이 읽어 보세요. 발음뿐 아니라 억양, 어조, 느낌까지 완벽히 따라 한다고 생각하면서 소리 내어 읽습니다. 따라 읽는 것이 조금 익숙해지면, 옆의 누군가에게 이 책을 읽어 준다는 생각으로 소리 내어 계속 읽어 나갑니다. 한 번 눈과 귀로 읽었던 책이기 때문에 보다 수월하게 진행할 수 있고, 자연스럽게 어휘와 표현을 복습하는 효과도 거두게 됩니다. 또 이렇게 소리 내어 읽은 것을 녹음해서 들어 보면 스스로에게도 좋은 피드백이 됩니다.

최근 말하기가 강조되면서 소리 내어 읽기가 크게 각광을 받고 있기는 하지만, 그렇다고 소리 내어 읽기가 무조건 좋은 것만은 아닙니다. 책을 소리 내어 읽다 보면, 무의식적으로 속으로 발음을 하는 습관을 가지게 되어 리딩 속도 자체는 오히려 크게 떨어지는 현상이 발생할 수 있습니다. 따라서 빠른 리딩 속도가 중요한 수험생이나 상위권 학습자들에게는 소리 내어 읽기가 적절하지 않은 방법입니다. 효과가 좋다는 말만 믿고 무턱대고 따라 하기보다는 자신의 필요에 맞게 우선순위를 정하고 원서를 활용하는 것이 좋습니다.

라이팅(Writing)까지 욕심이 난다면? 요약하는 연습을 해 보세요!

원서를 라이팅 연습에 직접적으로 활용하는 데에는 한계가 있지만, 적절히 활용하면 원서도 유용한 라이팅 자료가 될 수 있습니다.

특히 책을 읽고 그 내용을 요약하는 연습은 큰 도움이 됩니다. 요약 훈련의 방식도 간단합니다. 원서를 읽고 그날 읽은 분량만큼 혹은 책을 다 읽고 전체 내용을 기반으로, 책 내용을 한번 요약하고 나의 느낌을 영어로 적어 보는 것입니다.

이때 그 책에 나왔던 단어와 표현을 최대한 활용하여 요약하는 것이 중요합니다. 영어 표현력은 결국 얼마나 다양한 어휘로 많은 표현을 해 보았느냐가 좌우하게 됩니다. 이런 면에서 내가 읽은 책을, 그 책에 나온 문장과 어휘로 다시 표현해 보는 것은 매우 효율적인 방법입니다. 책에 나온 어휘와 표현을 단순히 읽고 무슨 말인지 아는 정도가 아니라, 실제로 직접 활용해서 쓸 수 있을 만큼 확실하게 익히게 되는 것이지요. 여기에 첨삭까지 받을 수 있는 방법이 있다면 금상첨화입니다.

이러한 '표현하기' 연습은 스피킹 훈련에도 그대로 적용될 수 있습니다. 책을 읽고 그 내용을 3분 안에 다른 사람에게 영어로 말하는 연습을 해 보세요. 순발력과 표현력을 기르는 좋은 훈련이 될 것입니다.

꾸준히 원서를 읽고 싶다면? 뉴베리 수상작을 계속 읽어 보세요!

뉴베리 상이 세계 최고 권위의 아동 문학상인 만큼, 그 수상작들은 확실히 완성도를 검증받은 작품이라고 할 수 있습니다. 특히 '쉬운 어휘로 쓰인 깊이 있는 문장'으로 이루어졌다는 점이 영어 학습자들에게 큰 호응을 얻고 있습니다. 이렇게 '검증된 원서'를 꾸준히 읽는 것은 영어 실력 향상에 큰 도움이 됩니다.

아래에 수준별로 제시된 뉴베리 수상작 목록을 보며 적절한 책들을 찾아 계속 읽어 보세요. 꼭 뉴베리 수상작이 아니더라도 마음에 드는 작가의 다른 책을 읽어 보는 것 또한 아주 좋은 방법입니다.

• 영어 초보자도 쉽게 읽을 만한 아주 쉬운 수준. 소리 내어 읽기에도 아주 적합.
Sarah, Plain and Tall*(Medal, 8,331단어), The Hundred Penny Box (Honor, 5,878단어), The Hundred Dresses*(Honor, 7,329단어), My Father's Dragon (Honor, 7,682단어), 26 Fairmount Avenue (Honor, 6,737단어)

• 중·고등학생 정도 영어 학습자라면 쉽게 읽을 수 있는 수준. 소리 내어 읽기에도 비교적 적합한 편.
Because of Winn-Dixie★(Honor, 22,123단어), What Jamie Saw (Honor, 17,203단어), Charlotte's Web (Honor, 31,938단어), Dear Mr. Henshaw (Medal, 18,145단어), Missing May (Medal, 17,509단어)

• 대학생 정도 영어 학습자라면 무난한 수준. 소리 내어 읽기에는 적합하지 않음.
Number The Stars★(Medal, 27,197단어), A Single Shard (Medal, 33,726단어), The Tale of Despereaux★(Medal, 32,375단어), Hatchet★(Medal, 42,328단어), Bridge to Terabithia (Medal, 32,888단어), A Fine White Dust (Honor, 19,022단어), Jennifer, Hecate, Macbeth, William McKinley and Me, Elizabeth (Honor, 23,266단어)

• 원서 완독 경험을 가진 학습자에게 적절한 수준. 소리 내어 읽기에는 적합하지 않음.
The Giver★(Medal, 43,617단어), From the Mixed-Up Files of Mrs. Basil E. Frankweiler (Medal, 30,906단어), The View from Saturday (Medal, 42,685단어), Holes★(Medal, 47,079단어), Criss Cross (Medal, 48,221단어), Walk Two Moons (Medal, 59,400단어), The Graveyard Book (Medal, 67,380단어)

뉴베리 수상작과 뉴베리 수상 작가의 좋은 작품을 엄선한 「뉴베리 컬렉션」에도 위 목록에 있는 도서 중 상당수가 포함될 예정입니다.

★「뉴베리 컬렉션」으로 이미 출간된 도서

어떤 책들이 출간되었는지 확인하려면, 지금 인터넷 서점에서
뉴베리 컬렉션을 검색해 보세요.

뉴베리 수상작을 동영상 강의로 만나 보세요!

영어원서 전문 동영상 강의 사이트 영서당(yseodang.com)에서는 뉴베리 컬렉션 『Wayside School』 시리즈, 『Holes』, 『Because of Winn-Dixie』, 『The Miraculous Journey of Edward Tulane』 등의 동영상 강의를 제공하고 있습니다. 뉴베리 수상작이라는 최고의 영어 교재와 EBS 출신 인기 강사가 만난 명강의! 지금 사이트를 방문해서 무료 샘플 강의를 들어 보세요!

'스피드 리딩 카페'를 통해 원서 읽기 습관을 길러 보세요!

일상에서 영어를 한마디도 쓰지 않는 비영어권 국가에서 살고 있는 우리가 영어 환경에 가장 쉽고, 편하고, 부담 없이 노출되는 방법은 바로 '영어원서 읽기'입니다. 언제 어디서든 원서를 붙잡고 읽기만 하면 곧바로 영어를 접하는 환경이 만들어지기 때문이지요. 하루에 20분씩만 꾸준히 읽는다면, 1년에 무려 120시간 동안 영어에 노출될 수 있습니다. 이러한 이유 때문에 영어 교육 전문가들이 영어원서 읽기를 추천하는 것이지요.

하지만 원서 읽기가 좋다는 것을 알아도 막상 꾸준히 읽는 것은 쉽지 않습니다. 그럴 때에는 13만 명 이상의 회원을 보유한 국내 최대 원서 읽기 동호회 〈스피드 리딩 카페〉(cafe.naver. com/readingtc)를 방문해 보세요.

원서별로 정리된 무료 PDF 단어장과 수준별 추천 원서 목록 등 유용한 자료는 물론, 뉴베리 수상작을 포함한 다양한 원서의 리뷰를 무료로 확인할 수 있습니다. 특히 함께 모여서 원서를 읽는 '북클럽'은 중간에 포기하지 않고 원서를 끝까지 읽는 습관을 기르는 데 큰 도움이 될 것입니다.

Chapters 1 & 2

1. C   It wasn't his job to pick up garbage. He was just supposed to pass out the balls during lunch and recess, and also make sure the kids didn't kill each other.

2. B   "I have to give it to Mrs. Jewls," said the man. Louis thought a moment. He didn't want the man disturbing the children. He knew how much they hated to be interrupted when they were working. "I'm Mrs. Jewls," he said.

3. A   "Oh dear, how shall I choose?" asked Mrs. Jewls. "I have to be fair about this. I know! We'll have a spelling bee. And the winner will get to open the door."

4. B   "Get that piece of junk out of here," said Maurecia. "Now, don't be that way," said Mrs. Jewls. "The computer will help us learn. It's a lot quicker than a pencil and paper."

5. A   But worst of all, his name wasn't Mark Miller. He was Benjamin Nushmutt. And he had moved from Hempleton, not Magadonia. But he was too scared to mention that to Mrs. Jewls. He was afraid to correct a teacher.

6. D   Benjamin didn't know what to say. He wished he really was Mark Miller. Mark Miller wouldn't be scared, he thought. He'd probably have lots to say. Everyone would like him. Nobody would think Mark Miller was weird.

7. C   Benjamin frowned. He looked at the white paper sack on Mrs. Jewls's desk. He couldn't tell Mrs. Jewls his real name now. She'd think he was making it up just to get a free lunch.

Chapters 3 & 4

1. D   "No, I didn't lose it," Mrs. Jewls said sternly. She showed the back of the paper to Bebe. Someone had written: MRS. JEWLS IS AS FAT AS A HIPPOPOTAMUS! (AND SHE SMELLS LIKE ONE, TOO.)

2. B   "Well, we'll show Ray," said Mrs. Jewls. She gave Bebe an A+. "There. I don't think he'll try that again." "Thanks!" said Bebe. "You may have a Tootsie Roll Pop, too," said Mrs. Jewls. Bebe took a Tootsie Roll Pop out of the coffee can on Mrs. Jewls's desk,

then returned to her seat. She proudly showed Calvin her A+.

3. A   "I wanted to talk to you about that," said Mrs. Jewls. "I think you're being unfair to Bebe. I think she often gets into trouble when really Ray is to blame." "Ray?" asked Mrs. Gunn. "Yes. I know you think he's a perfect angel," said Mrs. Jewls, "but some children can be angels on the outside and devils underneath." "Yes, that sounds like Bebe," said Mrs. Gunn. "I'm not talking about Bebe. I'm talking about Ray." "Ray?" asked Bebe's mother. "Who's Ray?"

4. B   Mac raised his hand. Mrs. Jewls pretended not to see him. "Oooh! Oooh!" Mac groaned as he stretched his hand so high that it hurt. Mrs. Jewls pretended not to hear him.

5. C   "Did you look under the bed?" asked John. "That was one of the first places I looked," said Mac, "but it wasn't there." "Did you check the dirty clothes?" asked Ron. "Maybe it was never washed." "I checked," said Mac. "Do you have a dog?" asked Bebe. "Maybe your dog took it." "No, my dog doesn't wear socks," said Mac. "Why didn't you just put on a different sock?" asked Allison. "Even if it didn't match?"

6. D   "Mac, what does this have to do with dinosaurs?" asked Mrs. Jewls. "Because that must have been the kind of watermelon that dinosaurs ate," said Mac.

7. D   Mrs. Jewls never finished her lesson about dinosaurs, so she had to assign it for homework.

Chapters 5 & 6

1. C   "This is a hobo," said Sharie. "I found him on the way to school." "Ooh, how neat!" said Maurecia. The hobo had long dirty hair and a scraggly beard. His shirt was covered with stains. His pants had lots of colorful patches. His coat was too big for him, but it wasn't as big as Sharie's coat. Sharie was a little girl, but she wore the biggest coat in all of Wayside School. The hobo wore old black shoes that also looked like they were too big for him, but that might have been because he wasn't wearing any socks.

2. B   "Did you ever try to get a job?" asked Calvin. "I tried," said Bob. "But nobody would hire me because I didn't wear socks."

3. D   "Maybe," said Bob. "But remember I told you I won the school spelling bee? Well, the day I won it, I forgot to wear socks. Think about it."

4. C   It was time for their weekly spelling test. "Everyone take out a piece of paper and a pencil," said Mrs. Jewls. "The first word is—" "Wait a second!" called Calvin. "I'm not ready yet." Mrs. Jewls waited while all the children took off their socks.

5. A   Paul sat in the desk behind Leslie. Once, a long time ago, he had pulled Leslie's pigtails. It felt great! That is—Paul thought it felt great. Leslie didn't think it felt

too good. But that was earlier in the year, when Paul was younger and immature. Now he knew better.

6. B   Leslie stepped back into the classroom. "I'm getting my hair trimmed tomorrow," she announced. "If you want, I'll save the pieces for you. It'll just be some split ends." Paul was so excited he forgot where he was. He quickly raised his head. It bashed against the window frame, then he bounced forward and toppled out the window.

7. B   She returned to the window, sighed, then leaned out backward. Her hands tightly held the edge of the counter as she looked up at the sky. "Grab my pigtails," she said, then winced. A big smile came across Paul's face. "Really?" he asked. "Just do it!" said Leslie.

Chapters 7 & 8

1. A   "Get back in your seat," ordered Mrs. Jewls. Myron reluctantly returned to his desk. I do live in a cage, he thought. I'm not allowed out. I have to stay in my cage until the bell rings.

2. B   Myron stood at the bottom of the staircase and looked up. "No!" he declared. "I won't go. I have to be free!" As all the other kids rushed past him, he eased his way around to the back of the stairs. As everybody else went up, Myron went down . . . to the basement.

3. A   With his arms outstretched, he stepped across the gritty floor. His hand struck against a large, fat pipe above his head. The pipe felt like it was covered with a thousand spiderwebs. Still, Myron kept his finger on the pipe as he walked, so he wouldn't get lost. As long as he stayed with the pipe, he knew he'd be able to find his way back to the stairs.

4. C   The man took a pencil and a piece of paper out of his attaché case. "So do you want to be safe, or do you want to be free?"

5. B   Joy sat at the desk behind Todd. Big deal, she thought. It's just a hunk of plastic that happens to look like a dog. But even though Joy didn't like Todd's toy, she decided to steal it.

6. D   "Awwww, how precious," cooed Mrs. Jewls. "He's the most lovable puppy I've ever seen." She kissed Todd's plastic puppy on its plastic nose. "I guess I can let you off this time," she said. "But try to keep him in your desk." She kissed Todd's toy again, then handed it back to him. "You can erase your name from the board, too."

7. A   "No, Mrs. Jewls is just a nice teacher," said Todd. "Here, let me show you the best part." He grabbed hold of the dog's tail and turned it like a crank. Suddenly the cute floppy ears stood straight up. The mouth opened wide, and the teeth grew into sharp

fangs. "Wow," breathed Deedee. Todd wasn't finished. He pulled the dog's nose and stretched out its face. The cheeks became thin and bony. The eyes were no longer sweet, but grim and frightening. "What a great toy!" said Calvin. The cute little puppy had turned into a mean, hungry, man-eating wolf.

Chapters 9 & 10

1. D   "Just milk," said Maurecia. "I brought my lunch." Miss Mush smiled and gave Maurecia a carton of milk. Joy was next in line. "And what would you like, Joy?" asked Miss Mush. "Milk," said Joy. Miss Mush smiled and gave Joy a carton of milk. "And what would you like, Jason?" "Milk, please," said Jason. "Just milk," said Dameon.

2. B   It was almost Ron's turn. He hadn't brought a lunch. He normally brought a peanut butter and jelly sandwich to school, but there hadn't been a single slice of bread in his house this morning. "I know!" his mother had said. "I'll give you some money and you can buy a nice hot lunch from Miss Mush!" She thought it was a brilliant idea.

3. A   This was the eighteenth day in a row that the special was Mushroom Surprise. It was called Mushroom Surprise because it would have been a surprise if anybody had ever ordered it. No one ever did—except Louis, of course. That's why they'd had it for eighteen days. There was always plenty left over.

4. D   "What's the surprise?" asked Deedee. Ron looked at Deedee. His face flushed and his eyes changed color. His whole body began to shake, like a washing machine on the spin cycle. Deedee was afraid he was going to throw up. She tried to get away, but with everyone crowded around, there was no room for her to move. But Ron didn't throw up. He stood up, put his arms around Deedee's neck, and kissed her smack on the lips.

5. C   Benjamin still hadn't told anybody he wasn't Mark Miller. His grades had never been better. Mark Miller is a lot smarter than Benjamin Nushmutt, he thought. When they chose up teams for kickball, he was always the first one picked. Mark Miller is a better kicker than Benjamin Nushmutt, he realized. The girls in the class liked him too. Mark Miller is better looking than Benjamin Nushmutt, he decided. But unfortunately, he knew he had to tell Mrs. Jewls his real name. He sighed, then slowly raised his hand.

6. C   "What's wrong, Mark?" Mrs. Jewls shouted over the music. "Why aren't you playing the tambourine?" "My name's not Mark," said Benjamin. "It's Benjamin Nushmutt. I'm sorry for not telling you before."

7. A   "Is something the matter, Mr. Kidswatter?" asked Mrs. Jewls. "Several teachers have complained about your music," said Mr. Kidswatter. "Their students are having trouble hearing." "I understand," said Mrs. Jewls. "Good," said Mr. Kidswatter. He

walked out of the room. "Okay, you heard Mr. Kidswatter," said Mrs. Jewls. "We'll have to play louder so everyone can hear. Uno, dos, tres, cuatro!"

Chapters 11 & 12

1. C   Across the playground, all the children quit their games when they saw D.J. Nobody could have fun when D.J. looked so sad.

2. D   Kathy glared at him. "Well, then how come you're so sad you lost that dumb watch?" she demanded. "I'm afraid a bird might think it's food and choke on it," said D.J.

3. B   Mrs. Jewls started the movie projector. Stephen turned off the lights. Dameon pulled down the shades. D.J. held the piece of black construction paper under his nose, because his smile was so bright.

4. A   Jason borrowed a pencil from Allison. When he gave it back to her, it was full of teeth marks.

5. A   He thought about asking Mrs. Jewls for a Tootsie Roll Pop. If I'm sucking on that, I won't chew Myron's pencil. And a Tootsie Roll Pop would probably taste better than Allison's socks. He didn't know for sure because he had never tasted Allison's socks. But before he could ask Mrs. Jewls, Mrs. Jewls called him. "Jason, will you come here for a moment," she said. "I think I know how to keep you from chewing pencils." Jason smiled as he walked to her desk. "I like the purple ones," he told her.

6. B   But Mrs. Jewls didn't give him a Tootsie Roll Pop. Instead, she taped his mouth shut with heavy-duty masking tape. She had to use a lot of tape, because Jason had the second biggest mouth in the class. "There," she said.

Chapters 13 & 14

1. D   Mrs. Jewls would start a new book today. She hoped it wouldn't be funny or sad. She hoped Mrs. Jewls would read a boring story with no jokes.

2. D   She pulled a tissue out of the box John had given her and loudly blew her nose. "There goes the foghorn," said John. Dana laughed into her tissue. She blew her nose again, even louder. "It must be a very foggy day," said John.

3. B   "Because I hate stories," said Dana. "They make me laugh and cry too much." "You don't hate stories, Dana," Mrs. Jewls told her. "You love stories. I wish everybody laughed and cried as much as you."

4. C   It was Calvin's birthday. His mother had made chocolate cupcakes with jelly beans on top. Mrs. Jewls passed them out to the class. "Hey, Dana," said Leslie. "I'll trade you my black jelly bean for your red one." "Okay," said Dana. Everyone traded jelly

beans. That was the most fun part of the party.

5. A   All day everyone had lots of suggestions for Calvin. they told him what kind of tattoo he should get, and where he should put it. A rainbow on his forehead. A flower on his cheek. An anchor on his arm. It was easy for the others to make suggestions. They wouldn't have to live with it for the rest of their lives.

6. B   "It was a real tough decision," said Calvin. "I almost got a leopard fighting a snake. But then my dad told me to think about it. He said it was sort of like getting a second nose. You may think you want another nose, because that way if one nose gets stuffed up, you can breathe through the other nose. But then he asked me, 'Calvin, do you really want two noses?'"

Chapters 15 & 16

1. C   Deedee hiccupped three times, then gasped, "I saw her!" "Who?" asked Louis. Deedee didn't answer—she just stared right through him. But everyone else knew whom Deedee had seen. Most of them had seen her too, during the last two weeks.

2. B   Who is she?" asked Louis. "A hippopotamus?" "No!" said Myron with a laugh. "Why do you say that?" "Because when a hippopotamus gets mad, it wiggles its ears."

3. D   "It wasn't funny," said Louis. "My mother always knew when I got in trouble, because I'd have bits of trash stuck in my hair."

4. A   He was in love with Mrs. Jewls. That was why he was always doing things for her, like passing out papers. He thought she was very pretty and nice. He thought she was smart, too. In fact, he thought she was one of the smartest people in the class.

5. C   "That's stupid," said Dameon. "How can I prove I'm not in love with Mrs. Jewls?" "Give her this," said Joy. She handed Dameon a paper bag. "Your lunch?" asked Dameon. "Look inside," said Maurecia. Inside the paper bag was a dead rat. Dameon knew Mrs. Jewls hated dead rats more than anything in the world. "Put it in her desk," said Joy.

6. D   "This is getting disgusting!" said the dead rat. It climbed out of Mrs. Jewls's desk and walked out of the room.

Chapters 17 & 18

1. A   "So read the story backward," suggested Mrs. Jewls. "That way the beginning will be a surprise."

2. B   "I couldn't leave the table until I finished it," explained Jenny. "And then I missed the bus." "What does prune juice have to do with anything?" asked Mrs. Jewls.

3. C   She put on her helmet; then her father drove her to school on the back of his

motorcycle. It was a very bumpy ride. "Put on your helmet," said her father. "I'll drive you to school on the back of my motorcycle."

4. B   Everyone in Mrs. Jewls's class loved it when they had substitute teachers. They loved playing mean and horrible tricks on them.

5. C   Benjamin frowned. He finally had the courage to tell Mrs. Jewls his real name. "Rats!" he said.

6. D   "My, it is certainly a pleasure to teach such happy students," said the substitute. "Who knows the answer to question four?" They all raised their hands. They all wanted to tell the substitute their names were Benjamin.

7. A   All day, everyone paid very close attention. They all wanted the teacher to call on them. Because as funny as it was when Mrs. Franklin called somebody else Benjamin, it was even funnier when she called you Benjamin.

Chapters 19 (1) & 19 (2)

1. B   Allison thought all the kids in Mrs. Jewls's class were silly, even Rondi, and Rondi was her best friend. Then there was Jason, who was always pestering her. That was because Jason hated her. Or else he loved her. Allison wasn't sure which.

2. C   "What's the name of your goldfish?" asked Mrs. Jewls. "Shark!" said Jason. Everyone laughed. Allison rolled her eyes. "It makes him feel important," Jason explained. "Where should I put him?"

3. D   "Have you gone crazy?" shouted Allison. She ran out of the room and down to the class on the twenty-ninth story. "Come quick," she said. "There's something wrong with Mrs. Jewls's class." No one heard her. She slammed the door, then continued down the stairs to the class on the twenty-eighth floor. No one saw her there, either. Tears streamed down her cheeks. Is the whole school playing a joke on me? she wondered. "It's not funny!" she shouted as loud as she could. She continued down the stairs, screaming anything that came to her head, hoping that someone, somewhere, would notice her.

4. D   "No one ever leaves Miss Zarves's class," said Nick. "How long have you been here, Virginia?"

5. A   She named every member of the class, including all three Erics. She didn't want to forget where she came from. If I forget where I came from, I might never get back, she thought.

6. D   "Ray, no talking please," said Miss Zarves. "Now, everyone please take out a pencil and some paper. I want you to write all the numbers from zero to a million in alphabetical order."

7. B   "Ben's new," said Nick. He pointed Ben out to her. Ben appeared to be about

Allison's age. She was glad about that. When the two-minute break came, she went over and talked to him.

Chapters 19 (3), 20, 21, & 22

1. C   In her mind she went through everybody in her former class. She didn't want to forget again. As she thought about each person, tears filled her eyes. She missed them very much. Even Jason. They were all so wonderful in their own special ways.

2. A   That's her plan! Allison suddenly realized. She shivered as it all came together for her. Miss Zarves assigns us lots of busy work so we don't have time to think. She makes us memorize stupid things so that we don't think about the important things. And then she gives us good grades to keep us happy.

3. B   Allison looked at her. She knew Mark was right. Teachers are experts at finding ways to punish you. And if Miss Zarves was the devil, who knew what she might have up her sleeve? Still, Allison had to take a chance. If she wanted to get back to Mrs. Jewls's class, she had to act as if she were in Mrs. Jewls's class.

4. B   Mrs. Jewls chose the biggest Eric. "Eric Fry, Mr. Kidswatter wants to see you."

5. C   Eric Ovens gulped, then walked inside. He sat in the little chair in front of Mr. Kidswatter's enormous desk. Eric Fry was nowhere to be seen. "Wh-what ha-happened to Eric Fry?" he asked.

6. D   Upstairs, Mrs. Jewls heard Mr. Kidswatter's voice resound over the loudspeaker. "MRS. JEWLS, SEND ME THE LAST ERIC!" "On my way!" said Eric Bacon. He hopped out of his chair and bounced down the stairs.

7. A   He turned the card over. On the other side, a left-handed handed person had written with a sharp pencil: Mr. Kidswatter is a Mugworm Griblick.

Chapters 23 & 24

1. D   Something terrible happened. Rondi grew two new front teeth. Rondi was afraid nobody would think she was cute anymore.

2. D   "Why not?" asked Rondi. "You said you liked me. If you liked me, you'd kick me in the teeth." "You know I can't," said Louis. "If I kick you in the teeth, then all the other kids will want me to kick them in the teeth, too."

3. B   "Terrence stole their ball," said Louis. "Make him give it back." "Her?" asked Stephen and Jason. "Me?" asked Rondi. Louis winked at her. Rondi's eyes lit up. "Okay, Louis," she said. "That's a good idea. That's a wonderful idea!"

4. D   They took a vote. Twelve kids thought she looked cuter with her two new teeth and twelve thought she looked cuter before. Three thought she should keep just

one tooth.

5. C   He looked at the grayish-white mound on his plate. He thought it needed more color. He squirted squiggly lines of mustard all over it. Then he added several dollops of red ketchup.

6. B   John's eyes filled with terror. "I—I just figured out who it looks like," he whispered. "Who?" asked Joe. "Mrs. Gorf."

7. A   "Ha! Ha! Ha!" said Mrs. Gorf. "Now I'll get you! You think you're so cute, don't you! Well, you won't get away from me this time!" She wiggled her ears, first her right one, then her left. "Quick, Joe!" said John. "Eat her!" The two boys dug their plastic utensils into the potato salad and shoveled it into their mouths as fast as they could.

Chapters 25 & 26

1. A   Stephen came to school wearing a three-piece suit: gray trousers, a gray vest, and a gray jacket.

2. C   "The more it chokes me, the better I look," Stephen explained. "See?" He tightened his tie.

3. B   Stephen pulled his tie tighter. "Now how do I look?" he asked. "Wow, you look great!" said D.J. "Pull it tighter!" Stephen pulled his tie even tighter. "How's this?" he gasped. "You look great and very important," said D.J. D.J. was wearing a toga made out of his bed sheet. "Pull it tighter!" said Bebe.

4. A   "Certainly," said Mrs. Jewls. "The tie didn't make you important. It doesn't matter what you wear on the outside. It's what's underneath that counts." "Underneath?" asked Stephen. "Yes," said Mrs. Jewls. "If you want to be great and important, you have to wear expensive underpants."

5. D   Mrs. Jewls tried very hard to ignore the voice. She didn't like giving busy work. Instead she tried to teach the children three new things every day. She believed that if they learned three new things every day, they would eventually learn everything there is to know. There are some classes where the teachers give so much busy work that the children never learn anything.

6. C   "We are going to learn three new things today," Mrs. Jewls announced. "How to make pickles, seven plus four, and the capital of England."

7. A   Paul jumped out of his seat. Those pigtails had once saved his life. Now it was his turn to return the favor! He pushed the vat of brine back the other way. He was just trying to push it up straight, but he pushed too hard. It poured all over Mrs. Jewls, drenching her.

Chapters 27 & 28

1. A   Maurecia looked all around for her lunch. She crawled in the dirt as she searched through the bushes. "Any luck?" asked Joy as she finished Maurecia's chocolate milk.

2. B   Maurecia smiled as she thought about it. "No, I better show it to Louis. He'll know what to do."

3. D   Mr. Finch nodded. "It was my life's savings," he said. "For fifty years I made pencils. I got a penny for every pencil I made. I hate pencils! But finally I saved enough money to quit my job and do what I always wanted to do."

4. C   "I'm going to open my own ice cream parlor," he said, then started to cry. "When I lost that money, I thought I'd have to start making pencils again."

5. A   "Mrs. Jewls, I don't need to take dancing lessons," said Eric Bacon. "I already know how to dance!"

6. B   "Dahnce?" asked Mrs. Waloosh. She looked very surprised. "Ve are not going to dahnce," she said. "We're not?" asked Ron. "No, Ronaldo," whispered Mrs. Waloosh. "Ve are going to tango!"

7. D   They all staggered out of the ballroom, cut up, bruised, and bleeding. "Next veek, ve valtz!" Mrs. Waloosh called after them. "So how did everyone like dancing?" asked Mrs. Jewls when they returned. "Dahnce?" asked Ronaldo, King of the Gypsies. "Ve didn't dahnce." "You didn't?" asked Mrs. Jewls. "No," said Ronaldo. "Ve tangoed!" Everyone cheered. "It vas vonderful!" exclaimed Kathy. "Fahntasteek!" said Terrence. Myron was sorry he had missed it. "I can't vait till next Vednesday," said Todd.

Chapters 29 & 30

1. B   Benjamin stared down at his desk top. He was very determined. Mrs Jewls would be handing out report cards at the end of the week. He had to tell her his real name before then.

2. C   "No, that's not crazy," said Todd. "I'll tell you what's crazy. What's crazy is that we all go to school on the thirtieth floor, and the bathrooms are way down on the first!" Everyone agreed with that, even Mrs. Jewls.

3. D   "Oh, this must be your lunch," said Mrs. Jewls. She gave Benjamin the white paper sack that had been sitting on her desk since Benjamin's first day of school. At lunch Allison headed down the stairs. "Mark!" she exclaimed. "Hi, Allison," said Mark Miller. "Long time no see." He carried a white paper sack just like Benjamin's. Allison was afraid she was back on the nineteenth story. "Don't worry," said Mark. "Suddenly everyone realized my name was Mark Miller and not Benjamin Nushmutt. And then Miss Zarves

gave me this bag and told me to take it to the hospital." "Is it your lunch?" asked Allison. "Look inside," said Mark. He handed her the bag. Allison looked inside. There was an ear.

4. C   Mrs. Jewls rang her cowbell. "Find your seats," she said. That wasn't easy. All the desks were crammed together on one side of the room. The building swayed, and the desks slid to the other side of the room.

5. A   Mrs. Jewls led the children out of the room. If there was a real fire, the children might not be able to see her because of the smoke, so she constantly rang her cowbell. There wouldn't be time to go all the way down the stairs, either. Mrs. Jewls led them up the ladder and through the trapdoor to the roof. If there was a real fire, helicopters would rescue them.

6. C   Mrs. Jewls rang her cowbell. "STOP RINGING YOUR BELL!" "Stop ringing your bell," said Myron. "Oh," said Mrs. Jewls. She stopped ringing her bell. Down below, all the students and teachers clapped their hands.

7. D   From all over the countryside, cows had heard Mrs. Jewls's cowbell and heeded the call. There were thousands of them. They filled the stairs and all the classrooms.

WAYSIDE SCHOOL IS FALLING DOWN

1판 1쇄   2015년 3월 16일

2판 3쇄   2024년 7월 1일

지은이   Louis Sachar
기획   이수영
책임편집   김보경 정소이
콘텐츠제작및감수   롱테일 교육 연구소
저작권   명채린
마케팅   두잉글 사업 본부

펴낸이   이수영
펴낸곳   롱테일북스
출판등록   제2015-000191호
주소   04033 서울특별시 마포구 양화로 113, 3층(서교동, 순흥빌딩)
전자메일   help@ltinc.net

ISBN 979-11-91343-02-1 14740